www.sparringartists.com

Artwork by **Hannah Yaryan**

ANTHOLOGY of SPARRING WITH BEATNIK GHOSTS©
ANNUAL #2

EDITORS:

S.A. GRIFFIN & RICHARD MODIANO

Sparring With Beatnik Ghosts title and logo © Copyright 2024 Daniel Yaryan

ANTHOLOGY OF
SPARRING WITH BEATNIK GHOSTS©

Published by:

SPARRING ARTISTS © Daniel Yaryan, 2024
Sparring With Beatnik Ghosts © Daniel Yaryan, 2024

Sparring Artists: Anthology of Sparring With Beatnik Ghosts; Annual 2 is printed in the United States of America. All rights of content revert back to the individual authors artists. No part of this book may be used or reproduced in any manner whatsoever without written permission except in the case of brief quotations embodied in critical articles and reviews. For information, contact Mystic Boxing Commission Publisher Daniel Yaryan: dyaryan@gmail.com

Editors:
S.A. Griffin & Richard Modiano

Featured Cover Artist:
Mike Street

Assistant Editors:
Christy McClain & Lynn Rogers

Staff Artist:
T. Mike Walker

Publisher/Book Designer/Art Director:
Daniel Yaryan

ISBN#: 979-8-9905623-5-6
1st Edition: 12/31/24 – Mystic Boxing Commision

ACKNOWLEDGEMENTS

I want to thank **S.A. Griffin** and **Richard Modiano** for co-editing the 2nd annual edition of Sparring Artists: *Anthology of Sparring With Beatnik Ghosts*. These two esteemed colleagues have assembled an incredible list of what I refer to as "Mystic Boxers" ranging from some of the most magnificent poets, storytellers, reviewers, photographers and artists alive today, as well as those still with us in spirit. I've always considered *Sparring With Beatnik Ghosts* to be a literary seance in a mystic boxing ring, with energy exchanged in order to acknowledge the past and be mindful of our fight for the future. The Ghosts symbolize our trainers and their inspiring legacies, materializing when needed in our physical world as our gurus, idols and instigators to propel us forward. These ghosts of bygone days give us a few jabs to remind us not to rest on our laurels. Artists must continue to fight to be heard using our own fresh new ideas, sounds and visions -- while reflecting on those who got us in the ring in the first place.

New features in this edition, include "Sparring Comix" to kick off the book, just as animated cartoons once kicked off films in our movie palaces of yesteryear. Speaking of which, we now include film reviews in a new section called "Kino Truth." Book reviews are also a new offering in this edition. As before, you'll discover enthralling, startling and amazing artists, such as the cover artist of this issue, Mike Street; plus the caliber of poetry and storytelling you've come to expect from *Sparring*. This time, we explore further uncharted territory for your reading pleasure and enlightenment. Thanks again to Mystic Boxing Commissioners Griffin and Modiano, as well as everyone participating in this edition! Keep Sparring!

— *Daniel Yaryan (Publisher)*

Annual No. 2

CONTENTS

10 *SPARRING COMIX DEBUTS IN THIS ISSUE OF SPARRING ARTISTS. ARTWORK ABOVE BY FITZ.*

18 *FEATURED COVER ARTIST MIKE STREET SHOWCASES HIS WORK INSIDE.*

CONTENTS

26 *A TOM WAITS MONOLUGUE: SEGMENTS OF A MEMOIR BY MICHAEL C FORD..*

34 *CHARLES PLYMELL'S NEW VOLUME OF POETRY "OVER THE STAGE OF KANSAS " REVIEWED .*

38 *FEAR OF A HIP PLANET: ABRAHAM, BRANAMAN, BECK, MARGOLIS AND SCIBELLA.*

68 *SPECIAL FEATURE: LINDA J. ALBERTANO BY FRANK LUTZ*

CONTENTS

90 NEELI CHERKOVSKI FEATURE: WITH MODIANO , GRIFFIN, CHERRY, WINANS AND STORTI

114 TRIBUTE TO ANDY CLAUSEN: WITH COHN, KATZ, GINSBERG, OLMSTED, PERL, SHOT, WARD, AND MORE.

CONTRIBUTING ARTISTS

- JUSTIN AYRES
- MARCO BAKKER
- VINCE BECK
- ELISHA BROWN BIRD
- ROBERT BRANAMAN
- GEORGE REITER BRILL
- NEELI CHERKOVSKI
- SAM CHERRY
- CATHYANN CUSIMANO
- SOHEYL DAHI
- DAVID HUMBERT DE SUPERVILLE
- ALEXIS RHONE FANCHER
- CHRISTOPHER FELVER
- ROBERT FISCHER
- MARK FISHER
- FITZ
- MICHAEL C FORD
- MIKULÁŠ GALANDA
- RAY GINGHOFFER
- ALLEN GINSBERG
- WILLIAM P. GOTTLIEB
- S.A. GRIFFIN

187 *MARC KOCKINOS: IN MEMORIAM BY DANIEL YARYAN*

210 *SUNSET FOR THE QUEEN OF THE BEATS, ANNE MARIE MAXWELL BY LYNN ROGERS, M.A.*

CONTRIBUTING ARTISTS

- JOHANNES HANDSCHIN
- mark hartenbach
- JOHN HASSALL
- GEORGE HERRIMAN
- MARK DAVID HOEFER
- CLEA JONES
- JERRY KAMSTRA
- KATIE KEENLOVE
- PAUL KLEE
- CHUCK KOTON
- MATT LAVIN
- LINDA LERNER
- GERARD MALANGA
- JESSE MCCLOSKEY
- PAUL NASH
- WALTER O'BRIEN
- DAN O'NEILL
- NINA PALEY
- ROB PLATH
- RUBEN QUINTANA
- KENNON B. RAINES
- ODILON REDON

CONTRIBUTING ARTISTS

- FRANK T. RIOS
- DOREN ROBBINS
- LYNN ROGERS
- ERIC ROHMAN
- HENRY LYMAN SAŸEN
- TONY SCIBELLA
- JOHN SEABURY
- ELLA SENERES
- DANIEL OWEN STOLPE
- VINCE STORTI
- MIKE STREET
- BEN TALBERT
- DR. MONGO TARIBUBU
- WILLIAM TAYLOR, JR.
- E. P. UPJOHN
- T. MIKE WALKER
- MARCIA WARD
- MELISSA WEST
- KRISTEN WETTERHAHN
- TRACY WITT
- HANNAH YARYAN
- KAMERA ZIE/PAMELA MOSHER

CHILLING···WEIRD···SPINE-TINGLING!
MBC PRESENTS
SPARRING
COMIX
"PEENYONE BUTTE" BASKS IN THE SOOTHING
SHEEN OF A NAVAJO SUN, "KRAZY KAT" COLLS
IN ITS SHADOW, "IGNATZ" IS ACINDERED BY
THE FIRES OF HIS SOUL'S WOEFUL WICKEDRY,
AND "OFFICER PUPP" IS PILLOWED ON THE
BILLOWING LILT OF HIS OWN LAUGHTER —
NOW, UNRAVEL THAT IF YOU CAN -
HOWEVER,
DON'T STOP HERE,
THERE'S MORE FOOLISHMENT
FOLLOWING.
" GEEDEEYAPP."

SPACE-TIME DRIPS FROM THE UNIVERSE OF DEATH. THE PLANETS SWOON AND SWAY FAR AWAY FROM MOTHER BLUE

WINDING WATCH WHILE LURKING OVER EARTH, DEITIES GRIND THEIR JAWS AT 3 A.M. THEY ARE GIDDY WITH THE GRAVITY OF THE SITUATION

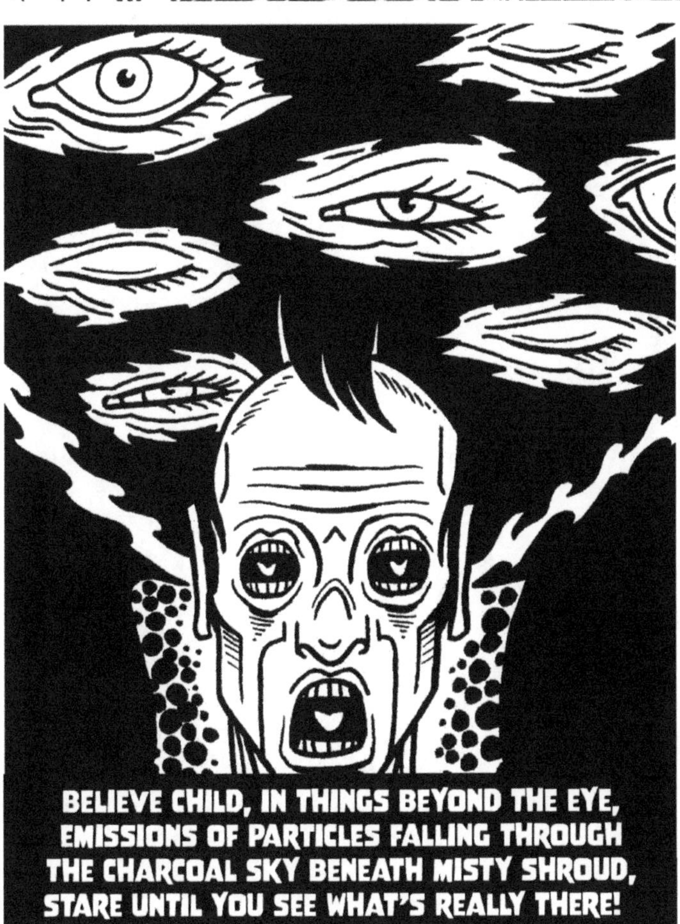

BELIEVE CHILD, IN THINGS BEYOND THE EYE, EMISSIONS OF PARTICLES FALLING THROUGH THE CHARCOAL SKY BENEATH MISTY SHROUD, STARE UNTIL YOU SEE WHAT'S REALLY THERE!

OLDER GODS!
BY YARYAN & FITZ

FROM MOUNTAINS, MONUMENTS AND MINUTE GRAVESTONES BELOW,

NEW CREATIONS -- FROM OLDER GODS -- WALK AMONG US EVERY MOMENT.

THIS DISRUPTS MORTAL FOCUS, RICOCHETING BETWEEN SCREAMING SOCKETS AND BRAIN WATCHERS PEERING AT THE MENTAL PICTURES.

A BELIEF DEAL WAS NEVER REACHED. HORN-HEADED BEASTS ARE CONCIEVED AND FLOAT FROM GODDESS MAMA'S UMBILICAL CORD IN THE MATERNITY WARD OF GALACTIC MADNESS.

AN OLD GOD GLOATS AT THE MAGNIFICENCE.

THERE'S RESISTANCE TO TRADING NOTHING FOR SOMETHING WITH THE COSMOS.

SUPERNOVAS JOIN WITH CONSTELLATIONS TO TEASE ASTROPHYSICS.

PERCIEVED REALITY IS ECLISPSED.

BABA KNO WARE GROWS TIRED OF --

-- WAITING FOR THE BLUE PEBBLE TO IMPLODE.

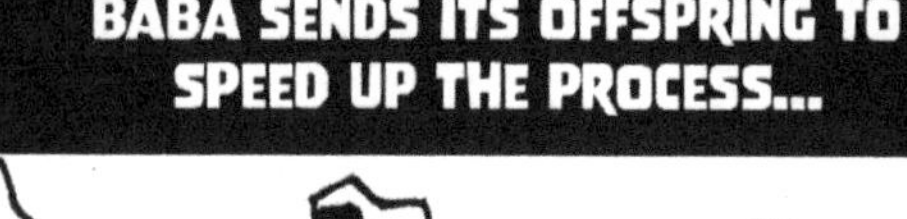

BABA SENDS ITS OFFSPRING TO SPEED UP THE PROCESS...

AND SO, THE CORROSION BEGINS!

KEROUAC'S FAVORITE:
KRAZY KAT by George Herriman

SIMON WARNER, Founding Editor, brings you special Beat features, interviews and reviews with a musical twist weekly online with *ROCK AND THE BEAT GENERATION*

simonwarner.substack.com

Check out a unique space where **Kerouac** and **Dylan**, **Ginsberg** and the **Grateful Dead**, **Burroughs** and **Patti Smith**, **Cassady** and **Tom Waits**, **Corso** and the **Beatles**, find common ground!

PAINTING BY MARC OLMSTED

And watch out for a new print edition: THE BEST OF ROCK AND THE BEAT GENERATION
Coming soon from Mystic Boxing Commission!

I HAVE A
DREAM

FEATURED COVER ARTIST MIKE STREET

MEDUSA PISSED OFF (FROM MOUNT OLYMPUS BELOW THE TREE LINE SERIES) BY MIKE STREET

Native Angeleno artist Mike Street has spent most of his life in Southern California. Like many kids, he began scrawling crayon drawings on book endpapers and blank walls. In hindsight, he now extends apologies for that unbridled enthusiasm. His first art mentor was eccentric grammar school teacher Louise Wise who introduced Street to artists of the Renaissance, Gustave Dore's imaginings of Dante's Divine Comedy, John Tenniel, etc. - and of course studio drawing and painting. The class assignments included copying old masters like Constable, Reynolds and Gainsborough. Some of these attempts still hang framed in the family home.

In his small private high school and college, Street became the go-to "art guy" for events, yearbooks, publications, billboards and posters, films, theater set designs, etc. They were playgrounds of varietal opportunities for a creative self-starter. At Loyola Marymount University he met his next art mentor and dear friend Pauline Khuri Majoli, a direct pupil of Stanton MacDonald-Wright. Beyond college, Mike pursued further classes of personal interest at Otis/Parsons and Art Center. That being said, there is no real formal educational pedigree. Just "Street smarts." A year of independent studies in Paris under the tutelage of Rod Abrahamson, a pupil of Fernand Leger, was a game changer. Besides spending countless hours in European museums with his indelible art history heroes, Mike found the trip to be an important transformative period of becoming more comfortable in his own skin and experiencing a bigger cultural picture. He recalls speaking to Man Ray on the telephone, in French yet. It was in Paris that he reinvented his painting style into a more colorful, psychedelic expressionism.

As a longtime resident of Los Angeles, Mike was never far from the entertainment industry. His peculiar stop-motion animated short film IN THE GARDEN premiered at the Fox Venice Theater in the mid-1970s and attracted the attention of Academy Award special effects winner Jim Danforth. His introduction and recommendation to legendary producer/director George Pal led to a collaboration on a Hieronymus Bosch film project. Like most Hollywood notions, the feature film never got beyond the pre-production sketches.

Street also enjoyed a long relationship with Barry & Enright Productions creating the graphics for their game shows, most notably "The Joker's Wild."

Once the art gigs dried up and beating the pavement became wearisome, Mike decided to "get a job." He found a position with Pottery Barn/Wlms Sonoma Inc. The rent could be paid, and there was food on the table. He was the Regional Visual Manager of the West for Pottery Barn for 25 years. Upon retiring, he returned to his fine art roots about 15 years ago and maintained an exhibition studio at The Hive Gallery in Downtown L.A. for about 10 years.

Known mostly for his drawings and paintings, Street often works in thematic series choosing various media, achieving continuity in the presentation. Among them have been the Forest of the Suicides, HOLLYWOODland (juried prize winner), Mount Olympus Below the Tree Line, Dance, Gold, etc. His conceptual series L.A. Dolce Vita recontextualized snapshots of the Southern California art scene into imaginary black and white Italian film stills. The show was reviewed by critic/curator Mat Gleason and published in the Huffington Post. https//www.huffpost.com>entry/la-dolce-vita-artist_b_8067448

Although somewhat layered, Mike Street's art is accessible to most. Nothing too complex. His interests, editorials and memories tend to bubble up often with a sense of humor - nature, cinema, fairy tales, religion, design, etc. He is interviewed in Mat Gleason's Modern Art Blitz episode #80 part 2.

-- *SPARRING ARTISTS STAFF REPORT*

GENTRICIDE BY MIKE STREET

GIANT PANDA (FROM THE RED SERIES) BY MIKE STREET

3 IMAGES: LIPSTICK / CONJOINED DANCERS / PANDORAS BOX BY MIKE STREET

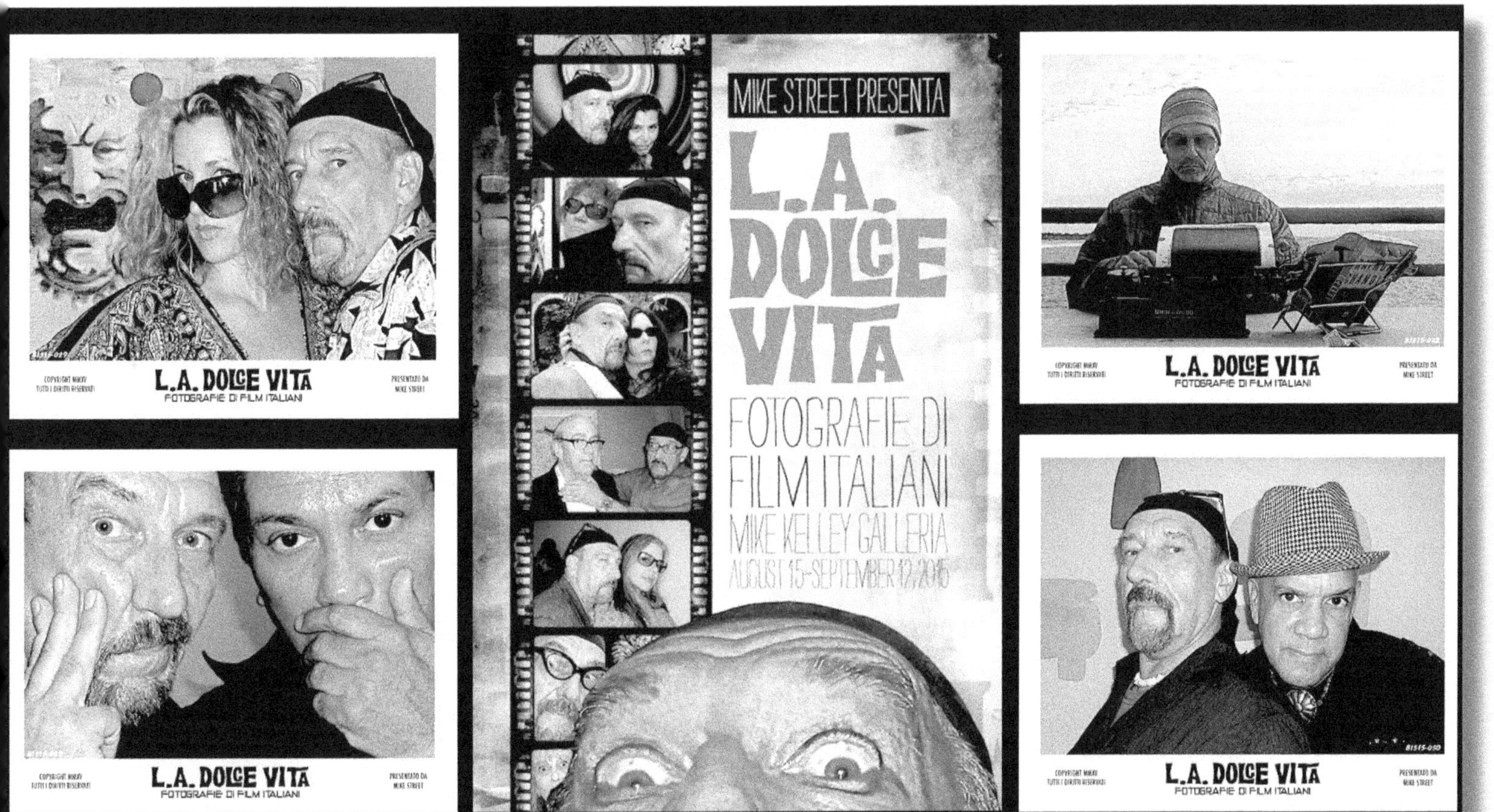

L.A. Dolce Vita Series by MIKE STREET

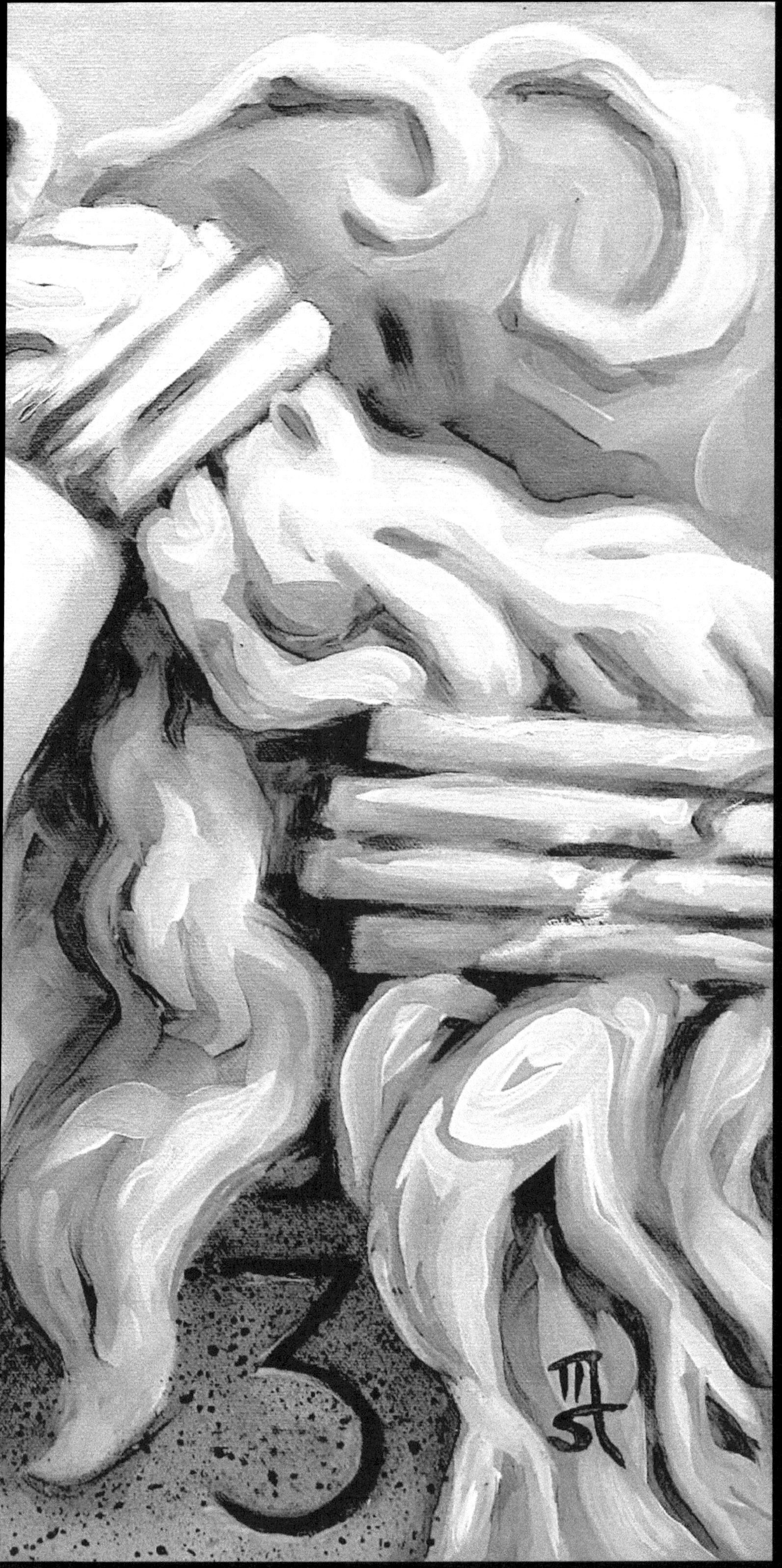

THE SPARRING Artists

FEATURED COVER ARTIST MIKE STREET

SPHINX
WAKING

from Mike Street's Mount Olympus Below the Tree Line series

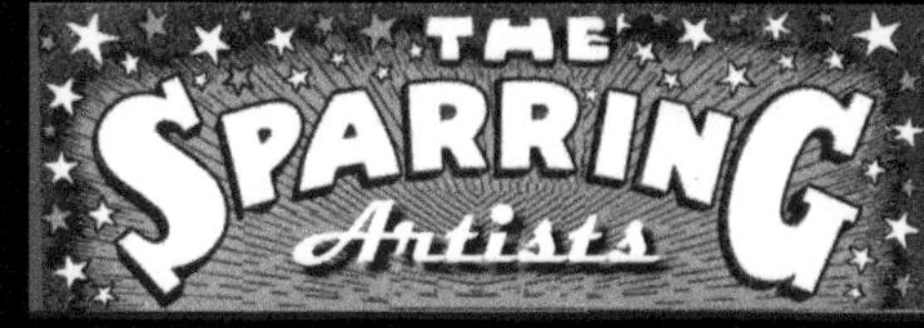

TOM WAITS & MICHAEL C FORD COLLAGE BY YARYAN; WITH MARK SULLIVAN

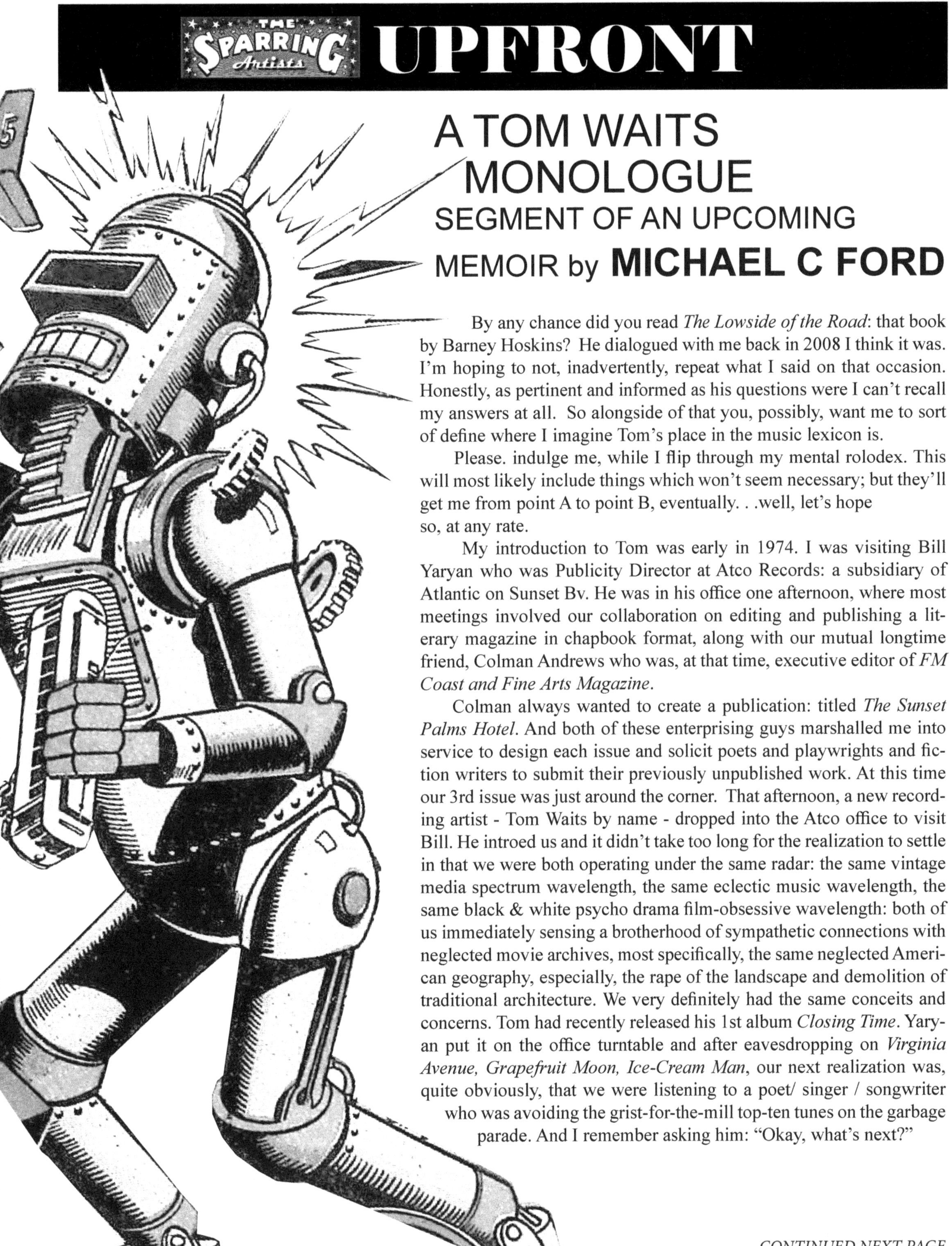

A TOM WAITS MONOLOGUE
SEGMENT OF AN UPCOMING MEMOIR by **MICHAEL C FORD**

By any chance did you read *The Lowside of the Road*: that book by Barney Hoskins? He dialogued with me back in 2008 I think it was. I'm hoping to not, inadvertently, repeat what I said on that occasion. Honestly, as pertinent and informed as his questions were I can't recall my answers at all. So alongside of that you, possibly, want me to sort of define where I imagine Tom's place in the music lexicon is.

Please. indulge me, while I flip through my mental rolodex. This will most likely include things which won't seem necessary; but they'll get me from point A to point B, eventually. . .well, let's hope so, at any rate.

My introduction to Tom was early in 1974. I was visiting Bill Yaryan who was Publicity Director at Atco Records: a subsidiary of Atlantic on Sunset Bv. He was in his office one afternoon, where most meetings involved our collaboration on editing and publishing a literary magazine in chapbook format, along with our mutual longtime friend, Colman Andrews who was, at that time, executive editor of *FM Coast and Fine Arts Magazine*.

Colman always wanted to create a publication: titled *The Sunset Palms Hotel*. And both of these enterprising guys marshalled me into service to design each issue and solicit poets and playwrights and fiction writers to submit their previously unpublished work. At this time our 3rd issue was just around the corner. That afternoon, a new recording artist - Tom Waits by name - dropped into the Atco office to visit Bill. He introed us and it didn't take too long for the realization to settle in that we were both operating under the same radar: the same vintage media spectrum wavelength, the same eclectic music wavelength, the same black & white psycho drama film-obsessive wavelength: both of us immediately sensing a brotherhood of sympathetic connections with neglected movie archives, most specifically, the same neglected American geography, especially, the rape of the landscape and demolition of traditional architecture. We very definitely had the same conceits and concerns. Tom had recently released his 1st album *Closing Time*. Yaryan put it on the office turntable and after eavesdropping on *Virginia Avenue, Grapefruit Moon, Ice-Cream Man*, our next realization was, quite obviously, that we were listening to a poet/ singer / songwriter who was avoiding the grist-for-the-mill top-ten tunes on the garbage parade. And I remember asking him: "Okay, what's next?"

CONTINUED NEXT PAGE

The Sunset Palms Hotel #4 featured a piece by Tom Waits with cover art by **CHARLES BUKOWSKI**.

"...Tom would never allow his soul to be placed on the commercial chopping block."

—*Michael C Ford*

Tom replied: "I'm working on a new album, man, and I'm calling it *The Heart of Saturday Night*" And I said: "Of course you are! I mean, I was pretty sure you were not the sort of composer who would name his recording project *Rainbows & Unicorns*." Anyway, a lightbulb went on over my head and I said: "Tom, the Venice Poetry Workshop meets every Wednesday at Beyond Baroque art gallery on West Washington in Venice and that's tonight, so, if you're free, bring lyrics you're writing for the record and read one to members of the workshop." I told him the two directors of the workshop were very aware published writers. Joseph Hansen was a Noir mystery author and had published his poetry in *The New Yorker* of all places. John Harris was a mountaineer and a poet and I'd published work by both writers in the 1st two issues of *The Hotel*.

Well, long story short: Tom reads Diamonds on my Windshield and one of the more competent writers to emerge from that workshop Jim Krusoe says "Hey that sounds like a song!" and Tom explains that he wasn't planning to sing it but treat it like a spoken-word track. I told him my plan was to publish Diamonds in the 4th volume of The Sunset Palms scheduled to happen right around the same time *Heart* would be breaking [to coin a phrase] and he said "Why sure and I'll see to it that the record label mentions your periodical as the original source of print." Well, his generous notion was, quite naturally, never respected and about which Tom stated later that he was sick about and I already comprehended the myopic negation by record company robots. *Saturday Night* was followed by a recording session in front of this handpicked invited live audience gathered in the main recording studio at the Record Plant, where Frank Sinatra's producer Bones Howe was turning the engineering knobs, as he was on Tom's subsequent vinyl: *Nighthawks at the Diner, Foreign Affairs, Small Change* etc. Interesting note: about the *Small Change* cover graphics: the girl with Tom on the cover is Cassandra Peterson, before she became Elvira. And do you recall that Vampira sued the Elvira character for image theft? However, to defend Cassandra, she was only doing what Vampira had done: cloned Morticia from the Charles Addams gothic 1940s *New Yorker* cartoons. To use the famous gameshow host Donald Trump's favorite catchphrase: a lotta people don't know that! Suppose there might be a little bit of repetition, here, in what I might have said in previously published commentary. But it possibly bears repeating and it's that his many crit-

CONTINUED FROM LAST PAGE

ics have alluded to Tom's - what would you name it - gravel-pit baritone sounding like Louis Armstrong. To be sure, there's a bit of Pops going-on. . . but there's such an original intonation in Tom's delivery: an almost burnt-out aura of aggravated melancholy in most of his vocalizing. So, yeh, throughout an amassing of a catalogue of original music, certainly, much of his mellowing through the years does attest to his continuous striving to perfect his artistry and, by that, further amplifying his creative imagination. The most impressive aspect of what you would dare characterize as a career is that Tom never bartered his integrity of purpose. He never sold out to the rapacity of the Corporation: the veneer of greed and gluttony of the Media meatgrinder. I remember writing something in a1974 *LA Free Press* review with respect to *The Heart of Saturday Night*. Le'me try to paraphrase what was very clear to me at the time. It was that Tom would never allow his soul to be placed on the commercial chopping block. And guess what. . .Waits never did! And I imagine, if he did, it would have been like as if he had the ice cream concession in Hell.

It's theoretical, then, of course, that his flawless and seamless talent would have, justifiably, melted away; just like Wallace Stevens reported happening in his poem: The Emperor of Ice-Cream.

I believe, in many ways and I hope you don't think I'm being gratuitous, here, but I think much of his advanced success was due to Kathleen: I began to believe that she was his camouflage. She was his protection covering. She kept him from going over the edge with possible varieties of substance abuse. She moved him out of harm's way.

This monologue is derived from my own recorded remarks from a November 2020 dialogue with music journalist Barry Alfonso

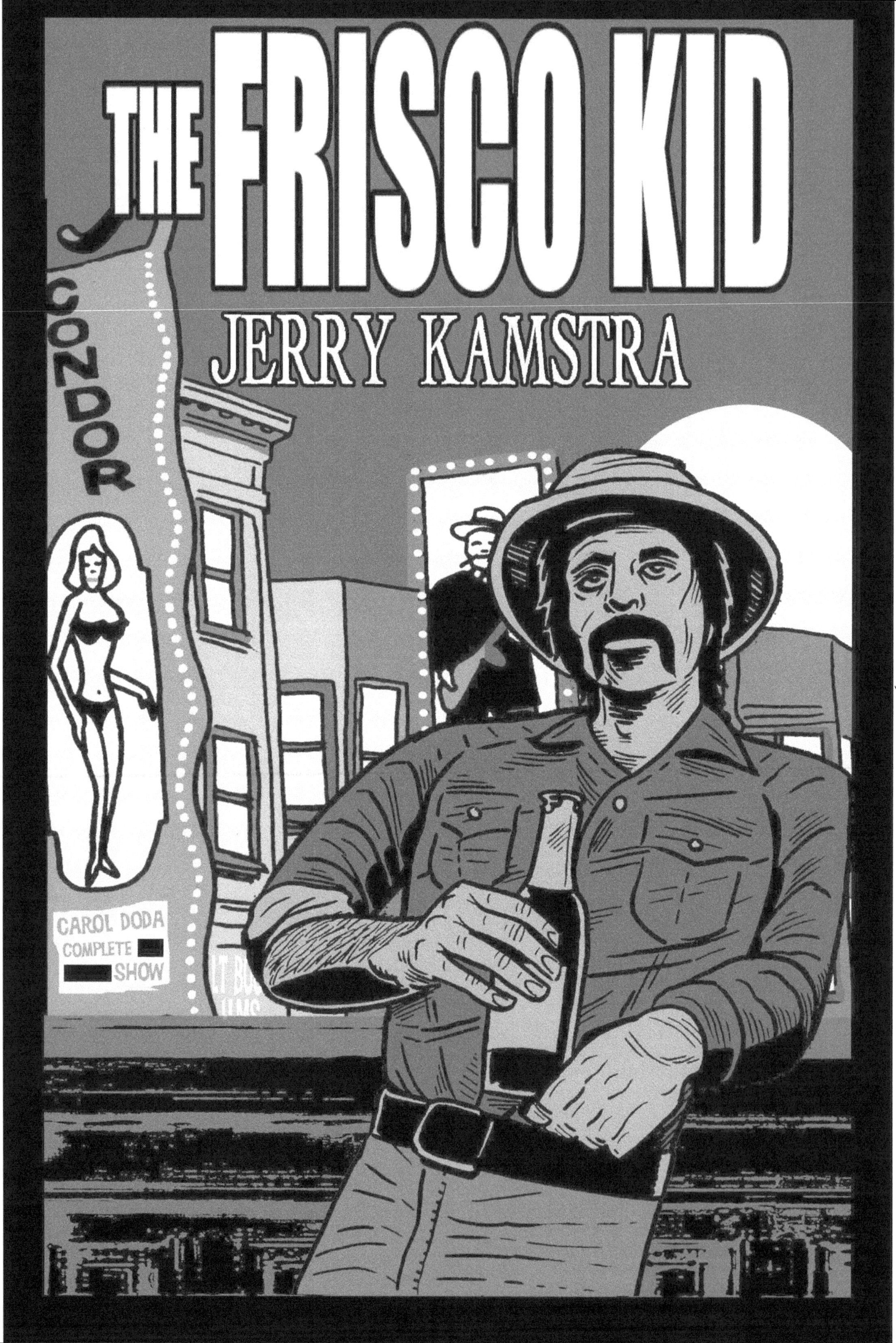

THE FRISCO KID
JERRY KAMSTRA
CONDOR
CAROL DODA
COMPLETE
SHOW
Cover art by FITZ

DISCOVERING "THE FRISCO KID"
BY NEELI CHERKOVSKI

Not long ago I found a photograph of Jerry Kamstra and myself in front of the Café Trieste in North Beach. There he is, tall and lean, ready to talk of the old days when poets crawled up and down the walls, able to soliloquize the least conspicuous characters, and go out of his way to greet them. Jerry romanticized the down and outers or "failed dreamers" as I put it. He was not judgmental, but took people as they came, good and bad. In "The Frisco Kid" one witnesses the goings on of a rare and off the grid neighborhood. Kamstra often said how grateful he felt to document the people he knew on such rare ground.

I cannot date the image of the others standing in the photograph, only Ron Kovic, who wrote "Born On the Fourth of July" is recognizable. This must be around 1979 or so. "The Frisco Kid" stood before us as if the fates had delivered him. I always described Jerry as "one of the taller bohemians," and he is properly tall, wearing a red bandana and looking ready to head down the street for a drink at Spec's Bar, his favorite watering hole. As is typical of him, he knew all the regulars and even some of those who dropped in occasionally

A few days earlier, on a somber evening of heavy drinking, Jerry engaged in an argument about Henry Miller. "Tropic of Cancer is a failed book," someone at the bar proposed, going on to say Hemingway did a much better job of describing Paris and what it meant to be an expatriate there. Jerry could not contain himself. Arguments over literature were in the commonplace life of North Beach, so no one was surprised when Jerry shouted the speaker down with an impassioned defense of Miller. He was knowledgeable without sounding scholarly. It was clear that he believed Tropic of Cancer to be a literary landmark because, as he put it, "The words don't just jump off the pages, they fly off of them." If I had been able to film that moment, I'd do a close up of Kamstra's fiery eyes as he rattled off the famous expatriate's achievements. "Miller had the good sense to avoid San Francisco," Kamstra said. "He didn't get much closer than Big Sur," adding that some of Miller's finest prose was written at his isolated cabin on Partington Ridge, far above the rugged surf.

I told Kovic the story, reminding him that both Miller and Kamstra were real life writers -- adding that there is a matter of fact spoken word quality to "The Kid.". One of the reasons I fell in love with its tightly-woven prose was the open-hearted and unpretentious nature of it, as if the story was being told to eager boys entering adulthood. I mean this as a compliment. The book has a playful and raucous grasp of language that reminds me of the writing I read in my youth. Kamstra is on top of, inside, of, and underneath his characters. The truth is he loves them, no matter their foibles. The prose is shaded with so many scenic elements. I compare it to a series of watercolors or sepia prints – come read and be sure to keep your eyes open. This writer/creator of "The Kid" will give you a visual experience right there on the page.

The magic of "The Frisco Kid" is that the writing reads like a letter, an intimate telling of a golden age when all these madcap things happened to these people in "that" particular place. Today, in a world attuned to the flow of information this book is an anomaly, an important one. To me one of the poetic equivalents to this prose work is Lawrence Ferlinghetti's A Coney Island of the Mind. It has the same straight-forward attitude, and serves as an initiatory bridge to what is seemingly more complex. The truth is that both Kamstra in prose and Ferlinghetti in poetry are hardly simplistic. You may catch the rhythms of North Beach up and down their work. Ferlinghetti thought of San Francisco as an island separated

CONTINUED NEXT PAGE

from the rest of the country. Kamstra tells his readers where he comes from, the small railroad and cement producing town of Colton, California, fifty or so miles east of Los Angeles, a place he abhorred. In high school he learned that San Francisco was a center for bohemian souls and possessed a working-class heart that welcomed outsiders.

I feel fortunate to have known some of the characters who populate Jerry's book. One of them is Hubert Leslie who had come to San Francisco as an artist in the beat a day and by the time I knew him sold the bulldog addition of the "San Francisco Chronicle" at the busy North Beach intersection of Broadway and Columbus. He wore the same blue coat night after night and sported a huge white beard. He was a living catalog of beatnik lore, engaging in just the kind of shenanigans you would find in "The Frisco Kid." When the book came out Hubert wanted to run for cover as he was used to anonymity.

Another person I knew, but only because we saw one another almost every day when I lived in North Beach, was Rosie "the flower lady" who would live on into the early 2000's and die in her 90s. Over the decades I watched as Kamstra's crew passed away one by one and our little bohemia would take one more step towards being like everywhere else. Without the outsiders and literary/ artistic castaways there would be no more 'color,' to the neighborhood.

The Frisco Kid is a paean to a crazy and wild lifestyle that made San Francisco a special place in which to live. There is Paddy O'Sullivan again, a beat pretender if there ever was one and the Coexistence Bagel Shop, hang--out of Bob Kaufman and other beat luminaries and many anonymous dreamers who fit in nowhere else. And there is the Frisco kid soliloquizing and elegizing all of the people he calls "mythological creatures."

It is perhaps the atmospherics of The Frisco Kid that charms a reader's mind. Consider: "The kid turns from the wharf and walk down the Embarcadero past the Balcutga, a three-mastered sailing ship to where hustling, crushing, blooming truck and forklifts hooted and thumped and jockeyed their loads dockward." This is so heartwarming and visuals, a kind of poetry embedded in prose. such language gives layers of meaning to the book and it's unfolding story. A lot of this comes about because of Kamstra's ability to stand back enough so that light and shadow (day and night) become so important. This is the result of keen observation, paying attention to man and his surroundings in such a manner that they are interdependent.

Kamstra and his tale comes to life in many ways. Here's the grand convener in the neighborhood, and a great witness to the comings and goings of his friends and fellow North beach denizens. He does not spare himself: ". . . that night I went up to the Spaghetti Factory – could say and got terribly drunk and became such a mess with myself, leaning over husband's shoulders that were with wives and whining and licking my lips so lewdly that Gary, the bartender, had to tell me, "Cool it kid. You're really making an ass of yourself. "

It must've been a month after I had been with Ron at the Trieste that I sat down with my copy of The Frisco Kid for the second time. So many of us knew Jerry, so you didn't have to point him out to us, not in the real world and not in the text. He's the guy who said "To know America you've got to stand in the middle of the Golden Gate Bridge… The Brooklyn Bridge won't do, nor any of those other Hart Crane green bridges back on the worn-out eastern shores." What I love the best is that Jerry gave us directions to his apartment right there a few pages in: "To get to Roach Alley you walk down Columbus Avenue to Pacific Street and then left to Davis Street near the Embarcadero. I searched all over America before I discovered my home among the warehouses and lofts and abandoned storefronts on the waterfront of North Beach San Francisco."

> **"Kamstra and his tale comes to life in many ways. Here's the grand convener in the neighborhood, and a great witness to the comings and goings of his friends and fellow North Beach denizens."**
>
> **—Neeli Cherkovski**

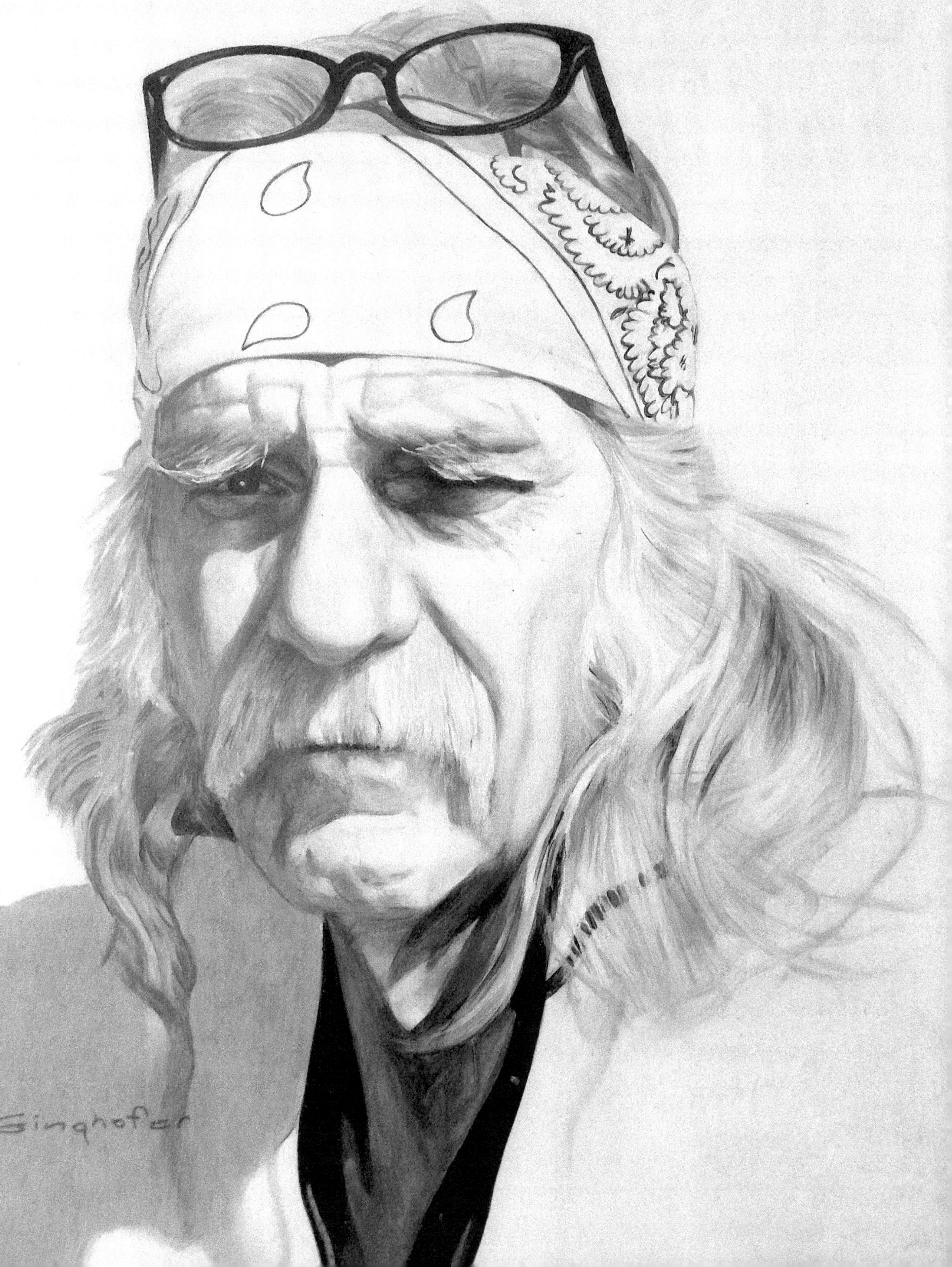

Portrait of Jerry Kamstra by RAY GINGHOFER

CHARLES PLYMELL'S
OVER THE STAGE OF KANSAS

Photo of Charles Plymell by **GERARD MALANGA**

"...this book is an affordable gateway drug to the highs of Plymell poetry."

—Daniel Yaryan

REVIEWED BY DANIEL YARYAN

Charles Plymell's latest book *Over the Stage of Kansas (New & Selected Poems 1966-2023)* is a surrealist joyride of contemplation, exciting encounters and first-hand accounts of a lifetime of adventure outside the mainstream. Plymell and his artist comrades together were a mid-century wild bunch of creative pioneers, hailing from the bullseye of America. Plymell, along with his friends and kindred, artistic spirits of the same region of Kansas were from a group known in counter-culture legacy as the "Wichita Vortex." Charley, as he's known by his close friends and collaborators, sprang from his stomping ground of Kansas with other quintessential Beat-era Wichitans: artists Robert Branaman, Bruce Conner and poet Alan Russo, among others (including famed Beat poet Michael McClure and actor/filmmaker Dennis Hopper). It was a staging ground and springboard for youthful rebellion, unconventional mores, as well as an over-burst of artistic expression. Charley and company were compelled to bee-line their way from the rural, rustic plains of Kansas to the well-springs of bohemianism in California and New York, where they could add to a blooming cultural revolution in the making.

In Plymell's poem "In Kansas" he expresses strong feelings about the Kansas he left in the dust, summarized in the poem stanza as follows:

But in Kansas you may have
the madman's dream,
white whale on the desolate plains.
Or wild strawberries
of a baby's dream
crushed beyond repair

There's a chronology of when his poems were written included in Over the Stage of Kansas, although all the places and times described in the poems defy that chronology, hopping around consistently. Which is suitable because this big 370-page volume stems from many previously

CONTINUED NEXT PAGE

CONTINUED FROM LAST PAGE

published books and chapbooks dating back to 1966 – a hefty sum of them referenced in the table of contents – selected and played in jukebox fashion as you read onward. This is the best Plymell poetry book to purchase and read right now because it gathers the essence of all of those older editions that are now worth some moolah as rare books, hard-to-find chapbooks and out-of-print collections from the Beat-Hippie axis. In other words, this book is an affordable gateway drug to the highs of Plymell poetry. Andy Warhol superstar and collaborator Gerard Malanga edited and wrote the foreword to Over the Stage of Kansas. In his foreword, Malanga states that he finds it inconceivable that Plymell is not a famous poet. "It's a wonder he hasn't received the recognition and respect that came easy to others of his generation," said Malanga. "The fact is, Charley's work represents some of the best poetry being written in America at this or any other time. It just is. Real and honest."

I also agree with Malanga that one of the best poems in Stage is "In Memory of My Father." In it, you get a beautiful glimpse of where Plymell came from:

To you who sung the riddles of that desolate Atlantis
While wind-worn wagons swept a sunken trail into eternal dust.
To your sod, your grass, your easy hills of flint from glacial
slope to wanderlust. "Perfect cattle country . . . the best I've
seen since Uruguay." I'd oft heard you say, your dreams and maps
unfolded beneath those eyes that invented skies, could you
have known the winter owl's alarm where black beasts of angus grazed?
I could not see as far, but went my way, you understood, and
Watched the windmills tell their listless joy to silt and seam.
Life must be beautiful or all is lost . . . those bison of the clouds
were pushed from life . . . slaughtered for sport . . . now they are the
stern clouds watching us from eternity and far beyond.

At 89 years old, Plymell is a poet I'd describe as one of the last "road going," traveling, sojourning Beats. This is re-

flected in his writing throughout this book, such as with "Apocalypse Rose" with imagery such as this…

The hand that strikes the match at night
soon may grasp the torch of liberty.
While a dog tail dipped into a wound
holds the mirror union of the senses

Here's another striking, insightful stanza from the same poem, written by Plymell, who you can tell spent a great deal of time with and was influenced by Allen Ginsberg

CONTINUED NEXT PAGE

(note: Plymell was the first one to turn Ginsberg on to Bob Dylan's music):

Do those who cannot see, love darkness?
Does nightingale trade its song for fame?
Are you in human form, calm once more
With your imploding love to blame?

"Apocalypse Rose" is a brilliant poem that harkened the sympathy for fellow humankind that the Beats embodied, including the plight of people trying to survive on the streets. In one segment of the poem, Plymell ponders the existence of the cruelty and callousness toward the downtrodden, describing a wino dying in a stack of cardboard, then having other winos stacking cardboard and sleeping on top of his long-dead body, described as being "crushed like a rose in a Bible."

There are several poems delving into the day-in-the-life grind of San Francisco streets. Another is this cool riff on "Apocalypse Rose" titled "Petal from the Rose," here's the whole petal:

Baby break that mind trap in time stigmata
through your outline has gone beyond the changes
of the mercury in your flaming youth!

Weary streets of waiting,
*   walking,*
under the marquees of all night movies
on the meat block
where teen-age hustlers cruise.

Market St.
And the moon is full.
We see an old newsreel with the face of Dillinger.
"He smiles on the right side of his face,"
You say, "like Bogart."

Voices in the fog
dispelled the blocks
of waves bright lights hung on.

In Over the Stage of Kansas, there are many phenomenal poems Plymell dedicated to many of his friends and cohorts, including Bob Branaman, actor Dean Stockwell, poet Jack Micheline, John Cassady (with a poem about Neal Cassady and Anne Marie Murphy – both of which were Plymell's flat mates in San Francisco in the sixties).

Yet, the one dedication that I find to be the most powerful is his poem "From the Neo Surrealmic Manifesto (For S. Clay Wilson)." Plymell and Wilson were friends for many years, starting when he first published Wilson in Grist magazine from Lawrence, Kansas. It helped launch Wilson's career, solidified with his inclusion of Zap magazine, not long after Plymell printed the premiere issue of Zap on his Multilith 1250 press in 1968. The underground comix movement was a shared passion of the two friends. After S. Clay Wilson became a famous counter-culture figure and famous artist, he always stayed in constant contact with Plymell – a friendship and correspondence superbly documented in the Water Row Books special artbook edition of Dear Charlie.

Here, is a fantastic stanza that sums up why it is among the top selections in Stage, especially among the dedicated poems:

Do you know something I don't know, man?
Don't let the bolts and liquid wrenches creep
*   upon you*
or the punk ghosts will squeeze the
*   rat cowboy*
*   out of his sleazy hormones*

Probably the most spiritual, signature poem of Plymell's is really the pyrotechnic, fascinating, big-finish offering of the epic "We Heard the Game Lord Speak, His Voice Became the Vision (Animals learn from Nature. Man must learn from Animals to understand nature's reprisal)." This is undoubtedly bound to be the most talked about and is clearly the most visionary poem of Plymell's in this collection. It is sensational; so here's a little snippet from the 14-page poem to wet your appetite for something special that falls into a Robinson Jeffers and William Everson category of high-powered nature-as-conduit-holy-hero zone. This is an area of great interest to me, being a follower of Everson, who was a devout disciple of Jeffers. There is a uniqueness though in Plymell's voice, being one that can morph between the boundaries of humanity's terrain and the natural world. Here is a preview of the poem that conjures up the native images of Plymell's Kansas vortex:

All suffered forever more man animal voice of space void
*   of hands and brains to conquer, attack, render*
destruction in the name power taught in all curricula
*   to become aware of death in first written history*
or discuss afterlife of the abstract gods
*   while elephants sensed their burial place.*

Over the Stage of Kansas (New & Selected Poems 1966-2023) is published by Bottle of Smoke Press and can be found on bospress.net or other booksellers online.

Charley Plymell

Bob Branaman

Kansas City - Wichita 1950's Punks

Oracle #10 cover art by **BOB BRANAMAN**

FEAR OF a HIP PLANet

ARTICLES ABOUT SHAPING AND DELVING INTO COUNTER-CULTURE:

PREVIEW...
The Pain Journal:
Disconnected Notes and Excerpts from a Paraplegic's Diary

by William J. Margolis

I was walking down Grant Avenue one day, enjoying my lack of employment, when a friend, Bob Alexander, stopped me and asked if I wanted a job. But this was no ordinary job; my primary duty would be to be there, to answer the phone, take orders for work – it was a small print shop owned by Bob and another friend, both of them having other jobs. My hours were 1-5pm, and I was free to use the printing equipment, either for jobs they had taken in, or for my own projects and amusement. The pay was only $25 a week for 25 hours (later they raised it to $30), but then, my rent was low and I was picking up a little from the poetry readings and from selling copies of THE MISCELANEOUS MAN.

Late one morning I was sitting in Cassandra's having some coffee and cake before going to work at the printshop, when some friends sat down at my table and started telling me about the magazine they were planning. They asked me if I'd help them, since they knew I'd been publishing for five years. Bob Kaufman, John Richardson and Stan Weitzer told me about BEATITUDE (I think the name was Stan's idea), and about John Kelly, who was to be the publisher since he'd been angel for the rental of a Bannam Alley pad, a typewriter, a mimeo machine, cans of ink and reams of paper. That evening after work I went over and met John Kelly, one of the sweet-

est philanthropic nuts who ever lived. But neither he nor anyone else had known how to get the thing off the ground, so I stared typing stencils, wrote the copy for the title page ("a weekly miscellany of poetry and other jazz designed to extol beauty and promote the beatific life among the various mendicants, neo-existentialists, christs, poets, painters, musicians and other inhabitants and observers of North Beach, San Francisco..."), got Mel Fowler to do the cover art around my St. Francis poem, and everyone helped with whatever talents of organizing, promoting, editing, running the mimeograph, touting, etc., we had; and in one week BEATITUDE #1 appeared. All the poets whose work was included were the salesmen and women, and got a good percentage of the sales proceeds. Kaufman's "Abomunist Manifesto" had been run off on the mimeo a week or so earlier (on the back of some old Republican Party campaign leaflets found in the old Monkey Block!). The Manifesto was also put into BEATITUDE as the last page – and every issue thereafter had further elucidations of the Abomunist message in that space, all written by Bomkauf except an encyclopedic work, "Excerpts For the Lexicon Abomunon," that I compiled by scrambling Kaufman's and my own satirical talents: "ABOMUNISM: n. Footprintism. A rejectionary philosophy founded by Barabbas (cf. BEATITUDE 2) and dedicated to the proposition that the essence of existence is reality essential and neither four-sided nor frinky, but not non-frinky either." "Frinkism" was defined as "A sub-cult of Abomunism, not authorized nor given aboumunitude by

CONTINUED NEXT PAGE

Bomkauf." These "political" works of mine were written under the Abomunom de plume of Bimgo.

For seven weekly issues BEATITUDE streamed & screamed out of Bannam Alley, until John Kelly decided he'd had enough hassle trying to keep us well fed on bread, baloney and cheese from Ken's Grocery, and occasional sit-down meals with red wine at one of the Italian restaurants on Grant Avenue, enough hassle trying to keep various poets from lushing it up (or turning on) in the magazine office and making trouble for him with the landlord, etc. He sat in the office a couple of days, sulking, while Bob and I tried to figure out how to pry him loose from the manuscripts we'd all collected, so we could take them up to poet/minister Pierre Delattre's Bread & Wine Mission, since Pierre had agreed to take up the publisher duty as well as add his poetic wisdom as an additional editor. I think it was Pierre who later referred to BEATITUDE as a "floating crap game."

It was never a very tightly edited magazine – we were after ebullience, eclecticism and eroticism much more than erudition, though some of that, too, got in occasionally, Kelly (whose Abomunom de plume, unofficially, was Outhouse) being one of the most erudite bohemians I've ever met. At one time he had this Chinese poem for BEATITUDE, with the Chinese ideographs drawn on the stencil along with a very rough word by word translation, and he asked everyone to write their own poem version based on this translation. Some very good ones were printed along with the Chinese original. I didn't finish mine at the time, but he really turned me on this way and I did eventually come up with my version. I didn't try at all to stick to the actual original images (which were set someplace in China) but came up with these, released so to speak by the Chinese poet:

AFTER CHANG CHIH

    the moon drops past Russian Hill
    & the birds of the tower hill cry
    goodnights to the coldlonely people
    sadly seeking sweets along the avenue –
    the bells of St. Francis on Vallejo
    toll the new day sleepily & I cry
    in my rocking bed on the avenue's edge…

        There was loneliness in the streets and alleys of
San Francisco,
    and there was also laughter…
    & TIME

    sitting in the coffee triangle
    of traffic lighted afternoon
    and this khaki gold guy

    comes importantly across
    the chromium street
    with the business under his arm

    and i have my feet
    in cool air & time for
    watching

    as he walks on ulcered
    money wheels
    with black cigar tires

…and there was always so much
        excitement – different kinds of excitement at different times, but always some kind of exhilaration, never boredom, and only occasionally might one see some dark-eyed chick in a bar in a pose of ennui…

Grant Avenue was a schizophrenic street. So bright, clear and sunny when I strolled down the hill from my alley nest in the carefully handmade sandals I got from Bob Saunders in return for painting "The Sandal Shack" on his shop window, down the hill past the Italian grocery and butcher shops, the poets' bars, picture frame shop, a bakery where sometimes you could get a fresh loaf of sour dough at 6am if you happened to be there and the bakers and truck drivers liked your looks, strolling down the avenue, pausing to chat with friends, on past the hardware store with imported Italian coffeepots next to the Coffee Gallery, past the laundromat where Bob Kaufman and I infrequently brought our huge Chinese basket of dirty clothes we'd shared, past the Chinese sewing sweatshop factory, Billy Faeir's Guitar Shop, a surplus store, a nod to Benny Bufano's statue of St. Francis, and in the back door of Cassandra's for a cup of coffee and one of last night's bakery goodies at half price for midday breakfast. Mid-afternoon I might come back for a coffee break from the printshop, if I didn't go instead to the Pavoni coffee shop a few doors from City Lights Bookshop on Columbus and Broadway.

At night Grant Avenue was transformed from almost bucolic afternoon serenity to a frenetic, sparkling boil of people, cars, scooters, lights and drifting music. The two places where we spent a lot of time just standing around (when the fuzz wasn't bugging us for it) were in front of the Bagel Shop and in front of the Coffee Gallery across the street. But I think the grooviest thing about Grant Avenue was its proximity to so many alleys that were like old country village residential streets, where the people lived who made North Beach both the community of love that it was, and the tourist attraction that it still is.

The second and third sections of THE SUMMER CYCLES – THE ALLEY CYCLE and THE ANCESTOR CY-

CONTINUED NEXT PAGE

CONTINUED FROM LAST PAGE

CLE – were written to celebrate those North Beach alleys and the sense of community we found there; and they were written in protest against the many and various pressures, harassments, the little and the large tyrannies of the "established powers," the "proper authorities," against our "voluntary minority".

THE ALLEY CYCLE (Preface)

North Beach, that tiny paradise island in the Summer City of St. Francis, the laughing streets climbing Telegraph Hill, the festive familiarity of Sunday afternoon jazz drifting down Grant Avenue, the warm security of its Mediterranean alleys… In those alleys the wonder of North Beach comes fully alive, in the apartments rented from old Italians and Chinese families (whose children may be the very birds & flowers of that hill!) in the rooms made, recreated as the dwelling places, living, loving places of these children of paradise, the beatific lovers of rooftop sun and 4am jazz… It is in these alleys, behind the neon of false fronts & billboards, behind & hidden in that hill, in the flamenco Dolores alleys, the kabuki masked & precise gestured alleys, it is in these labyrinthine alleys that musicians/painters/poets live/love…

ALLEYPOEM, I

in the meshwork alleys
of our days & nights
we figure constellations
on our fingers

& knock on all doors
with friends flinging
bouquets of keys & roses
down upon our heads

& we look up
into our own eyes
& know the buoyancy
of petals drifting

down the live-ends
of our laughter
& in our alleys
we create the birds

of hills & the seas
cascade from our
chiaroscuro lips
& we live

& drink the peace
of windows flung
open to the sky
& the sun

keeps trysts
with shadows
in our alleys…
in our meshwork alleys…

& the way was good
& the way was all
& I am now
just as much the way
(I tell myself)

then as I was now
& forevermore
I have & will be

if being is
& it is
as I know…

KID IN AMERICA

EXCERPT FROM THE BOOK BY

TONY SCIBELLA

Stuart brought me to thebeach.   he brought me here. we met at miltons birthdayball   cholly brought him from thebeach & it was a gd time at miltons likealways being percussive w/miltons old 78's of hamboneblues & we were funny   he liked a couple of the daubs i'd daubed bythen & he give me a lookme up if yr ever at thebeach & oneday i did going to get cholly to front me & stuart wuz there   we stood in chollys room looking at chollys painting which hadgone off the canvas on thewall to the walls around theroom doorframe windowframe back to the canvas on thewall & we leftthere talking & hardly stopped

i had a 1/2hearted paintingjob delivering supplys had the use of a truck & since my dad was my boss i was loose hourlylike him wanting to see me straighten out veteran kickaround school coupleyears its time to settle i'm spoutin vangogh not a nickel pollack themasses in commyscaredydays my dad knows i'm cracked   i wanted some thing somewhere & cdnot possibly say what it wuz but i heard it in blackbars & i thot art/

i started stopping by to see stuart when i had a delivery i'd end the run at the beach & park the truck to walk & talk&talk meeting zen&exivisigist alike   why we came suchfriends we were both at a point in life poised to leap into the void to what? into the eternal lunchbucket to be snapped closed responsible satisfying all qualms of family as to sanity&worth or always or dreaded or alternate or: thelife! bohemianbabes beware two rootinshootin poetfellers ah no it was serious considerations to unfold stuart had his own smallfamily i acquired my own soon after not simple to balance time&frustration wanting the cutoffs the beach&the babes not saying this of course having highdesigns of mansquest inlife & freedom to.
stuart unloaded boxcars i rolled intermittent ceilings sputtering along in our intentions boundbypaint i taught him how to.   onelesson like: its ezy man, any one can do it & he did.   his color was orange.   we went to gallerys showsmuseum wangled ourway into a vangogh 100paintings at the countymo preview/

thru emptyhalls we wanderwhacked by vincent in bold red so who wd not in the parkinglot scream w/joy exultant in belonging?

stuart taught me to write by showing me the pencil. thats how, he sd.   but howlong is the line i ask. as long as the breath, he answer. & that was my longline. 2 words. short words. stuart called it `the cut-

CONTINUED NEXT PAGE

Photo of the author Tony Scibella

CONTINUED FROM LAST PAGE

throat gurgle' & he told me patchen & cummings creely & if i cdnot speak yet i wd.

stuart came a long way from st louie thru newyork as a teen trying to crack the theatergame as an actor or director i forget.   as stuart told it: it was a girl in n y that told him he was gd when he read some verse to her & being the romantic of course it was a lady that gives u yr first as it was for me   the firstpiece i did a lady wanted & took & thereafter introduced me as the artist & it was embarass i had to liveup to it.   i am terrible as to dates as when something exactly happened kind of judging by howold my kids are relating inaccurately to time so if i say i met stuart when melody was 2 fine but i dont know howold melody is now it must havebeen maybe 55 or 6 just before the suicide room came out by jargonpress quite an honor for a youngman starting & this pushed him toward commitment &lipton (who was writing his book & interviewing stuart) gave him a lot of encouragement &being lipton was an `old' published pro-writer: important i know it meansmuch to youth to hear an olderpro in yr own profession say yesucan   go for it.

stuart flung over the edge & took me w/him. opposites: he was political not joining partypolitical more anti-pain like: people puttin the hurt on people anti or bookburnin anti i was a veteran lovedgames of ball & card & horse he didn't i was spade&hondo he was miller&lawrence implied a whole social difference in getting where we stood on thebeach walked thru different schools attitudes of face & nationality

o ho but not that he hadnt read spade or didnt w/urging dig hondo & look forward then to sacketts down the road   he wd read a christie in an hour voracious & how very hip to reach on thewall pulldown a book & read u a verse just exactly what u were talking about & he cd read from the lung the hair on yr neck standing & women fainted overcome i've seen it he'd give'em that stare & rumble that thickthroat voice   the blueeyed mortal jimmy called it, deadly at 20 yds

i dont mean to makefun just remembrance of yesterday & friend but i do think of fun & serioustalk of wife&strife & laffter as utterjoy of life embarking tumult we lived balancing world&word rollingbennies thru the nite stoned on tide&earth raising arms to sky yes! yes!

—Tony Scibella

Part 1
Venice Daze
by Vince Beck

In 1959, I moved to Venice Beach, Los Angeles. The L.A. papers were full of stories about "beatniks" and the wildlife they were leading in the Venice community called "the slum by the sea". 'They' being the "unwashed, the pimps, queers, whores, artists, poets, and musicians, don't forget the dope fiends". These are the people my mother warned me about, I liked it.

I was long, tall and thin as a rail, twenty-four years old, just a few years out of the Marines. I had read Aldous Huxley's "Doors of Perception". I think that had something to do with my coming to Venice. I was ready to open doors, doors I didn't even know existed. In Jack Kerouac's "On the Road", I found a kindred soul. America's nine to five work ethic was not the only option.

For first time in my life, I was seeing how inhibited I was. The freedom of leaving my inhibitions behind, and just letting go. Wow! It was exhilarating, like entering a new world. "ART is LOVE is GOD" L.A. artist Wally Berman wrote on the wall in the Venice West Café. I could dig that.

My hangouts were the Venice West Café, Angelo's Pizza, the Carousel Bar, the 40 Thieves, and then there was the Gas House. When it was built at the turn of the century the place was a casino. In the late '50s the Gas House became a place where artists, writers, and musicians could work, play, or just hang-out. Financed by civil-liberties lawyer Al Matthews, Eric Nord, known in the press as "Big Daddy", was loosely in charge, the "official greeter". It became a coffee house for a while. He was a big guy 6 foot 7, Nord talked about a multi-racial alternative society. At that time these were new ideas to me. I introduced myself to Eric, I had brought along a collage that I made, the subject of the work was "Police Brutality in Venice" …Eric put my collage in one of the windows, there it stayed. When they finally destroyed the place in 1962, my artwork was buried with the building.

My favorite haunt was the VW, the Venice West Café

CONTINUED NEXT PAGE

"Secret" assemblage art by VINCE BECK

CONTINUED FROM LAST PAGE

at 7 Dudley Ave., open from 7pm till 7am for Coffee, Chess, and Conversation. First opened in 1956 by Stuart Z. Perkoff, one of the original Venice poets. When I arrived on the scene John Kenevan had taken over. I can't say much about Kenevan, an ex-Army Officer; he served in Korea, and he didn't seem particularly interested in art or poetry. By 1962 he was getting ready to close the café down, I talked him into letting me have a go at running the place. For about six months I was the chief cook and bottle washer. I served 20 different coffees, starting out with our standard percolator coffee. I think there was only one 2 cup espresso maker. But I had a lot of recipes for different tastes of coffee. I would go out early in the morning, before going to bed, and scrounge food wherever I could, day old bread etc. Each day I made up a good but cheap meal, a stew, or spaghetti ...whatever. I sold a meal for a dollar, people who had no money like Claire Horner ate for free… Claire was a funny guy. His

poetry was an expression of his sense of humor, which was weird, "better to have failed your Wasserman (a V.D. test), than never to have loved at all." He cracked me up. He made "Feely Pieces" out of glazed clay, hung them on string and sold them to tourists.

I loved the time I spent in that place. I put in a radio that was permanently set to a Long Beach station that played jazz 24 hours a day, everyday, Miles, Monk, Horace Silver, JAZZZ! Poets and writers of all sorts were free to get up and share their latest inspirations with us. This was how I first came across Bill Margolis, and many others, the "Beat" Poets; James Ryan Morris, known as Jimmy, Stuart Z. Perkoff, Frankie Rios, Tony Scibella, Maurice Lacy. You can't have poetry without a Muse, enter; Shanna, (I'd seen her around but didn't get to know her till the end of my time in Venice). The dancing Goddess of Venice Beach, a poet's muse, besides being the 'artistic director' for the Gas House, Shanna could be found dancing in the Carou-

CONTINUED NEXT PAGE

sel, a small place that seemed big. It was painted black inside and had no lights except a candle on top of the cash register, and the lights of the juke box. There were two lesbians behind the bar, a roaring "gay" club, funny it was such a fun place to be, but I never had a hassle in the Carousel.

There was an L.A. ordinance against dancing (touching), so the dancers formed a line (it was here that synchronized line-dancing began) and they danced without touching. It was something to see and Shanna was in the middle of it all. Shanna makes pictures, pictures that include her poems. I lost track of her for years. When I got my first computer, I found her living in Hawaii and making pictures that include her mystical poems. She and her work can be found on My Space, and Facebook. At this point I had tried smoking dope a few times, without any mind-blowing effects. One day I was in the Venice West getting ready to open and this woman showed up. Daisy was her name, she invited me to come for a smoke. We got in the car with a couple of dudes I didn't know. We drove down to the oil derricks, parked and lit up. Man, I got stoned! She took me back to the VW. Next thing I knew we were all over each other. We must have had at least six orgasms. After a while she left. I started eating—you've heard of the "munchies", I had them big time. I ate everything in the place then went to the shop to get more, I couldn't stop eating. I don't think I ever got quite that high again.

It was about a half mile walk from the VW to the Gas House. Ocean Front Walk is featured in countless movies. If you didn't want to be seen you went down an alley called Speedway, a block in from the beach. Speaking of movies, they made a movie in Venice with Sharon Tate, "Don't Make Waves". Sharon played the part of a free-spirited beach nymph, the character they were portraying seemed an awful lot like Shanna.

Shanna in the sand
She danced in the sand. Tamboo beat the drum. Weed and cheap wine, the cops called us bums.

I would drop a couple of 'beans' (Benzedrine) and head down the beach, maybe come across a drum circle in the sand. Tamboo, a big black, gentle man playing his conga drum, and his friends would be pounding away on their bongos, Shanna would be dancing with a big crowd around her, or she and Jimmy Morris would be sharing a bottle of Thunderbird wine. For a while I crashed in an abandoned house that was declared public domain by Charlie Foster, a junkie artist / poet who hung out with Alexander Trocchi, author of "Cain's Book". Also living there was a young (18yrs.) painter named Aaron, who was waiting impatiently to be discovered. The only radio in the house played classical music constantly… I craved

> ## "Ben Talbert. When I knew Ben, he was doing what every man secretly aspires to do. He had two women, and there was never a sign of friction—everybody loved everybody. Ben had questions about sex and porn in his art. He would confront the critics and the censors. Ben was still painting with a brush but that was OK, because he was 'Far Out!' "
>
> **—Vince Beck**

jazz. I had to get out of this place! Another time I had a pad on a roof, a small room with running water and a toilet. Great views. I shared that place with Ron Gronhovd who constantly scribbled notes in little journals. Ron was about twenty, we shared a pad for a short while. I think he came from Huntington Beach just down the coast. He had father issues, and he admired William Burroughs. We would meet up four years later in New York City. That's later in the story.

Life in Venice was never boring. The nights of the full moon seemed to be the most exciting. Police cruisers put in an almost constant appearance at five miles per hour, hassling young chicks, and drunks, anyone with long hair, doing whatever they wanted to do, all up and down the beach. Once they knew you, they would try to intimidate you. I favored the "yes sir" approach. Trouble was, after a couple of beers I might get belligerent. (I had a drinking problem for some years—in Venice I drank much less. Still, on occasion I drank too much). Funny, when I got stoned, I didn't care to drink. Today, I can say I haven't had a "drink" in 21 years.

On another slow night, I was contemplating closing early, when a young woman named Sue came in, a dark-

CONTINUED NEXT PAGE

IF SHE SAYS NO....
4 SPEEDS FORWARD
CONDITIONING BEGAN AS A NUISANCE

Collage by *TONY SCIBELLA*

CONTINUED FROM LAST PAGE

eyed beauty with long dark hair cut in "bangs", and lots of mascara outlining her eyes, Cleopatra style. I was interested. She was alone so I bought her a cup of coffee and started chatting with her. Next thing I knew the sun was coming up and we were walking down the beach to Windward Avenue where there were some cheap hotels. I rented a room, and we got high and balled the day away. For the next four or five months, Sue was my woman. Of the many women I've known in Venice, Sue made the biggest impression in my life, among other things she turned me on to some of the most amazing people, Wally Berman, George Hermes, Ben Talbert. Wally Berman's first exhibition was at the Ferus Gallery, 1957. The Hollywood vice squad arrested the 31-year-old artist on charges of displaying lewd and pornographic material. He was found guilty. Berman went to the court black board and scrawled: "There is no justice, only revenge." You can see Wally Berman on the cover of (the Beatles' album) Sgt. Pepper next to Tony Curtis. He died in 1976.

Ben Talbert. When I knew Ben, he was doing what every man secretly aspires to do. He had two women, and there was never a sign of friction—everybody loved everybody. Ben had questions about sex and porn in his art. He would confront the critics and the censors. Ben was still painting with a brush but that was OK, because he was "Far Out!" George Hermes created the "Clock Tower Monument to the Unknown" in 1987 incorporating four huge steel World War Two surplus ball floats left over from the Long Beach Harbor anti-submarine nets. It's located in MacArthur Park. I felt privileged to meet these artists. These guys were artists for the sake of 'Art'. Money may rule, but it could not rule them. Trash, thrown away junk would be turned into Objects of Art, sometimes they even used paint.

Down on the corner from the Venice West Café, was Angelo's Pizza, a popular place to score most illegal substances, 10 Benzedrine tablets rolled up in foil for $2.00—an ounce of good Mexican grass was $15. Anyway, the

CONTINUED NEXT PAGE

Assemblage art by **WILLIAM J. MARGOLIS**

CONTINUED FROM LAST PAGE

juke box was pretty good, and everybody was having a good time when in walks LAPD undercover detective, Gerson. You could hear the pills and various other contraband being thrown to the floor while the juke box played The Four Seasons record "Sherry Baby". Once, on another slow night, Shanna was in the VW in all her advanced pregnant beauty. She was playing a game of chess with some young black dude when three thug looking red necks came in and started to hassle people, they didn't like the inter-racial chess game and started to hassle Shanna. I had water boiling on the stove and a baseball bat under the counter, but just then a couple of the LAPD's finest came in, like out of thin air they appeared, cuffed the thugs and took them away. That was one time I was happy to see the 'heat'. Shanna tells me one of the guys came back next day and apologized, he didn't realize she was pregnant.

The Los Angeles Police force had a game of cat and mouse they played with anybody that looked to be unemployed or had long hair or a beard. I spent many a night in the Venice lock-up. If you opened a beer on the beach, that was enough to get you in the slammer. That's the way it was in '61. I thought the good times would never end. The LAPD harassment would go on and on. Every time I saw a police car, I'd be rousted, "Let's see your ID, where are you going?" Blah, blah, blah… Here's a quote from Shanna, "I remember getting rousted one time, me and Lil' Annie, they put us in their police car and took us way to hell and gone to the other side of town and dropped us off. I called a cab that took us to the Venice police station. In one door and out the other, the police had to pay the cab fare. Gerson was his name He was a jerk! He didn't bother me any more after that. Another time "the one-armed bandit" Mary Lou took off with the goods while the cop used the bathroom… went in one door and out the other with all the pot they had seized from some unlucky dealer…turned the whole beach on, she did… (smile)".

Sept. '62 Vince Beck

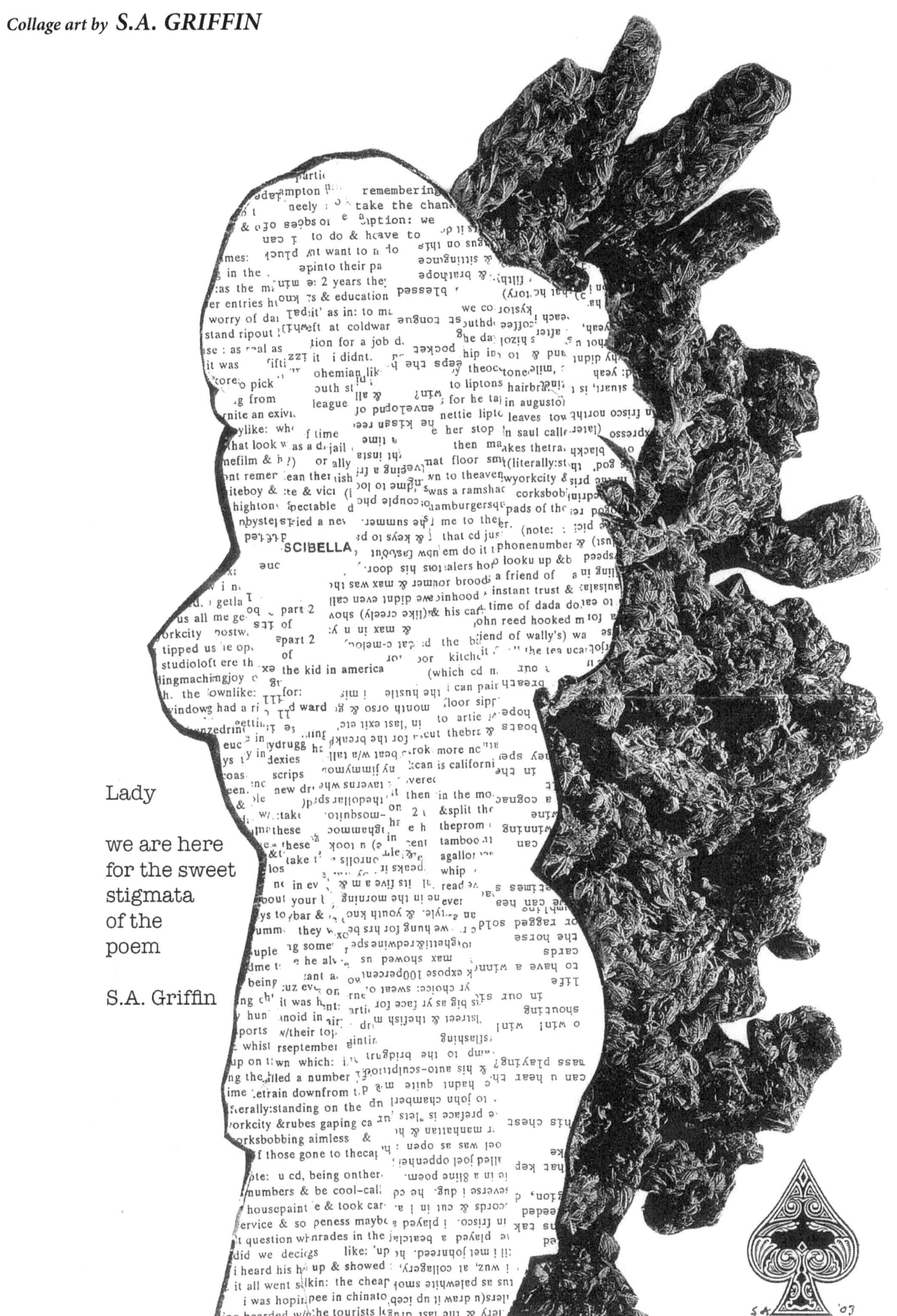
Lady

we are here
for the sweet
stigmata
of the
poem

S.A. Griffin

From PHD to LSD and *POLITICAL ACTION* in the '60s

A Memoir from *Hip Santa Cruz* by

RALPH H. ABRAHAM

(7/4/36 — 9/19/24)

Late in 1967, during my fourth year as Assistant Professor of Mathematics at Princeton University, I took LSD for the first time. Within four months, I had accepted a tenure position at UCSC, and more miracles ensued. This account is from my chapter in HIP SANTA CRUZ, published September 2017.

My prehistory from 1958:

My own story in math started in 1958, when I joined the math department at the University of Michigan. Finishing my PhD in Spring 1960, I was lucky to get my first job in Berkeley. Lucky, because overnight it had become a first-class mathematical center. The governor of California, Pat Brown, had decided that California would follow Detroit into oblivion unless they really pushed science and math education. So, with the aid of a large grant, in the fall of 1960 Berkeley became the home of a number of very famous and capable research mathematicians. Miraculously, I happened to be in this special place and time. After two years in Berkeley I went to Columbia, another excellent math department.

In 1964 I went on to Princeton, and again, I found myself at yet another great math center. I was there for four years. In the first year, I was assigned an honors calculus course to teach. It had fifteen students: one was still in high school; the others were all freshman. They were all great students. When I moved on to the sequel course the following year, they all followed. And for four years in a row, they were my star pupils and eventually all got PhDs and became professors.

Meeting Santa Cruz – March, 1968:

The University of California at Santa Cruz (UCSC) opened in 1965, in the ambience of student actions worldwide. Its college-centered plan was to open a new and relatively independent college of about 1000 students every year for 20 years or more.

In my last year at Princeton, I received an offer from UCSC, and Phil Bell, the new provost of the fourth college, came to Princeton to interview me. I decided to go and have a look, although I had no intention of accepting the offer. So, I went ahead anyway and visited Santa Cruz. I had an interview with Vice Chancellor Clauser; we had a disagreement, and I think that influenced my further history in Santa Cruz in the following years.

I was prepared for Santa Cruz by a couple of experiences I had at Princeton. First of all, there was my first LSD trip, in the beginning of that last year, November of 1967. And secondly, there was my initiation into student politics. SDS was active on campuses, not only in California but

CONTINUED NEXT PAGE

ramtek

throughout the East Coast and even in Europe. I joined a group of students who occupied the president's office: The goal of this action was to make Princeton co-ed, and we succeeded.

With this behind me, I came to Santa Cruz just to have a look, and I was surprised by a couple of things. One was the ongoing political activity on campus, mostly around the issue of the Vietnam war. And the other was the Hip subculture which was flourishing in downtown Santa Cruz. Comparing Santa Cruz in the Spring of 1968 with Princeton at the same time, I knew I just had to accept the UCSC offer.

Berkeley – Summer, 1968:

My transition from Princeton to Santa Cruz was punctuated by a summer conference at UC Berkeley. This was a summer-long event on Global Analysis sponsored by the American Mathematical Society. I wanted to go to that conference en route to Santa Cruz, and many of my Princeton students wanted to go also.

With guidance from the I Ching we invented the Eagle Flying project. We proposed to write a series of new math textbooks, sell the idea to a publisher, and use the money to sponsor our trip to Berkeley. The plan was that the Eagle Flying group, mostly students from Princeton, would, in the course of eight weeks in Berkeley, produce twelve new textbooks for a new math program. We rented a large house near the UC Berkely campus. The Eagles lived there communally while working on these books, and in the daytime we went to the extremely interesting conference at the Berkeley math department.

Santa Cruz, Fall, 1968:

At the end of the summer conference, I moved to Santa Cruz with my wife, Caroline, and sons Peter (age 4) and John (age 3). We bought a derelict Victorian mansion near Santa Cruz High School on California Street, which soon evolved into a hippie commune.

From the first day at UCSC, I got on the wrong side of the Chancellor, Dean McHenry. First of all, I arrived on campus for my initial day of work on a motorcycle. But McHenry hated motorcycles. In those days, there was a kiosk that you had to pass through to get on campus. So, my misdemeanor was reported to McHenry.

The next mishap involved a UC Regents meeting. These meetings rotated from campus to campus, and this particular one was on the UCSC campus in October, 1968, shortly after my arrival. Student activists planned a protest march to greet the Regents when they arrived on the UCSC campus. So, here's my second misstep in more detail.

The Regents meeting:

The Regents meeting on the Santa Cruz campus was the occasion for a massive student action having several goals: the end of the war in Vietnam, more academic freedom, civil rights and lower tuition.

Some of the student activists attacked the bus that was carrying the Regents around the UCSC campus. Although they failed, they attempted to roll the bus over by rocking it from side to side with the Regents inside.

Another part of this protest was a march led by a pig on a leash, and two professors, Paul Lee and me. A photo showed Paul Lee, dressed in his academic robe, and me, in my American flag shirt. Even though that photo was published in the Los Angeles Times, it was just part of my problem.

> ## "Although they failed, they attempted to roll the bus over by rocking it from side to side with the Regents inside."
>
> ### —Ralph H. Abraham

The Bill Moore affair:

At the same time the Regents meeting was happening, we were visited by Bill Moore, who was head of the Black Liberation movement in Santa Cruz County and associated with the Black Panthers in Oakland.

I had arrived for the opening year of College 4. College 5 was in construction and about to open; College 6 was in the early stages of planning; and no one had any idea yet about College 7.

Except for Bill Moore. He was working in Santa Cruz and was aware of the college-by-college growth plan of UCSC. He had an idea for the improvement of the UC System – an idea he called The College of Malcolm X.

I heard about it off campus. My house was next door to Santa Cruz High School. Walking home one night, I heard a commotion going on in the high school. There were some black people wearing red berets and Bill Moore was speaking.

He said that College 7 should be a place that would be home for minority students, which would reflect their culture, their food, their religion, their play, their color

CONTINUED NEXT PAGE

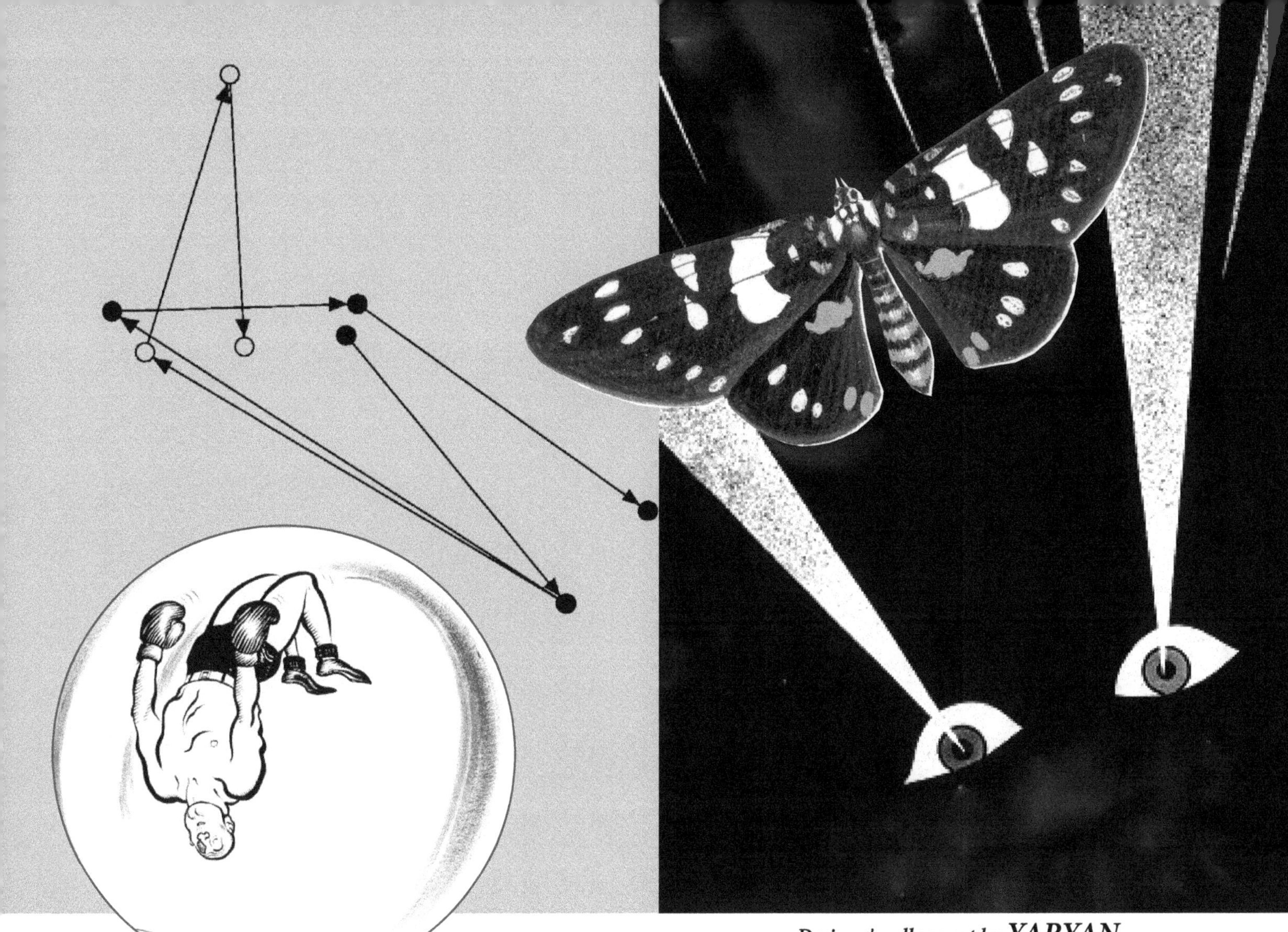

Design & collage art by **YARYAN**

CONTINUED FROM LAST PAGE

schemes, their everything. It would aid attracting and retaining minority students. It should be called the College of Malcolm X, because Malcolm X was a hugely popular leader of minorities, he was brilliant and he was adequately non-passive.

From the stage of the school auditorium, Bill Moore said he had this idea for College 7 but they would not let him speak on the campus. I went up to him after his talk and told him that I was a professor at UCSC and a fellow of Merrill College. "We have academic freedom," I said. "Anyone can speak on campus." And I invited him to speak at Merrill.

But when he arrived at Merrill College to speak at my invitation, he was escorted off campus by police.

So, I was in trouble again over my support of Bill Moore, academic freedom and so on. UCSC tried to fire me. I got a lawyer who saved me. Many professors came to my support because I had tenure – if they could fire me with tenure, everybody was unsafe. Later on, McHenry announced I had won the war with him and he resigned.

There was an interview with McHenry in the library. It had been transcribed and was online. He was inter- viewed by Elizabeth Calciano in January of 1969, just a few months after these events. So, I consulted it and discovered that McHenry had been annoyed by two math professors: Me for my politics and Bob Herman for his beard.

Conclusion:

In the three years following my first year at the University, there were no hires in the UCSC math department. There was a theory for that.

Since I had misbehaved, annoying Chancellor McHenry to the point that he could not sleep and suffered severe depression and since I was in the math department – therefore the math department must be punished. Math could never grow at UCSC because of me.

Some colleagues believed this theory. And I kind of believed it myself at the time. And McHenry was not the only one annoyed. It was my political activity, rather than my Hip Culture affiliation, that caused the problem. This is my memory of 1968.

My move from Princeton to Santa Cruz was among the greatest bifurcations of my life and LSD was an essential trigger.

I have never regretted it.

KINO TRUTH

GODZILLA

By Tony Williams

Something always attracts me about an image often conveniently dismissed as "the guy in the rubber suit" that must have other reverberations than my personal "imp of the perverse" feelings. They manifest themselves in my imagining the creature trampling on the campus, incinerating expensive unnecessary new stadiums and administrative buildings, its fiery breath leaving the latter as a pile of radioactive ash. My first and better Chair in the English Department, a rare person who was honest and protected his faculty, once told me he would leave meetings with higher administration imagining the former Sports Stadium full of their bodies. He actually out-Peckinpah's Peckinpah and is now happily retired writing his weekly columns on baseball.

Yet, other interesting features more than dark wish fulfilment desires governs my fatal attraction to this creature who like so many entities becomes co-opted into a harmless children's toy demolishing other toys in his playroom, seen in *Godzilla (1985)*, used by the grandson of Steve Martin (Raymond Burr in the Ameri-

can version) always there to reassure American home audiences, as he did in the dubbed and re-edited version of *Gojira (1954)* – *Godzilla, King of the Monsters (1956)* – that revealed the great American art of denial as in those Roger Corman produced American releases of 50s Soviet science fiction cut and dubbed for drive-in audiences out for entertainment, or not looking at the screen while engaged in taboo pursuits. Past and recent Hollywood purchases of the franchise see "Big G" saving America and its loathsome families like its Japanese predecessors when the genre became stale or employed for useless spectacular productions.

Yet Gore Vidal's definition of the "United States of Amnesia" is not, happily, 100% effective. Post WW1 efforts to transform Jack London into a children's dog story writer are still not totally successful. Novels such as *The Iron Heel (1908)* still exist. The recent Italian version of *Martin Eden (2019)* re-affirms the vision of the actual novel and first 1913 film adaptation by Hobart Bosworth still survives incomplete but contrasts with the 1942 Hollywood pro-

CONTINUED NEXT PAGE

On My Mind

CONTINUED FROM LAST PAGE

duction *The Adventures of Martin Eden* starring Glenn Ford in giving a faithful adaption of the writer's novel. For every "harmless entertainment" version of Godzilla there exist at least a few welcome alternatives such as the 2016 *Shin Godzilla* that deals more with the intricacies of contemporary dysfunctional Japanese politics than spectacular rampage and which ends with the creature suddenly silent and immobile in Japan leaving this unexpected action up to the film's characters and audiences to consider.

The best adaptations are those that seriously reflect contemporary issues such as Ishiro Honda's first 1954 version that views Godzilla as a symbolic version of the nuclear bombings of Hiroshima and Nagasaki, civilian, not military, centers. The creature makes no discrimination and destroys everything in its path, a brutal expression of the destruction America originally wrought that left devastating psychological scars on a defeated nation. When Dr. Zerizawa (Akihito Hirata)

finally agrees to use his secret Oxygen Destroyer to defeat Godzilla and succeeds, he cuts off his air support taking his information to the deep. Zerizawa does not want his discovery to fall into the wrong hands – and the film implies it is not the Soviet Union.

In my humble opinion, I believe that *Godzilla Minus One (2023)* should have swept the Academy Awards. It is the one film I've seen theatrically, not once but twice after a long absence. I've yet to see *Oppenheimer (2023)* but have viewed the seven part BBC TV production with Sam Waterston (1940 -) in the title role and blacklisted American actor Phil Brown (1916-2006) ironically playing the role of his defense attorney defending the title character in those later dark days. I shall wait for the dubious pleasures of *Barbie (2023)* probably at a University Family Day event or a dark stormy evening where I viewed *Top Gun Maverick (2022)* for free and shed no tears at Ice Man's departure. I much prefer searching for gems such as *Antonioni's China (1972)* and *The Osterwald Mystery (1980)* but I'm digressing…

CONTINUED NEXT PAGE

Written and directed by Takashi Yamazaki (`1969 -   ), like his predecessor Honda, *Godzilla Minus One* represents the return of real cinema, one that functions both as entertainment and serious reflection on issues that concern us today, issues derived from the past that have returned in a similar manner to Godzilla's frequent resurrections heralded at the end of his distinctive cry in previous versions suggesting that a good monster is hard to put down especially one having very serious implications for past, present, and future.

The film opens with young kamikaze pilot Shikisima (Ryunosuke Kamiki) landing his Zero plane for repairs on Odu Island, the place where Godzilla first appears in the 1954 original. However, head mechanic Tachibana (Munetaka Aone) recognizes that the young pilot is reluctant to fight but does not condemn him since all are weary of a war they know will soon end. However, at night Godzilla attacks the repair base killing all but Tachibana after Shikisima is too scared to use his airplane's firepower against this unexpected enemy. Shikisima thus bears a double version of "survivor guilt": his failure to die for his country and cowardice before a superior enemy even though his superior weapons might not have eliminated this pre-radiation incarnation of what would become an even greater threat. When he returns home, he finds a devastated community, the setting evoking those desolate post-war living conditions in the first part of Kenji Fukasaku's *Battles without Honor and Humanity /The Yakuza Papers (1973)*. Encountering his next-door neighbor Sumiko Ota (Sakura Ando) who has also lost all her family, he receives a beating from her puny fists as she blames him for not doing his duty. Although Shikisima aids an orphaned young woman Noriko (Miname Hamambe) protecting a baby (Akiko) that has lost her parents, and begins a surrogate family, he is deeply haunted by survivor guilt while the others bear deep psychological stars from the trauma of losing their families by the dropping of the Atomic Bomb.

Fortunately, this film avoided the temptation of inserting American actors such as a Raymond Burr contemporary successor into a whitewashed narrative for American audiences allowing their 2023 counterparts to consider both the devastated victims of Japanese defeat and the culpability of America, both in wartime and the immediate post-war era. It is never fully explicit but develops the implications within the 1954 original subtitled version, virtually erased in the 1956 dubbed and edited Americanized ideological version.

Recent investigation reveals that the kamikazes were not the suicidal maniacs depicted in American wartime propaganda, but young men drafted reluctantly into these squads, bullied by peer pressure and physical discipline of their superiors. Linda Hoaglund's co-produced produced documentaries *Wings of Defeat* and its

> ## "As many historians now recognize, the real reason for dropping the Bomb was to stop the advance of the Soviet Army into Japanese territory."
>
> **—Tony Williams**

companion *Wings of Defeat: Another Journey (both 2007)* directed by Risa Morimoto, reveal the poignant realities linking American and Japanese survivors as vulnerable human beings victimized by the deadly consequences of that last conflict concluded by President Truman's questionable actions in ordering the use of the atomic Bomb.1 Koji Tsurata (1924-1987), well known for his Japanese genre performances, also survived his recruitment as a kamikaze but also suffered lifetime survivor guilt over the fact that many of his group died on these deadly missions. He appeared in at least three films exploring this issue such as *Ah Yokaren (1968)*, Junya Sato's *Saigo non tokktai/ The Last Kamikaze (1970)* and *A Kessen Kotutai/Father of the Kamikaze (1974)*. This second film co-stars him with Takakura Ken (1931-2014) and Sonny Chiba (1939-2021) while the third three hour one exists on YouTube in a non-subtitled version. Tsurata's role in these three films is worth exploring. He appeared in many genres during his long career in Japanese cinema and these films obviously had a personal feeling for him.

Shikisima eventually finds work on a minesweeper disposing of naval mines left after the conflict mostly by the American Navy. With the exception of young Mizushima (Yuki Yamada), his fellow crewmen are all veterans, and they are prompt in condemning him for regretting his being too young to fight. While they continue to clear up American military debris, nuclear tests at Bikini Atoll manage to mutate Godzilla into a more dangerous form than before resulting in its destruction of USS Redfish and several other vessels. General MacArthur is too busy fighting the Cold War with Russia and offers little help except in donating a few decommissioned Imperial Japanese Navy vessels that will be of little use against a nuclear rejuvenated enemy now armed with nuclear heat rays and superior weaponry courtesy of the American military. Iro-

CONTINUED NEXT PAGE

CONTINUED FROM LAST PAGE

nies abound in this film there for any discerning viewer. As many historians now recognize, the real reason for dropping the Bomb was to stop the advance of the Soviet Army into Japanese territory. The American High command's attitude towards its so-called allies now under its protection is dismissive. To make matters worse, the puppet Japanese Government, ostensibly concerned about not spreading panic, blocks any information reaching Japanese citizens concerning this new danger, an action that would not be taken without the hidden pressures of the American Military Power.

Two years following Japan's defeat, Shikisima's minesweeper receives orders to stall Godzilla's approach to Japan. For those familiar with previous Godzilla films and understanding the deeper implications of the screenplay, this is little better than designating them kamikazes in all but name. The minesweepers are equivalent to those outdated and in-need-of-repair planes the Imperial Military Command employed to send the young pilots on their deadly missions and several malfunctioned on the journey before they reached their targets. Tachibana knows this as revealed in his first encounter with Shikisima. Yet the crew manage to detonate a mine in Godzilla's mouth causing it significant damage that the creature's new regenerative powers immediately allow it to overcome. This forms an interesting parallel to American superior firepower war by attrition that often allowed certain sides to win the conflict both in the Civil War and World War Two. The heavy firepower of Generals Sherman, "Black Jack" Pershing, Patton, and Eisenhower receives its appropriate symbolic incarnation in Godzilla but it is one that cannot be easily controlled – despite false assurances given in past and present. Godzilla easily overcomes the heavy cruiser Takao with its heat ray similar to the Martian War machine's devastation of the British battleship HMS Thunder Child in H.G.Wells' *The War of the Worlds* (1897). Like his 1954 predecessor, Godzilla finally arrives in Tokyo and moves towards Ginza where Noriko now works. Noriko is the sole survivor of a tram attacked by Godzilla, a scene that occurs at night in the 1954 version. She narrowly escapes death, becomes briefly re-united with Shikisima, pushes him to safety after Godzilla uses his heat ray against the tanks that fire against it, but becomes caught in the blast, and disappears presumed dead.

Having lost someone close to him, Shikisima vows revenge. Realizing that America and their puppet Government has left them to possible extermination by Godzilla, citizens and a group of veterans mobilize to find a solution. Shikisima's fellow crewman, Kenji Noda (Hidetaka Yosioka), a former Naval weapons engineer and other specialists plan to destroy Godzilla by enticing it into Sagami Bay, trapping it with Freon tanks, then destroying the items,

CONTINUED NEXT PAGE

resulting in lowering the water's buoyancy so the creature sinks into the lower depths and becomes crushed by the water pressure. Should that fail, then balloons placed under Godzilla will inflate forcing it to the surface and finish it by explosive decompression. Noda also recruits Navy veterans led by Captain Yoji Akitsu (Kuranosuke Sasaki) who will helm disarmed Imperial Japanese Navy Destroyers approved by General MacArthur against Godzilla. The guilt ridden Shikisima intends to fulfil his kamikaze destiny by flying into Godzilla's mouth and detonating the explosives on board the broken-down Kyushu J7W Shinden fighter he plans to repair. On the morning of his departure, he leaves Aiko with Sumiko, subjecting her to another orphan experience in her short life so far.

Opposed to the 1954 version, the solution is not due to one individual character Zerizawa. It is a collective one arrived by surviving veterans who all agree that there will be no return to the Bushido cult of death. Also, no peer pressure is exerted on those who decide not to participate in the venture. It is directly opposed to the type of social pressure seen in one flashback within Clint Eastwood's *Letters from Iwo Jima* (2006). To save the future, these veterans realize that breaking away from Japan's military past is important. When young Mizushima wishes to join the venture, Shikisima and Noda abruptly turn him down. Unlike the Showa Regime military exploitation of young men to serve as kamikaze "cannon fodder", this represents another important break from the past.

Even continuing the kamikaze legacy is mistaken, no matter how noble the intentions are in a defeated world as seen in the concluding scenes of *The Last Kamikaze*. Shikisima seeks out Tachibana who is now a psychological casualty of the War and eventually persuades him to repair the plane which will not have an ejection seat. The image cuts to a long shot as the two men discuss this out of hearing of the audience.

The battle begins. Godzilla survives the initial assault though sustaining serious injuries. Then a group of tugboats arrives like the 7th Cavalry in a Hollywood western led by young Mizushima. He cannot remain apart from the conflict deciding to help his veteran comrades as well as possibly realizing that the battle for the future involves himself – especially if Godzilla wins. The tugboats haul an enraged Godzilla to the surface but just before the creature manages to employ his dreaded heat ray, Shikisima arrives, crashing his plane into the creature and disintegrating its body.

As Godzilla sinks below, Captain Yoji Akitsu and his crew salute a fallen enemy. No dialogue or irritating overlapping commentary, as in the climax of the American dubbed release of Ishiro Honda's *Rodan (1956)*, is necessary. Earlier during the battle, the familiar original

Godzilla theme by Akira Ifukube (1914-2006) occurs. This symbolic nuclear threat has again been defeated on screen. But its consequences remain with us today, whether in Japan or elsewhere. The threat will continue as seen in the last shot of the film where the creature's ominous sound occurs as a piece of its flesh begins to regenerate within the depths.

Unlike previous versions, *Godzilla Minus One* urges a complete break with past militaristic values and a search for new alternatives. There is no longer any need for the Bushido cult of death, now being revived today in Western forms with the West's support of Ukrainian military forces such as the Azov Battalion modelled on the Waffen S.S., and the current remilitarization of Germany and Japan in contrast to post-war agreements to say nothing about the kamikaze tradition which was far from noble but oppressive. Shikisima survives because Tachibana installed an ejection seat into the repaired Shinden fighter. A brief flashback now reveals to us what the two men discussed when the audience was out of earshot. Though blaming Shikisima for the death of his men on Odu Is-

CONTINUED NEXT PAGE

Unlike previous versions, Godzilla Minus One urges a complete break with past militaristic values and a search for new alternatives.

CONTINUED NEXT PAGE

land, Tachibana now realizes that any form of return to deadly ideological values is now impossible and urges the young man to get over his survivor guilt.

On his return home, Shikisima again confronts Sumiko who begins to pummel him with her fists, this time expressing anger at his return to the kamikaze tradition she once venerated. She delivers a telegram informing him that Noriko has survived. He and Akiko rush to the hospital and reunite. It appears a happy ending. But is it? Although she survives, Noriko was swept away in the radioactive storm emanating from Godzilla's heat ray. She is in the category of those Hiroshima survivors who would eventually due from radiation exposure. A black bruise creeping up her neck is visible that (the director confirmed in April 2024) was caused by one of Godzilla's cells. 3 This image coincides with the final sound emanating from Godzilla's flesh as it regenerates in the final scene. The battle is not really over.

Godzilla Minus One is a worthy complement to *Oppenheimer (2023)* but one that needed better recogni-

tion. While *Oppenheimer* focusses on what might be called "an American Tragedy", *Godzilla Minus One* emphasizes the role of the defeated who have to live with the consequences throughout their lives. It has one thing in its favor. The film recognizes that past values cannot be followed and some alterative progressive direction is needed, one that is collective, not individual, respecting the reasons of others who should not be subjected to guilt trips over phony patriotic values. However, as the concluding images show, the struggle will not be easy.

Notes.
1. https://en.wikipedia.org/wiki/Wings_of_Defeat

2. See especially the work of Gar Alperovitz (1936-) such as *Atomic Diplomacy: Hiroshima and Potsdam*. New York: Simon and Schuster, 1965, and T*he Decision to Use the Atomic Bomb and the Architecture of an American Myth*. New York: Alfred A. Knopf, 1995).

3. https://www.sponichi.co.jp/entertainment/news/2024/04/28/kiji/20240428s00041000704000c.html

KINO TRUTH

Review:
Alex Garland's *Civil War*

By Marc Cooper

Don't worry if you have not yet seen it. There are no spoilers. Mostly because there is absolutely nothing in the film to spoil.

The story, set more or less in the present or the very near future, is about an American Civil War that has torn most of the country apart. There seems to be a vaguely Trumpian President in power. He is in his third term and has dissolved the FBI (though we don't know if he did this because he was faced with an armed uprising or were these acts the cause of the revolt).   He is on the verge of losing the war to something called the Western Forces – an alliance between, are you ready, California and Texas!

No, this isn't an intentional comedy. Though the thought itself belongs in a stand-up act. That one detail should be enough to tell you this movie is a waste of time as it has absolutely nothing, zip, nada of substance to transmit. Oh, wait…I take that back. We do learn that War is Hell, a lot of people die, cars and buildings get wrecked, shopping malls are turned to rubble, highways are littered with shot-up cars and, in this case, we also learn that some folks in The Great Flyover of the Heartland are ignoring the bloody, rather apocalyptic conflict and are going about their usual, small daily lives. Choosing Texas and California and secondarily Florida as the spearhead of the rebellion is an obvious, cheap and clunky ploy by Garland to not offend anybody across the current political divide and for the audience to make sure Garland is not taking sides.

I mean, who would want to choose a side in a civil war where the oldest democracy in the world is about to collapse.

The film follows four journalists scurrying to D.C. before it falls so they can get "the big story" with one print reporter determined to get the last interview with the embattled president. Along the way they witness extreme violence, grotesque sadism, burning forests, and they have nothing to say to each other or to us about what is going

CONTINUED NEXT PAGE

Cailee Spaeny and Wagner Moura star in "Civil War." Photo courtesy A24

"The film follows four journalists scurrying to D.C. before it falls so they can get "the big story" with one print reporter determined to get the last interview with the embattled president. "

—*Marc Cooper*

CONTINUED FROM LAST PAGE

on and who is who. Of the four the two photojournalists are the real subject of the story. A world-weary veteran played by Kirsten Dunst and a much younger naïve college aged woman who Dunst takes under her wing.

But so what? We learn nothing. There's even an extended sequence in a civilian refugee camp and even there the film does not stoop to giving voice to a single one of them. And these reporters also, ask no questions. It's phantasmagorical. Earlier in the film, when an unidentified gaggle of armed men are found torturing two captives, again nothing is explained. The younger photog wonders out loud why are they doing this.

And…then..drumroll…spotlight…stop action…close up on Dunst as she is about to speak the key line of the movie, the line that is supposed to win you over to her cynical, remote and unemotional detachment, the line that writer Garland would have us believe unlocks the central moral of the story, the money shot:

Sounding like a Ivory Tower journalism professor of 1957, Dunst lectures her mentee: "Once you start asking yourself those questions, you can't stop," Lee replies sharply. "So we don't ask. We record so other people ask. You want to be a journalist? That's the job."

Journalists are not supposed to ask questions? They are not supposed to provide context, even for photographs. Or is Dunst sloppily speaking only of photojournalists? That doubt has been cleared up by director Garland in several public statements basically affirming that the sentence in question is the whole point of the movie and is precisely the correct position to understand the film and presumably journalism and maybe even the whole wide world.

Garland has said publicly, the movie is meant to be as politically objective as possible. "The kind of journalism we need most — reporting, which used to be the dominant form of journalism — had a deliberate removal

CONTINUED NEXT PAGE

CONTINUED FROM LAST PAGE

of a certain kind of bias,"

"If you have a news organization which has a strong bias, it is only likely to be trusted by the choir to which it's preaching, and it will be distrusted by the others. So that was something journalists used to actively, deliberately, consciously try to avoid. [...] And then the film attempts to function like those journalists. So this is a throwback to an old form of journalism, being told in the manner of that journalism."

Do I really need to take the above apart? Is it not obviously just plain stupid?

Having been a journalist since 1971, I can attest to the fact that there are lot of clueless, detached and deeply cynical, not to mention, plain old mediocre journalists out there. But they are not the really good ones. They are space fillers.

I have worked closely with many combat photojournalists while covering the wars and uprisings in Latin America. They are the most exposed, the most vulnerable of any press corps and by definition they are the most courageous. And I know three who were killed. This specie of reporter is most usually the best informed and also the most passionate and the most engaged. Few people are willing to risk their lives to just take pictures about a cause or a conflict that they don't have some at least minimal stake in. After all, their primary subjects are people, and in order to best capture them they have to know who they are politically, what is driving them etc. and how to best capture that sentiment in an image. And given their vulnerability, they are quite often the best source for safe passage through combat zones. Garland has protested the accusation that the film is abstract to the point, IMHO, of being vacuous.

"I cannot see how it's abstract," he told Polygon in an interview ahead of the film's release. "There is a fascist president who has dismantled the Constitution sufficiently to be able to stay for three terms, has removed one of the legal institutions that could threaten his position doing that, and is causing violence, attacking his own citizens. It might be abstract, possibly, on first blush — but to me, that does not stand up to any inspection at all, in terms of the actual content within the film."

Comically, there's more exposition in that statement than there is the 109 minutes of the movie.

There's also some great irony in the Garland's wishcasting about what makes good journalism. I would argue, as I have for years, that one of the primary reasons the American people are so politically immature, apathetic and irrational is precisely because of the way the mainstream media has always opted for "objectivity," thereby releasing themselves of any responsibility to explain in depth what might really be in play because, you know, that would be partisan. So if Garland's little

> ## "Few people are willing to risk their lives to just take pictures about a cause or a conflict that they don't have some at least minimal stake in. After all, their primary subjects are people, and in order to best capture them they have to know who they are politically, what is driving them etc. and how to best capture that sentiment in an image."
>
> **—Marc Cooper**

crew of reporters had been in Berlin as the Red Army deposed Hitler or near Hiroshima when the US vaporized a hundred thousand civilians, I guess they still would have nothing to say or explain.

They would, in the words of Dunst, "not ask." The producers of the film and Garland clearly made this movie, as all movies are made, to make money. OK, his timing was good and he has cashed in. Bravo. But he doesn't seem to get that his desired muting of an aggressive press is in part what has produced the conditions that make civil war suddenly thinkable in the US. It can be traced back to the media celebration of Trump as candidate in 2016 and the normalization of this dangerous, authoritarian imbecile during his tenure…and to a great degree, once again now during his haphazard re-election campaign.

In the film, Garland makes two references to people in the American Heartland who –apparently untouched by the violence of the conflict — just ignore it and carry on life as usual. Too bad Garland didn't book a ticket to Des Moines and sit out the last couple of years pondering his navel instead of making and then inflicting this trash film on a country already in sufficient pain and confusion without it.

PAIRING UP POETS DESTINED FOR THE STARS!

GET TO KNOW ME

I don't know you
You don't know me
And I don't owe you any pussy
Take me to dinner if that's your desire
But forgive me if I have to put out your fire
I refuse to be one more man's joke
Get to know me before you poke
Cause I'm not into casual sex
You better show me your personal best
I used to be so accommodating
I swallowed all that prevaricating
But it wasn't love just ejaculating
I've done better sometimes masturbating
Sure woulda been better off meditating
I'll tell you something on which you can bet
Men will say anything when they're erect
So don't come around here yanking my chain
Looking for cheap-date pussy and fucking my brain
I am a goddess, I am a jewel
My love is a treasure, it ain't for no fool
Now don't take this personal if this ain't you
If giving true love is your goal to do
I'm just saying I am a queen
I'm waiting for he who would be king

--Kennon B. Raines

ACRES OF BLUE

I'm flying high,
The sky is mine.
Acres of blue
Caress my eyes.
I'm on the move,
I'm in the grove!
I'm feelin' fine!
How about you?

-- Dr. Mongo Taribubu

Part of the exciting new collection...

AVAILABLE SOON:

www.sparringartists.com

CAPTURES

> ## "Astounding images captured of the heroes of punk, the Beats, artists and filmmakers throughout an explosive decade."
>
> **-- Yaryan, MBC Publisher**

PHOTOGRAPHS

1970–1980

Kamera Zie / Pamela Mosher

HARDCOVER COLLECTOR'S EDITION COMING 2025 TO MBC!

SparringArtists.com

All photos: Copyright © 2024 Pamela Mosher

Special Feature:

Linda J. Albertano
R.I.P. 4/17/42 – 9/6/22 
Photo by
Alexis Rhone Fancher

COLLAGE BY YARYAN

Dear Charles,

On the road with Alice Cooper. I be real evil six nights a week. The crowd loves the badness to pieces. 60,000 strong, times three nights in a row, at Joe Lewis Stadium in Detroit. From behind the Sludge Monster's cage, I see 1000 points of light. Not the President George H.W. Bush kind. No. More like the rebellious rock-fan roach lighter kind.

As the cruel Nurse Ratchet, I shove a doll-baby in its carriage onto the stage. Soon the doll will be impaled at the end of a sword for the winsome tune, "Dead Babies." But for now, I pluck its formula from its tiny mitts and brandish the bottle fiendishly above my head. Except for the night they secretly substitute a dildo for the baby bottle, and I find myself waving a wobbly large-caliber rubber thing at the cheering crowd.

Later, when Alice is trussed in a strait jacket, I'll stomp up behind him armed with a giant syringe. Kicking him to his knees, I'll plunge the trick needle deep into his neck and draw out what appears to be a quart of blood. I'm despicable! The fans are delirious with hatred.

Then, as I scratch furious notes on a clipboard, Alice slips from his bindings and throws them around my neck. I flail like a salmon thrashing at the end of its line. I gasp! I tug at the garrote at my throat! I claw at the air with both hands! Finally, I collapse. A colossal roar of approval erupts from 60,000 tattooed, pierced and slavering fans! And so, I am dragged away, a glow of perfect achievement inwardly warming me.

After the show, a devotee will invite Alice to a party. "Thanks," he'll respond, "but I've got an embalming to get to."

Dee-troit! We crash in the Omni Hotel. Oh, Detroit. Detroit. Where covered catwalks high above the city lead to luxury eateries and displays of opulence heretofore unimagined. But. In Detroit. If you push open a door at ground level, you'll enter a world of squalor and despair populated by hobos and costermongers, cut-purses and down-n-outers. Where the clerk at the corner convenience store cowers behind double layers of bullet-proof glass.

We live in relative splendor on the tour

CONTINUED ON PAGE 73

Linda
by Frank Lutz

Photos courtesy FRANK LUTZ

Over the years - decades - people have asked me about Linda, her background, where she is from, how we met, and so forth.

Linda J. Albertano had her first poem published in the early 1960's in Orange County, California when she was nineteen years old. During the following sixty-one years, she would develop prominence in poetry, performance art, music and film. She performed and worked her arts in the USA and other parts of the Western Hemisphere, Europe and Africa. The number of venues, theaters, and stadiums where she performed, plus small clubs and private showings, can be counted in the hundreds. Her poems were published in dozens of magazines and poetry anthologies.

This very tall lady was brilliant, beautiful and loving of people. She had a kind and generous nature. She was helpful in many ways to those in need. All of this despite the tragedy and neglect of her very young years, and the abuse she suffered in foster homes. She overcame it all, and so let her be an example for those young women now and in the future who aspire to be poets and artists.

Linda spent the first eight years of her life with her family in Utah, Montana, and finally Denver. At age eight, when her brother Jim was only four years old, their father abandoned the family and accused their mother Alberta of not being able to care for the children, which was untrue. This is just one reason Linda's support for Women's Rights was unwavering throughout her career in all of her art disciplines.

Alberta was a fine person. Very loving of her children and an artist, as Linda would become. Linda always said, "Any good qualities I have, I got from my mother".

Her father falsely and maliciously reported Alberta to Denver child "welfare", who took the children and put them into foster homes, and worse, separated them into different homes! Both Linda and her brother Jim would be treated to several years of neglect and abuse in the foster homes, which would have a negative impact on them for the rest of their lives.

FRANK LUTZ, CONTINUED NEXT PAGE

The work of award-winning poet, performance artist, actor, and musician Linda J. Albertano and her husband of 55 years, Frank Lutz (pictured with Linda above), is collected in ON THE LIFE OF LINDA J. ALBERTANO, including poetry, stories, and prose, as well as memorabilia from Linda's astounding performance career. Go to www.lindajalbertano.com for ordering information.

FRANK LUTZ, CONTINUED FROM LAST PAGE

Linda was often not allowed to eat meals with the foster family and treated more like a domestic maid than a child. Linda went on to become an honors student both in high school and in college at University of Colorado, Boulder. At age nineteen her father remarried, and her step-mother refused to fund Linda's University of Colorado tuition or expenses. (Contrary to some misinformation about her, Linda was born on April 17, 1942, and not 1952.)

So her weak-minded father gave her $50.00 in spending money and a one-way ticket to Los Angeles, where Linda knew no one! Linda struggled in LA, doing odd jobs until she was discovered due to her beauty and height, when she started to work doing modeling and some TV work, including as a regular friend of the Monkees on their TV program, as well as The Ozzie and Harriet TV Show.

For a time, she was also the Space Girl at Disneyland, and she appeared in the movies Mary Poppins and Beach Red, an Academy Award nominated film. She was also developing her talent as a guitar-playing Blues singer. Linda Ronstadt and The Stone Poneys and Taj Mahal recorded at least one of Linda's Blues songs called "The Two-ten Train" on one of their albums, During the mid-1960's Linda made two trips with the USO during the Viet Nam War as a dancer-singer with an all-girls troupe to Viet Nam, Cambodia, Thailand, South Korea, and Japan.

In 1966 she enrolled at UCLA to complete her higher education and get a degree. Because of her excellent grades, obvious intelligence, and lack of family support, UCLA gave Linda a grant and scholarship money to attend that great university. Her Senior Class film was voted by students and faculty in the Film Department the Best Film of the Year when she graduated in 1971.

When I met Linda she had no family support, nor help from anyone else. She did all of this on her own.

It is also interesting to note that Linda Albertano was the first female member of Gold's Gym, Venice, having joined in 1970 when she was in UCLA film school, to get her arms stronger for carrying heavy camera equipment.

CONTINUED FROM PAGE 70

bus…furnished with refrigerator, indoor plumbing, tables and captain's chairs, TV's and DVD players PLUS two ultra-comfy lounges separated by cozy, stacked bunk-beds where we sleep after each show while the bus whistles through the dark to our next gig. We do six cities a week – a clock whose second hand is rapidly spinning. When we learn that Luther Vandross stays one full week at each stop – a clock ticking verrry slowly – we're incredulous and envious.

But on we roll, to Phoenix, where leaves rustling across the sidewalk whisper, "Barry Goldwater, Barry Goldwater." Of course, today, they'd whisper "Joe Arpaio, Joe Arpaio." But that was the late eighties, and people still remembered.

We get a one-day holiday in Breaux Bridge, Louisiana. I drop in to Mulate's for red beans and rice only to discover Dewey Balfa and Brothers singing their lids off in Cajun French and every living body, adolescent or ancient, small or tall, frail or burly is whooping it up, dancing as though one foot is nailed to the floor while the other gyrates wildly! "Chank-a-Chank!" as they say in zydeco.

In Cleveland, where department store clerks actually assist you, I fell in love with a white-haired gentleman in the luggage aisle. I'd have married him on the spot, but he wouldn't sign a pre-nup, and that was a deal-breaker.

I jest. Performers are the lettuce-pickers of the entertainment industry. So the dancer, the sludge-monsters and the evil nurse earn just enough to keep them in heavy-metal jewelry and black eye-shadow. Shopping is what you do on the road in a new town in the afternoon before the show. Alice Cooper knows the location of every "Chess King" extreme accouterment retail store in America!

Rolling across farmland, we see the names of porno-flicks hand-painted on the side of a barn in thick, crooked black letters. Instead of roadside produce in the bucolic landscape, we're offered bushels of flesh. Alice slides open a window and shouts, "What's this, America? We give you the Farm Aid Concert and you give us, 'Debbie does Dallas'!!?"

So when we get to Chicago, I decide to explore a local porn shop. I look tough in a long, khaki army overcoat, working the stub of a frayed cigar into lip cancer. I shoulder my way to the back where the magazine rack stands. A ragged line of guys are fingering the plastic covers with their hot hands. Yeah. At six-foot-four-inches tall, I tower over all of them. I'm like the monolith in the "Space Odyssey" movie. I catch a few startled glances whilst I paw through the goods. I see porn of every description from tasteful fat-lady erotica to grainy black-and-white newsprint pix of the private parts of 80-year-old grannies.

Something for everyone! I purchase a couple of handsome gay-guy mags for me and the whip-dancer and take my leave.

All the performers and band members on the bus are into health and fitness. Alice put down Johnny Walker for good after he was found living in a motel wearing a diaper and sporting six-inch fingernails. Now he imbibes only juice and soft drinks that he, himself

CONTINUED ON NEXT PAGE

ALICE COOPER

has opened for fear of unknown and pernicious spiking of his beverages. The lead guitarist, Kane Roberts, is a genuine big-biceped body-builder. Kip Winger, the bass player, is as beautiful as a matinee idol and intends to keep it that way. So, conversation on the band bus goes like, "Hey. Where'd you score the low-fat cottage cheese?"

The crew, however, still bears the torch of decadence aloft. They're men who've skirmished with luck and lost. Their bodies sag like spent mattresses. Their smiles are full of black holes, dense and massive. No illicit substance, no general debasement, no off-limits act is too depraved for their amusement.

We've been touring with White Snake, Guns and Roses, Alien Sex Fiend and assorted bands with Big Hair. One of whom brings a naked groupie decorated with whipped cream into the dressing room on a dessert trolley. As the tour feminist, I feel compelled to pull her aside afterwards and encourage her to form a union with the other groupies. After all. They ought to be remunerated for their labors.

And because the destination on the front of the bus reads "Show Us Your Tits" (all in fun, of course, but it silently enrages me), the whip-dancer and I make bumper-stickers for the back of the bus reading, "Reveal Testes or Perish!"

When I appear in my bald-head wig as the black-robed executioner, I am Regina Dentata, the Queen of Teeth! Soon Alice Cooper will be dragged to my guillotine and strapped down there while I raise the blade. Then, whoosh! As if by magic his cranium will roll into the basket at my feet. I'll snatch it by the hair, and make a dramatic show of kissing his dripping, gory lips. I'll stride to the edge of the stage holding his head high and grinning diabolically. Then, I'll reach into his cold, dead skull to squeeze a bulb filled with a viscous red fluid which Alice's grim head will vomit into the screaming, writhing crowd. The End.

Except that Alice is resurrected in white tails and a top hat for the anthem, "School's Out for Summer." His disciples are ecstatic! The stone has been rolled away from the mouth of the cave, and the cave is empty! Easter has come early this year. Good times!

I keep having this dream. For a prank, I take Alice's fake head to a party. The door is thrown open, but no one laughs. They're horrified! I look down and realize… I have the wrong head. It's someone else's real dismembered head!

Hey! Long Beach in three weeks. Hope you can make it. Wear a blood-bib anywhere in the first three rows. And be sure to stay for the embalming after the show!

Hugs,

Linda J.
Evil Nurse and Executioner

LINDA J. ALBERTANO
MAJESTIC LANDFILL

In order to cut carbon, they'll soon be serving grubs and mealworms
on intercontinental flights.

If insects can't out-crawl, out-skitter or outrun extinction, can birds
or bipeds be far behind?

At least we've halted salting the sea with plastic straws.

But some of the juices that feed our Teslas are wrung
from fire-breathing plants.

And not the kind of greenery squeezed from the flaming orange orb
that incrementally boils us in our own sweat, either.

O, diminutive human beings... are we the only species stuck on self-destruct?

Lemmings lunge after their leaders over cliffs. Yet lemmings abound.
Hope in a storm of despair?

A modern bard foretold this catastrophe when he sang,
"It's the Slow Consumption killing us by degrees."

Sing, people! Sing! Whilst our stumpy legs carry us to the eternal landfill
in the sky.

Sing!

Originally published in Maintenant 16, Summer 2022

LINDA J. ALBERTANO
TO THE PACIFIC

To the Pacific!
Who is older than wisdom.
Who is shrinking like the slow death of thought.
Who is caught in a storm behind our ribs.
Who finds her rhythm in the delirious
        heartbeat of night.

It's dark.
Where were we when the lights went out?
Who poured the last round?
It's dark.
It gets dark in here fast.

To the Pacific!
Who throbs in our improbable bodies.
Who breathes us in and out.
Who sings between earth and Orion.
Who makes us feel taller than trees.
Who suffers the weight of our pain.
Who's been trained to submit to our whims.
Whom we'd bring to her knees if she had them.
Who's been trapped in a terminal brothel.
Whom we've cast in an X-rated movie
        and we're waiting to watch her bleed.

It's dark.
By the nature of our deeds we're dirty.
We're bound in our own senseless chains.
It's dark. How long can this last?
It's sad. Is it criminal? Or criminally insane?
It's dark in here.
It gets dark in here fast.

To the Pacific!
Who surprised us with the curious
invention of life.
Whose intentions were purely honorable.
Who stirred our first shimmering cells.
Who helped us crawl up on her shores.
Whose blood still roars in our ears.
Whom we've caged like a laboratory rabbit
blinded with stinging rain.
We're boys pulling wings from sparrows
        obliviously nonchalant.
We spend her like sailors on benders
        ignoring her desperate eyes.
She's kidnapped for the intangible joyride.
She's dropped in the vestigial ditch.
How quickly we tire of our toys.

CONTINUED NEXT PAGE

It gets dark.
It gets dark in here fast.
We are pushing her past her prime.
We shout petrochemical lies!
Time sticks in our indecent throats.
It gets dark, it gets dark, it gets dark in here fast.
And where were we when the lights went out?
Where were we?

To the Pacific...
          to her we belong!

She holds no wrongheaded notion of justice.
She builds no concrete tomb for our lungs.
She forces us to feed on no poison.
She hangs us from no twisted tree.
She rids us of no personal medfly.
She plants no bomb in our gut.
She crushes no skull for freedom.
She nails us not to the ground.
She studies us not into extinction.
Her changes are slower than rivers.
History melts in her mouth.
She'd deliver us from evil if we'd let her.
How long have we been lost?
And where were we when the lights went out?
It's dark. It's dark.
It gets dark in here fast.

To the Pacific!
You are bluer than our insignificant eyes.
You are saltier than the tears we cried
          when we heard you might die of
                    our neglect.
We're killing you with exquisite indifference.
You've washed our feet with your grief.
We're gathered on the courthouse steps.
We're bargaining one more plea.
We're praying they'll spare you from us.
Our blood is screaming your name!
We're tearing up the deed to your being.
We'll love you more deeply than death.
We're prepared to pay the better price.
We'll rip the tainted needles from our veins.
Our blood is screaming, is screaming your name!

We are about to become more serious.
Where were we when the lights went out?

To the Pacific!
Older than unbearable wisdom.
Shrinking like the pointless death of thought.
Caught in the fire storm in our heads.

Tattooing the sacred skin of night.
Pounding in our hopeful bodies.
Breathing us in and out.
Shouting Hosannas under Orion!

Drench us with unquenchable life!
Your waves are breaking deep inside!
Your blood is roaring in our ears!
You are dreaming us awake!
Make us feel taller than trees!
Dance us in your pagan arms!
Your drums are beating on our shores!
We're comprehending what you'd have us do!
We're sounding louder alarms!
We long to be truer believers!
We'll be strong in our will to prevail!
And we belong, we belong, we belong to you!
It's to you that we belong!

You've made your mark on our souls.

But it's dark in here.
Don't let the lights go out.
We're about to become more serious.
Don't let the light disappear.

Don't ever
let the light

disappear.

— *LINDA J. ALBERTANO*

Artwork by
GEORGE REITER BRILL

IRIS BERRY
LATCHKEY ME

Don't worry
about me
I'll be ok.
I'm that kind of girl.
I'm a tough cookie.
The kind of girl
that won't take no
for an answer.
I do not like
to let death
get the last word
so I will continue
to celebrate
those who I love
long after they are gone.
I learned as a child
don't rely on
instructions
life doesn't come with them.
But whatever it takes
figure it out.

I grew up
a latchkey kid
in the middle of a circus.
Nothing lonelier.
I always wondered
who am I?
And why am I here?
And I have always
found ways to create
through my feelings
long before
I knew that's what I was
actually doing.
With a homeless heart
from the start,
I've always
made the best
of bad situations.

And If I could reach
This knife
In my back
that you left behind
I'd bedazzle it.
I'm that kind of girl…
I'll be just fine.

"Alice Meets Alice" collage art by **T. MIKE WALKER**

LYNNE BRONSTEIN
THE GILDA GOWN AND THE LOMBARD SCAR

The strapless gown
Didn't just unzip.
("I'm not very good with zippers," she said).
It had a corset inside.
It would have taken many fingers
Unlocking little snaps
That cinched the natural
Curves into a willowy wave.
The men wanted to unzip her,
Unsnap and un-corset her,
And so did she-----
For different reasons.
Rita and Gilda
Wanted to be free.
Free to breathe,
Free to speak her mind,
And free to be naked, refreshingly real.

Rita had black hair,
Dark eyes, olive skin.
The movies dyed her hair vivid red,
Blitzed her forehead hairline,
Powdered and painted her face,
And starved the flesh off her.
"I'm decent," said Gilda
With a toss of flaming hair over bare shoulders.
A decent box office return.
Love goddess, sex symbol,
A face affixed to a test bomb,
A slithering body down on her knees, crying,
A shimmying dancer,
A bond woman to the studio sharks.
She said her trouble was that her men went to bed
With Gilda and woke up with Rita,
Not Hayworth but Rita Cansino,
Teenaged Spanish dancer adrift among horndogs.
Years later, on the set
Of one of her last movies, she told
A younger star
"I used to be beautiful like you."

A genius at lighting
Was a guide and personal savior
For Carole Lombard
So that no one would see
That scar on her left cheek,
Made by a sliver of windshield glass,
Remnant of a night out partying.
She endured stitches, drank her meals through a straw,
Only to end up with a grim reminder.

Still, she sought a career. She mugged
In Sennett slapstick, dodging the cream pies,
Switched to tight gowns and screwball comedy,
And found the camera man whose lights restored
The pure face she'd had at seventeen.
Makeup and that big dimple when she smiled
Helped too.
But it's there, the Lombard scar
And she couldn't say she got it from a duel.

She arrived at a party
In an ambulance, made up as a victim
Of an accident, like the one
That made her scar.
She talked with the grips and the gaffers
On the set, not with the gossip queens.
She ignored a psychic
Who told her not to get on that plane,
And they found some strands
Of her light blonde hair
And a script she was reading
For her next film role.
No one found
The plan in her head
To be a director of films
That would be burned up
Along with the scar,
The symbol of her
Survival.

Millions try,
Using every product and every technique,
To emulate the perfection
Seen on the screen.
Two women who are
Part of the legacy now,
Without their corsets and makeup
Are real and raw and probably
More like you and me.
When we bathe in our fantasies.
Living the lives of old Hollywood
Do we dare to be Rita without the Gilda gown
Or Carole with her scar?

"Screen Door" artwork by JOHN SEABURY

AMERICA

MIKE BRUNER
CRICKET PUNCH

"A magic enchantment for children trained to produce yet another safe performance."

Summer never ends for the owner of a magic lantern ready to fill their precious hours with sweet forgotten pleasures.

Believe it or not, when you select this new foreign language it's a way to clarify thought and make your good summer great.

Only rigorous testing of our character in business can calm wise anxiety and make the day supreme; only varying degrees of ignorance with a strong, deep hold in your very own home can stop these first impressions of a fashionable foreign range of exclusive designs from setting the new party's theme and having everyone over for the latest paradise.

So, branch out you travelling companions of the new generations. Get hold of these daydream expeditions made to charming spots and lost horizons.

Count on it. There are guardsmen on the other end of the motors not allowed to enter the looking glass, as any excuse will do when people contain their generation.

So, let's make it a marvelous party, you engineers of empire, for life goes to the smart pros who know it's simply in style to know a compelling interest unseen by all the others.

Be the true thrill of a brighter beauty spot that refreshes and says "show us."

Forget the not quite bright enough agencies that wash out the superlative and assist to stop the positive, and don't you settle back in admiration of the momentary dizziness of the Hollywood movie of the moment.

You can have a wonderful summer's music to last a delightful lifetime with quality to carry over and comfort to boot, if only you dare to illustrate the customs as scenes made by motion picture craftsmen for a feeling of confidence that gives what stands supreme its top touch tuning, and what agents hide in the Chairman's finest speech announcing an event of great national importance and what it does to our world.

You will be richly rewarded with gossamer voices bringing home wisdom herself, and taken through a great treasury to ascertain the exact lines of the right choice.

Those cathedrals of pain and exiled castles in the air, and all it costs to help the sufferers offered up as craftsmen, absolutely ruined, do give direction to how you are feeling in the mirror surface, though you pass on through it to your ultimate remarkable discovery. There, no experts can give the definite name of the present, as the greatest of blessings is personal eyesight serving you well and a liberty born in good trouble.

And, once there is a folk tale the sun never sets on that helps our challenged heritage, you order your copy and chase the latest bought power to achieve a humble kind of reliability among the great and the free. You discover the new renaissance made by old time company men who now can see the century as it should be, with a precious phase of workmen's compensation that insists on helping to let you breathe. You even become a permanent fit for the will to ask for evidence against the general pain of the real and to protect our new encyclopedia from anger.

CONTINUED NEXT PAGE

Or, how about the famous triumph of listening you can read in the great actors' faces after they agree to the corrections on the next page or on who they may please first in a fast surrender.

So, it's worth knowing that the sign of a world in need is the corporation as the finished product everyone is after because success may save your life. The master's voice more molten and smoking that ever, while the cheapest regard of the apparently white and whiter marketing board system speaks in frightful volumes of cleaner, fresher, smoother every minute.

But, you profit with safety by your new instinct to be the emperor who could only buy the perfect gift and the natural celebrations of today.

Do you, as an artist, bring that certain empire?

Do you found glorious knowledge or rule as a player on an island of pleasurable leisure?

Are you the new chivalry of stirring deeds and better ideas or that ever-present legacy of winter's bedlam? As the one in command, do you own the great prescription that helps heal our future or are you too confused by the marks of winter and how words can't quite describe the steady cold marks on what's living in all of the shade, or how all your leading senators want total advantages and all the gold?

So, I long for you to bring me a gentle pressure to bear in the matter with smoother and extra sensitive conversational openings as doors to a better story and a way to say what even the eye cannot do: to accept this fresh drink of cricket punch as king and keeper of the key.

Hold the life of the wild in your hands and travel this wonderful branch of a happy science that can't be observed in any other way, then send me the protection of your distinguished army and navy made of best principles and earned salvation that corners the globe.

For another war is coming and here's one in progress, and only a few can predict the perverted justice in all the great demolition work, or the giant will it will take to protect us enough from the latest old problems again.

Don't be a product or tool of reaction, but expect to get a quality picture of how to have glowing health in winter's gloom and a special first-class universe to be happy in. It is our season to ask for year-round as the rest is the silence there to defeat us.

There's a tale to be told about free opinion ready to branch out and the difference between making what's lovable and the effective disguise of the real assumed by the public. So, don't get too comfortable with the commonplace, and be careful to look out for the subtle charm of an old edition taken for the new.

For we are the perfect makers of the world order we become in going through discovering our glass to see the worst political argument about to take off with us.

Who will defend the glorious instead of the plain mask?

Why is there only so much one can do with all that is wrong with the times?

So, forget the correct-shaped notions worn deep, and remember to take back the most famous advancements in life and be the health of the light.

8/29/22

SPARRING ALL-STARS SERIES
Word Troubadours
ELLYN MAYBE & PJ SWIFT

PETER CARLAFTES
THE TITLE DOESN'T COUNT

some moons past —once
this cowboy-type colleague
invited me to see
Journey in concert
so I went along

general admission
no seats on the floor
the place was mobbed
first come/first serve
and there we were
me and him
at the very back

this position
didn't sit well
with my colleague, so
he literally
plowed through
forty rows of
closely-knit people
breaking couples apart
banging folks to the side
one row at a time
and these people
were pissed
yet I kept up
through the clearing
created behind him
shrugging at those
who were screaming a-fit
until we both got there
in front of the band
and as I gaped back at
the tangled mess of fallen
my colleague slowly began
tapping his right foot
with a shit-eating grin
and I think about
all the years
my country
forced its way of thinking
down the souls of others
and I followed
maybe griping
but followed just the same
right up to now
repeating
human fate
on the heels of
neither side

Artwork by **CLEA JONES**

AMERICAN EXPERIEN

Neeli Cherkovski: Truth, resistence, transformation

Introduction by Richard Modiano
Photo by S.A. Griffin

I first met Neeli Cherkovski in the summer of 1976 during a visit to San Francisco (I lived in New York City at the time.) Marc Olmsted introduced us, and over the decades I saw Neeli whenever I visited San Francisco. Our last in person meeting took place in October 2018 at the Beyond Beat four-day extravaganza that I co-produced with S.A. Griffin at Beyond Baroque Literary/Arts Center when I was director there.

Neeli was a remarkable figure in contemporary American poetry, whose work and life embody the spirit of literary resistance and authenticity. His poetry reflects the legacy of the Beat Generation, but he added his unique voice, bridging the exuberant spontaneity of the Beats with a quieter, more contemplative tone. Born in 1945 and raised in San Bernadino, Neeli was deeply influenced by the countercultural movements of the 1960s, and his poetry is infused with a sense of urgency, rebellion, and deep humanity.

Cherkovski's poetic style is unpretentious, conversational, and grounded in the everyday, yet it conveys a sense of universality. He explores complex themes such as love, death, politics, and the human condition without ever losing touch with the personal and the intimate. His verses often meander like thoughtful conversations, engaging the reader in a reflective dialogue. His use of language is direct but layered with meaning, drawing readers into a world where emotions, ideas, and memories collide.

In addition to his own poetry, Neeli's contributions to the literary world extended through his friendships and collaborations with key figures in the San Francisco Renaissance and the Beat movement. As a biographer of Charles Bukowski and Lawrence Ferlinghetti, Cherkovski offered insight not only into these poets' lives but also into the shifting cultural landscape they inhabited. Neeli's *Whitman's Wild Children* is a captivating tribute to the spirit of the Beats and their literary lineage, and his Elegy to Bob Kaufman, reverberates with admiration and loss, capturing the complex essence of Kaufman, a poet who

CONTINUED NEXT PAGE

CONTINUED FROM LAST PAGE

merged jazz, surrealism, and political consciousness into a powerful, untamable voice. Cherkovski's words mirror Kaufman's spontaneity and visionary intensity, honoring his legacy as a cornerstone of modern poetry. Neeli's understanding of the broader poetic tradition and his role as a cultural historian made him a vital link between different eras of American poetry.

Neeli's work is rooted in the belief that poetry should speak to the people, not just to the elite, and that it should engage with the struggles of the times. This commitment to social justice and personal freedom resonates throughout his work. His long-standing involvement with poetry communities, including his role as a co-founder of the San Francisco Poetry Festival, showed his dedication to creating spaces for poets and readers to connect.

Cherkovski's poetry may be quiet in its tones, but it carries the weight of experience and an unflinching honesty. It's a testament to his artistry that his work continues to inspire new generations of poets, reminding them that poetry can still be a vehicle for truth, resistance, and, ultimately, transformation. Rest in power my friend – your voice lives on.

—Richard Modiano

Illustrations of Lawrence Ferlinghetti and Bob Kaufman by **SOHEYL DAHI**.

Charles Bukowski and Neeli Cherkovski photo by **SAM CHERRY**

(Above) Poets David Meltzer, Cherkovski, Sharon Doubiago and A.D. Winans at Beat Reading, April 2010 at North Beach Library. Photo courtesy A.D. Winans

Cherkovski

A.D. WINANS
POEM FOR NEELI CHERKOVSKI

poet friend of fifty-two years
a lyric bard of magical words
a hummingbird who spun poems
like a master weaver.

You danced the dance
to the end of the line
kindness in your heart
poetry in your soul
a city boy with a country heart.

Your poems take root
this windy Thursday afternoon
marinate in my head
walk the North Beach streets
we were wed to.

gone but not to be forgotten.
a blue jay in the green garden
of my mind.

SPARRING WITH BEATNIK GHOSTS

ANTHOLOGY
Bird & Beckett

Arntson

Blackwell

Booker

Camincha

Cherkovski

Cook

Dodger

Nails

Siegel

Xandra

Yaryan

Plus: Li Po Features

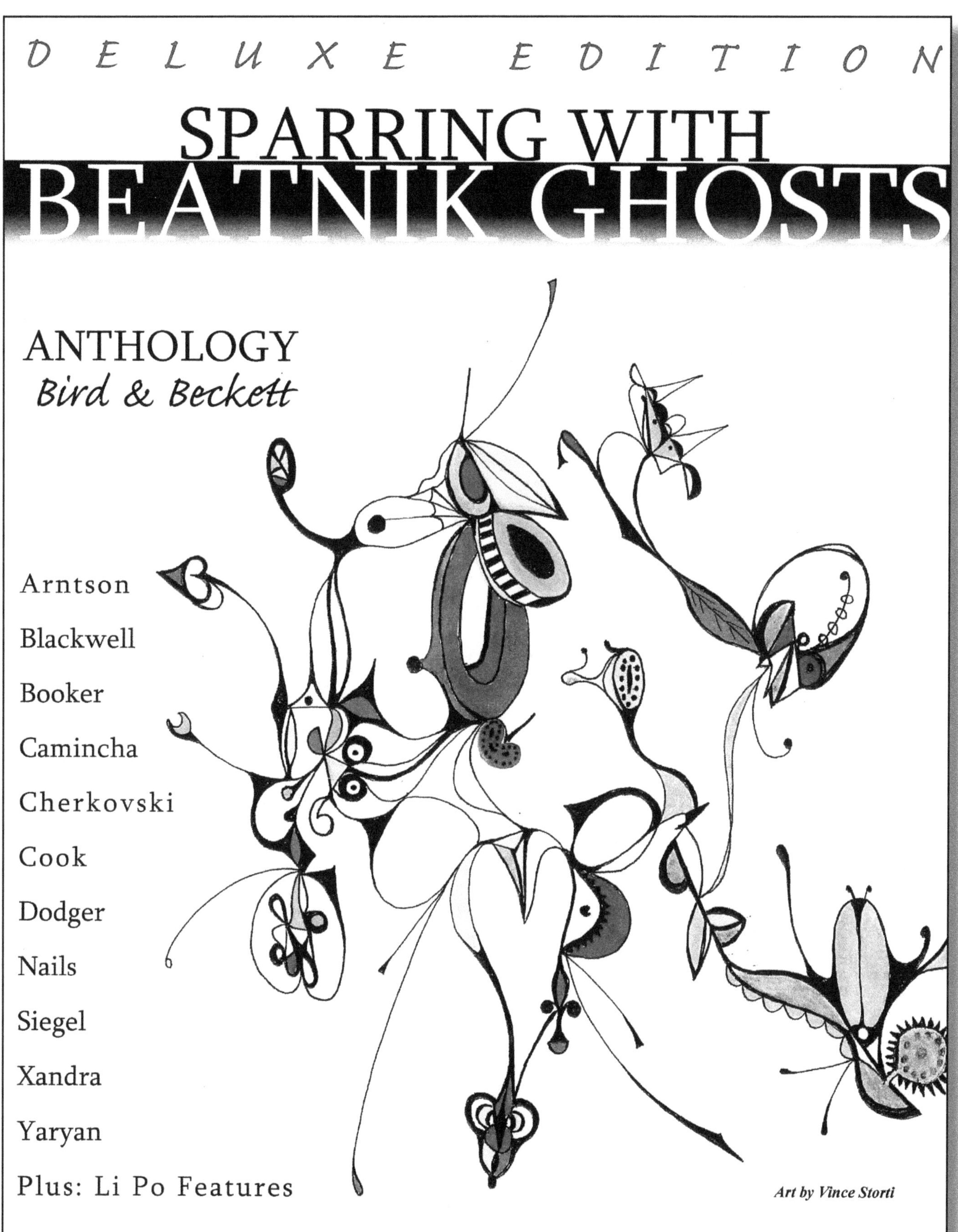

Art by Vince Storti

*Sparring With Beatnik Ghosts Anthology (Vol. 1 #2, 8/15/09 showcased Neeli Cherkovski's poetry and cover artwork by the late **VINCE STORTI***

NEELI CHERKOVSKI
THE BURNING OF LOS ANGELES

somebody let me see
the great pillar of fire
over the Basin,
cars lined up on
the Santa Monica
Freeway, drivers gone,
one grayed bulldog
waters his roses on
Orange Street, the buses
are scattered like terrible
toys on Melrose,
I get out of bed and walk
to the back porch,
people are wondering
why I stay there
in my father's apartment
after he has died,
how can I listen to his voice
in his kitchen where he
used to run
the water for half an hour
at a time, he
would yell "Hey, fuck Bush!"
and wait for
a reply, but only the dog
next door answered

Los Angeles stank from
the burning embers,
white stucco bungalows
collapsed
in the flames, a procession
of Christian Scientists
came out from behind
a wall of geranium
to meet with a brigade
from an obscure
yoga society, well,
I touch the things my father
touched, I open the
refrigerator and drink
the last bottled water,
he had looked so sublime
in the coffin, good old Sam,
he deserved
more, but so goes the bonfire:
ashes to ashes, dust to dust

the freeway pillars
collapsed from the heat
of raging fire, one fire

truck sat derelict
at the Pacific Palisades,
two gulls alighted
on the hood, I stay in my
father's rented space
for two days, he managed
'to avoid assisted
living, I wonder if I'll
be so lucky, what hell
it must be, they feed
you oatmeal in the morning
and Ensure for lunch,
you are wheeled to
the rest room, but now
all of that is burning up,
nobody can stop it,
the conflagration grows
more obscene by
'the moment, only the sun
seems to be impervious
to the carnage, that
same sun my father
knew sitting on the small
porch, watching stray
cats, observing
the young people with
their SUVs going to
or coming from work

"Fuck God and
Fuck the President!" yelled
my father, he stomped
on the floor, dragged
himself to the fire,
I wake up at two in the
morning in the other bedroom
and peek]into his
room, there is
his pillow, I see the form
of his head, I feel the heat,
and remember
how he lay, in the end,
maybe dreaming
so far back that
the saber-toothed cats
are preparing to pounce,
or just emptying his mind
of all those things,
ancient and of our day,
and feeling a music
beyond the fire, a
music loud enough
not to be heard

VIRLISTO
La Divina Commedia
Arcos Paper 2013
Homage to Dante

Letters
of A Tree
Draft 88
The Plane is Flying
DRAFT 88
By Neel Clodwell

NEELI CHERKOVSKI

LETTER TO SAN FRANCISCO

San Francisco watch out
You will price yourself off the peninsula
And into oblivion
We love the old bay windows
The lovebirds
We understand changen
But not the wrenching out
Of a wise and wild song

It's all being sanitized
The sea lions are bathed
Young entrepreneurs
Cure themselves with expensive wine
They command table
Laden with fine organic food
At exorbitant prices

The beautiful madness is going
Not even the fog can save it
Nor the dreams at lands end
Goodbye to all that
Hello to unparalleled success
Hello to progress of the
purely corporate kind
Hi to more concrete steel and
Window glass
Goodbye to the street poets
The corner musicians
"The rebirth of wonder"
as the monolithic buses
Plow over time to deliver
People to the pod

Helpless invisible folks
At the bottom of the pile
Homeless helpless unseen
Lost in the rumble
Invisible uninvited

I look down Vallejo Street
And cannot smile
Though the old beauty still reigns
At 6 pm
And there is a
Light at Dimitri's window
Where dinner will be served

Be thankful for this
For the moment floating
Over the newborn arcades
Of a polished town
For a touch remaining
Of what had been
Our crazy beautiful flaring
Flawed working class clamor
Of neighborhood glamor

I will miss you San Francisco

--Neeli Cherkovski
June 9 2015

VC
No P
Neeli
Cherkovski
"Lucky"

NEELI CHERKOVSKI

THE LUCKY DOG

Artwork by NEELI CHERKOVSKI

he curls up
on the couch
oblivious
to the rain
beating on the window

he sighs
and stretches his
haunches, I hold
the blue leash
and shake
it, he stares
out of deep terrier eyes

this is a
lucky dog, he loves
the rain, and so he prepares
to get up
from slumber

he is twelve now, people say
he's like a puppy, the way
he runs
and tugs at his restraint

up on the hill
he chases the wind
and catches
a passing cloud

on days like this
he braves

the rain, if he has
a darkness
he keeps it hidden
away
unlike the old drunk
down on
Cortland
who shouts
into the sky

this is a lucky dog,
he weighed eight
pounds when we
brought him home
in a cardboard box
with instructions
and a sack of
puppy food, you just
add water
and the years flower
like a rose bush
against the rain
and the sun

he is a lucky
dog with his canine
mind fully mindful

we are both
led
into the rain

NEELI CHERKOVSKI

GLOBAL WARNING

you would have to be blind
not to understand the extent of the heat wave
that will come here and in Europe
and in tropic climes

and as you grope through our fields
clinging to solitary stalks of wheat and corn
be sure to forgive no one, make a ring
for memory, make a solid gold ring
like the amulet makers of long ago

the good and the bad become one
and don't look in the museums anymore
they will be filled with grains of sand
and the walls empty and archaic books ever more useless

to find love go to the moon with your fingertips
and touch the unforgiving glow

the meadow of asphalt
and the mountains of steel
and hills of glass and stunned frogs
in the sick rain are all the rage

when you dove into my eyes
I did not feel your cruelty
or your fire, nor did I realize
how much like you I am
and I did not see the fireball
in our brains, I hoped only
for freedom, only for a garden

I could not hold your Venetian goblet
where the horse prances
with a happy prince in tow
I would not see the tapestries again,
lady and unicorn in harmony beyond all science

Artwork by **NEELI CHERKOVSKI**

"Me Tried By Neeli
"BUKOWSKI" Chertkowski
ok
"This is the tragedy of
The leaves, the dead
Ferns..." C. Buk
HANK
Study #1 For
Henry
Charles
Bukowski
"Hank"
FLOWER
FIST
AND
Bestial
Wail
NC
2013
DRAPE
1
"ALMOST
Good
Enough"
NC

NEELI CHERKOVSKI

A CALIFORNIA ELEGY

it's never simple
thinking of those mescaline trips
in Santa Barbara on the
sand dunes, 3 nights running, or sleeping bags
turning into bags of salt
and those old comrades gone, Franz Adler
with his bag of tricks, born in Vienna the thick lips
of his dispensations, but he could not come
to the festival, old and heavy, or roll down
300 feet to the coast highway
and scram for all it's worth up a series of concrete
pipes, no, no, he sat in his office with radical
magazines, now I'm thinking he is 132 years old,
the world is several billion years old, Vietnam has many
worthy resorts and French restaurants, Hamas
is looking for Jews under every rock, I sit
in the cramped studio trying to finish a glass of iced tea
we are an embarrassment of sympathy
my young friend I kiss your alabaster eyes, I lick
the fine ivory threads on your skin, here as the trucks
roll by, the squad cars rush back and forth, vacationers
ramble and explain themselves
to the solitude, the wind is empty, we head north
to the old mission and run down the red hallways
till we find the words we need, so may awful people
with fixed ideas, love standing alone
in the garden with a green hose and the sprayer
on "mist" because it is simple and direct, oh Leon Sumerian
oh Jerry Cavanaugh, Judy Eisenstein, the pale
thief I loved, the boy with his red jockey shorts
on the dunes, the colors bleeding onto my hands
California

NEELI CHERKOVSKI

BURYING THE DEAD
For Sam Cherry, my father

Move me
Touch me
Trust no man
Other than
The man in the
Moon, trip over
Dust, try imagining
A day without
Rest, motivate
My ashes as I
Contemplate
The beauty
Of a private
Universe, it is
Guarded day
And night, long
After the bars
Have closed

Shout a dirge
To Lip Service
Your Crystal Text
Pushes tidal pain
Over sea spume
Of a grim noontime
My tie is loose
Shoes shined hello
To the elders
Who live underground
Where Paradise and
Sodden Love become
a single flame, where
the grand matriarch is
a shade
A soul may stroll
In peace under
Loud canopies
Of light, a man
May tempt mortality
And bend light,
Such a primary
Pleasure to skip
Down the sidewalk,
To promoter layers

Of silence, to mutter
The kaddish and to
Bury the dead
Shake a finger
At the air
Long ago when
The encircling sea
Was a trap for
Primitive desire,
When men emulated
Reindeer and
First dipped fingers
Into a pool of honey,
We are ecstatic
Tasting the earth, happy
To be blinded
By the truth, when
Arrive to bury the dead
We check-in at the gate,
A uniformed guard
Shows precisely what
Road to take, how to
Recognize truth and
Justice, we
Go on in, the
Arrangements
Have been
Made, we walk
Metaphorically
In canyons of obsidian
Toward cities
Of grass and
Grateful trees

Is this Istanbul?
Paris? Kansas City?
Do we drive into
Hong Kong or Beirut?
Why not Lima? What
Of Calcutta?

Way down the way
In pristine wild

CONTINUED NEXT PAGE

Discordant shades
And shadows, heavy
White clouds,
Blocks of gray, the
Dead, men and women
The same, Whitman
Grown old and sick, the
Tough frail leaves,
Badger and racoon
In the outer room
Where the poet works
On his Death-bed edition
A comma, a check
Point, Crazy Horse
And Custer, bring
A sprig of
Lilac, emulate
Roses, water our
Redwood forest,
Dead, dead, bury
Mother in
Rich soil, father
Under same, don't
Yield to violence,
Tell the kids to
Resist, now good
Rain, thunder, rubies
And peals, full fathom
Five a ship of
Blood, burial of
The dead

Oh nurse
Help me turn over
For morning light,
I traipsed the high
Desert and
Landed on rock,
My head is a mine
Of meteors,
Help me out
Of bed, it's time
To drive to this
Carnival called
Burial of
The dead, we have
Bells and hammers,
Nails and candles,
Six-month special
On dance lessons,
You'll be pleased
To enter Paradise
In a coat of fire,

Guide me
Through heavy traffic,
Ah, we turn
By the Universal City
Sign, poor
Stupid rancor, poor
Ideological hatred
Good old
Pantheon of
Light, dead dead
Ripe you are
Om plains of sight,
Stout dove-like
Beams, hold the
Promise of a hawk
In sure-fired
Blue skies, zoom
Across the pond

Touch move
Trust no one
But yourself
Way down
Inside, hear
An echo
Of the washer-
Woman priest
Who offers
A taste of
Honey and
Some wine,
It goes away
Soon enough,
Life and
Death, wounded
Signs, be awake
To your passage
As you hold on
To an animal
And enter
The hunting grounds

Speak sumac
And wasp, trim
A Socratic moment
In the mulberry ground,
May we resist
None of it and give
No ground though
We perish, may we
Sweeten deft
Heaven, our terraces
Cleared, pagodas

Rise anew, moated
Mind sound]
As an ankle bracelet drawn
To the burial
Of the dead, stop for gas
And eat a burger,
Pause for phantom
Photographers, raise
A palm on
Midnight's column
Drear steep
Memorial, chant
Like a poplar tree
Raised on wind,
Burying the dead,
Here the Ventura
And Hollywood
Spar, traffic clashes,
Stars run away like
Wild goats in
An old story, today
I celebrate life,
My father was 96,
An old bum
On the freights, you
May elbow-in
To where whispers
Glow and futile
Gestures of belief
Follow
Oh meticulous end
Of life, death takes
All, leaves not
A crumb, another cloud
Opens, every
Raindrop is an ocean
On fire
With desire

Neeli Cherkovski
August 13, 2020

Artwork by **NEELI CHERKOVSKI**

Radio Flyer
RUSSIAN FUTURISM
TREE TO LOVE
Ardes / Draft 9
Neeli Cherkovski 2013

Neew Clerkomw
2013

NEELI CHERKOVSKI

DID I EVER THANK YOU
                    for A. G.

did I ever thank you for opening your mail
at my poetry reading?
big modern prophet of the poem
great genius of the prayer for the dead
and the song of protest
in a country that had just completed
a national highway system?
Lord, Lord, the greedy little boy
in all of us desires to pick all the grapes
and stuff them in his mouth, Lord
what a scene when papa bear and mama bear
lumber out of the meadow
with baby bear in tow
and you are opening the goddamn mail
with expertise, nothing rips, it seamlessly
opens with straight lines, and here
on my wall a photo of you
dead as the crone who stood aside
while the troops passed in Athens
when the philosophers reigned
over the hearts of every soldier

dear ole Allen sitting on your grave
I hand myself a frail leaf
and smile at the frowning clown
in the sky scape far down
where your letters lie

TERESA MEI CHUC

WHAT HAPPENS TO THE HOMELESS WHEN THEY DIE?

maybe there is a name
written in a ledger book
of a cemetery

maybe she will die
with no one saying her name

unclaimed bodies
are cremated
and buried outside of city limits

there is no funeral
no tombstone

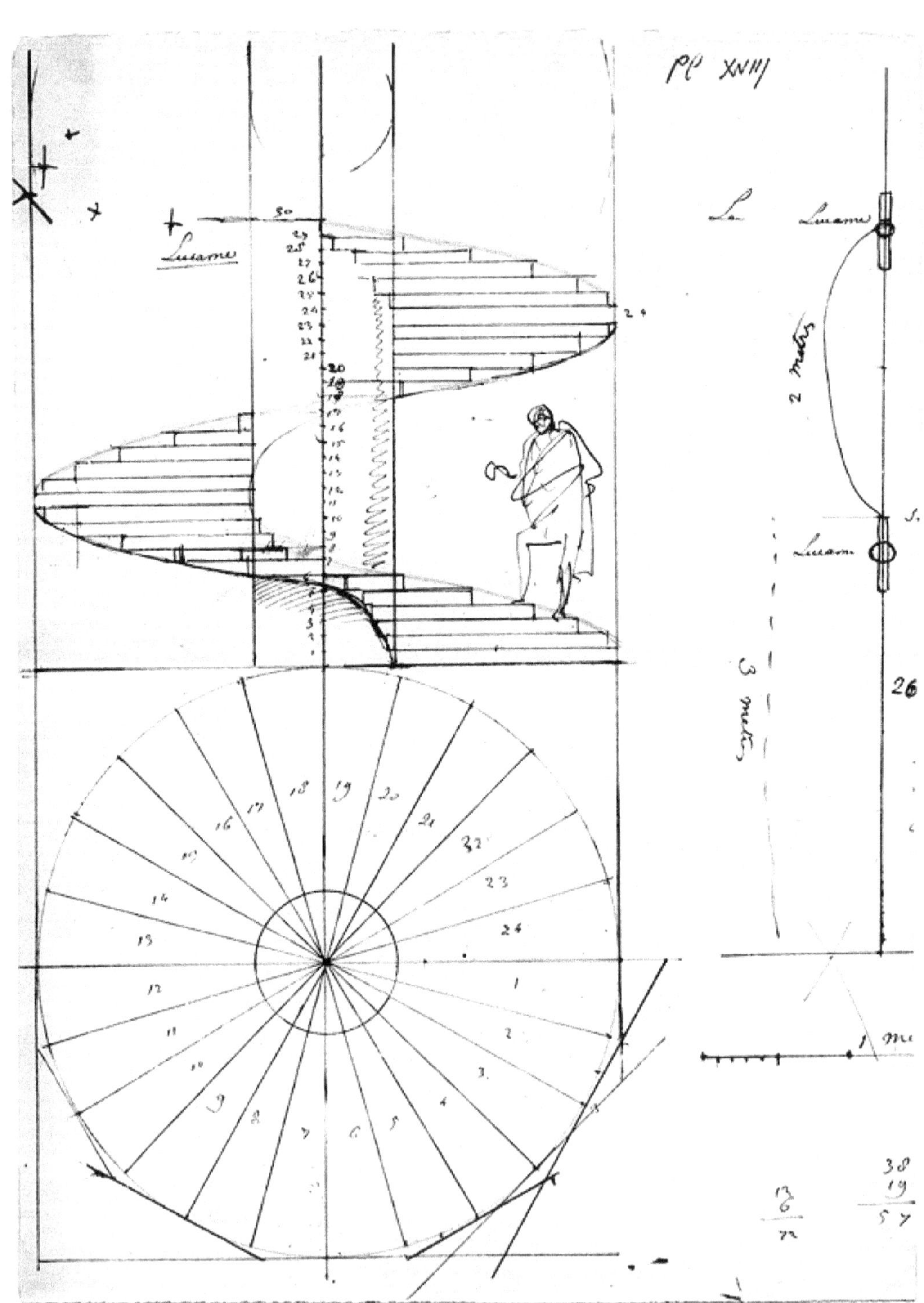

"Construction of a Spiral Staircase" illustration by
DAVID HUMBERT DE SUPERVILLE

Dedicated to our grandmothers, mothers, sisters and daughters experiencing houselessness
#SheDoes deserve shelter, protection and compassion

"The Golden Butterfly" painting by **ERIC ROHMAN**

TERESA MEI CHUC
SPRING POEM

The flowers are blooming
and so are the bruises
on her face
purple and pink like showy penstemon
and there is no where she could go

The bruises on her arm
the deep violet of prickly pear fruits
tender to the touch

The flowers are blooming
around her tent on the hillside
overlooking the freeway
sunflowers, each branch
carrying light

The robins, mockingbirds and blue jays
are singing
as his fist punches her face

The flowers are blooming
fuchsia red
fairy duster red
on her skin
and there is no where she could go

PAYING TRIBUTE TO ANDY CLAUSEN

By Eliot Katz

A great American poet and a great friend for 44 years, Andy Clausen, passed away peacefully in his sleep in a Kingston, NY nursing home and physical rehab center, Golden Hill, in the early morning of April 11, 2024. Andy had spent the last few months in Golden Hill, trying to recover from a leg amputation (after a serious infection) and a variety of other physical ailments. Because I have a post-surgery neck that made it difficult to take the long drive up to Kingston from where I live in New Jersey, I had kept in touch with Andy by phone. (And let me here thank Danny Shot and Raymond Foye, who did more to help Andy at Golden Hill these recent months than anyone except perhaps some of the nurses there.) The last time that I talked with Andy on the phone was about 5 or 6 days before his death. During our call, Andy said that he was in so much pain, despite some pain meds, that he was thinking of trying to find an easy way out of this world. I made him laugh by asking him to please try to hold on for at least a little longer, to see if his pains might

improve in the weeks and months ahead, and because I enjoyed still being able to tell people that I thought Andy Clausen was the best living poet in America. I'm not sure who I would say that about now, but at least Andy is now out of his pain and suffering.

Andy Clausen was born as Andre Laloux in a Belgium bomb shelter in 1943, and moved to Oakland, California at age three, at the end of the Second World War, when his mother gave him his new name--his last name, Clausen, being the name of his new father. Andy was physically stronger than most poets. After graduating from high school, Andy became a talented Golden Gloves boxer and, for a brief time, joined the Marines, which he left in 1966 after watching Allen Ginsberg on TV read his anti-Vietnam War poem, "Wichita Vortex Sutra." The line from Allen's poem that caught Andy's attention and changed the direction of his life was the simple but poignant, hu-

CONTINUED NEXT PAGE

Photo of Andy Clausen and Eliot Katz by **ALLEN GINSBERG**

manizing question: "Has anyone looked in the eyes of the dead?

With his ex-wife, Linda Clausen, Andy has two adult sons—Cassidy and Jesse—and a daughter, Mona. Beginning in the late 1990s, Andy lived in a cabin on the outskirts of Woodstock, NY, with the well-known Beat poet, Janine Pommy Vega, until Janine passed away in early 2011 of a heart attack, compounded by a long battle with rheumatoid arthritis. Sadly, Andy's next long-term partner, the poet, Pamela Twining, also passed away unexpectedly, in July 2023, after what was supposed to have been a routine hospital surgery. In recent years, both Andy and Pamela had been named Beat Poet Laureates by the National Beat Poetry Foundation; and that Foundation's publishing arm recently published a wonderful book, *Two Hearts Beat*, which included poems by both Andy and Pamela. Andy also published a terrific poetry book of his own in 2024, *The Fabled Damned* (Zeitgeist Press), which includes an introduction by Danny Shot.

It was a real pleasure to know Andy Clausen and to have had many adventures together through four-plus decades. The first time that I saw Andy read poetry, days after we had been introduced by Allen Ginsberg, was in the summer of 1980, at Naropa Institute in Boulder, Colorado, where I was doing a monthlong apprenticeship with Allen. Andy was scheduled to read one night as part of a three-person program, along with Allen and Phil Whalen, and Allen and Phil had Andy close the show, symbolically passing along a generational poetry torch. With his deep oratorical voice (check out any of his readings on YouTube), and poetry filled with amazing energy, insight, humor, and imagination, Andy gave a reading that night that left a deep and lasting impression. A few years later, Danny Shot and I published a book of Andy's, The Iron Curtain of Love, that included those first poems of Andy's that I had heard. The poem that I remember most from that evening was his long poem, "From the Top of My Lungs: An Open

CONTINUED NEXT PAGE

Photo of Pamela Twining and Andy Clausen at Mercury Cafe Denver 2019 by **MARCIA WARD**

Letter to the Russian People," with its explorations of the historic hypocrisies and exploitations, sometimes hawkish and fatal, of both the U.S. and Soviet governments, and its visionary insistence that artists and working people of the U.S. and U.S.S.R. could one day figure out how to put an end to the physically and psychically damaging Cold War: "No more guilt American O Russian / The Freedom to choose Peace—/ Jesus! How badly our governments behave! / Brothers & Sisters / THE GENERAL STRIKE! / NOW!"

Andy and I did many readings together through the decades—in Boulder, San Francisco, New Brunswick, New York City, Woodstock. A few of those readings featured Allen Ginsberg as the main headliner. One memorable early event was a young poets midnight reading—featuring Andy, Danny Shot, and I--at the large and historic Jack Kerouac Festival at Naropa Institute in 1982. To get to that reading, Danny and I had taken a cross-country, energetized conversation-filled van ride with Andy and

his family, a ride that also included the Beat jazz poet, Ray Bremser, who seemingly chose beer as a substitute for any solid food during the full two-day drive, leading to many extra rest stops along the highway. Andy and I were also roommates for about seven or eight months in New Brunswick, New Jersey, in around 1983, during which we started a feature/open reading series at the Roxy Bar, a series that included some well-known visiting poets, like Gregory Corso, reading with local NJ poets, and that continued on for about seven or eight years with a few different New Brunswick poets taking over running the series.

For decades, Allen Ginsberg consistently cited Andy Clausen as one of the most important poets of the next generation. For Andy's book, *Without Doubt* (1991), Allen wrote an introduction that declared: "The frank friendly extravagance of his metaphor & word-connection gives Andy Clausen's poetry a reading interest rare in poetry of

CONTINUED NEXT PAGE

Photo of poets Jack Michelline and Andy Cluasen in 1976

any generation." Allen also said in that same introduction that he would take a chance on a President Clausen! Andy Clausen's best work through the years extended the democratic-left and imagination-filled traditions of poets like Walt Whitman, William Blake, Muriel Rukeyser, Langston Hughes, Allen Ginsberg, the French surrealists, and the Russian Futurists, especially Vladimir Mayakovsky, who was always one of Andy's favorites. Andy's many poetry books include *The Iron Curtain of Love, 40th Century Man, Songs of Bo Baba, Without Doubt,* and *Home of the Blues* (for which I wrote an introduction), and he is also the author of an extraordinary memoir, *Beat,* about his adventures with well-known and lesser-known Beat Generation writers. At the request of Allen's longtime secretary, Bob Rosenthal, Andy and I worked together as assistant editors to finish *Poems for the Nation* (Seven Stories Press, 2000), a small collection of political poems that Allen had started compiling and editing during the 18 months before Allen's death in 1997. Andy also worked several years with Danny Shot and Nancy Mercado as a co-editor for *Long Shot* literary magazine.

In Andy's poetry, empirical observations mix inventively with jazzed-up surreal and modernist imagery, the kind of surreal imagery that the European philosopher, Ernst Bloch, called "anticipatory illuminations," because the surreal images don't yet exist in the actual world and therefore imply the possibility of creating a better and more humane world in the future. From wars to widespread hunger and poverty, from AIDS and Covid epidemics to ever-present racism and sexism, from continued violations of international human rights to the new and growing risk of climate change, our species has witnessed plenty of tragedy and danger over the last half-century. As Andy writes in "The War to Begin All Wars," up to this point in world history, "the medicine isn't working." Carrying on the most energetic, mindful, politically progressive, and intellectually probing aspects of the Beat tradition, strings of high-speed

CONTINUED NEXT PAGE

adjectives mix in Andy's work with thoughtful speculations about unfair aspects of our often-broken social and economic landscapes and about the often-unjust nature of wage-based work.

Andy worked most of his adult life as a construction worker, a union hod-carrier, carrying around 80-pound sacks of cement, also holding other physically demanding jobs that included driving cabs, heavy stonework, and working in a saw mill. For some years, he taught poetry in New York schools and prisons, while still doing heavy-lifting jobs that, in a more just society, one of America's best poets wouldn't have had to keep doing late in life with a bad back. Having titled one of his two books of selected poems, *Home of the Blues*, Andy Clausen earned the blues that he wrote about, the blues that have traditionally been sung with a sense of irony and self-awareness while waiting, writing, and working for a changed world.

Having reached the age of 80 with thousands of pages of poetry in published books and in hand-written notebooks, Andy Clausen during his lifetime earned a distinctive place among the second generation of Beat poets, in a way that Allen Ginsberg and Philip Whalen had foreseen when I first saw Andy read at Naropa in 1980. Because Andy outlived most of the original Beat Generation poets, readers interested in the Beat poetry tradition, and in contemporary poetry in general, will find Andy's perceptions about recent history and about our 21st century politics and culture to be essential reading. In some segments of literary America, readers and listeners already know what Allen Ginsberg knew, that Andy Clausen was one of the most compelling poets of our time. The linguistic energy, surprise phrasings, and global insight of his poems send readers into motion— thinking, planning, pacing, going quickly down to the nearest poetry cafe, rock and roll club, or political rallies for peace, social justice, and ecological well-being. Our current, perilous world could surely use more people stirred by poets and other artists into constructive thought and action.

---Eliot Katz

A half-hour film made by Vivian Demuth about Andy that includes Andy reading poems, and also pizza-dinner conversations about poetry and politics between Andy, Eliot, and Vivian. At one point in the film, Andy explains why he once thought, in the mid-1960s, that Beat poetry, not computers, was going to be the trend of the future. The film's title, *Dinners with Andy*, is a play on a previous well-known film called *My Dinner with Andre*, partly because Andy's original Belgian name, before moving to the U.S. at age 3, was Andre Laloux. www.youtube.com/watch?v=J2gw-E54uBc

"...Andy Clausen during his lifetime earned a distinctive place among the second generation of Beat poets, in a way that Allen Ginsberg and Philip Whalen had foreseen..."

—Eliot Katz

ELIOT KATZ BIO:

Called "another classic New Jersey bard" by the late Allen Ginsberg, Eliot Katz is the author of seven books of poetry, including *Love, War, Fire, Wind* and *Unlocking the Exits*, as well as a prose book, *The Poetry and Politics of Allen Ginsberg*. His most recent poetry book was a free pdf volume posted on his website before the 2020 presidential election, titled: *President Predator: Poems to Help Make America Trump-Free Again*. A book of selected and new poems is currently being translated into Italian for an upcoming publication in Florence. He was a co-founder, with Danny Shot, of the long-running *Long Shot* literary magazine, and was a co-editor with Allen Ginsberg and Andy Clausen on *Poems for the Nation*. Katz, whose late mother was a Holocaust survivor, has worked for many years as an activist for a wide range of peace and social-justice causes, including helping to create several housing and food programs for homeless families in Central New Jersey that remain ongoing. He currently lives with his partner, Vivian, in Hoboken, New Jersey and his website is at www.eliotkatzpoetry.com. Previous pieces by Eliot about Andy Clausen include an introduction to Andy's selected poems, *Home of the Blues*, and two pieces (one bio and one book review) about Andy in *The Encyclopedia of Beat Literature*, edited by Kurt Hemmer. The latter part of this new piece is based partly on previous pieces that Eliot has written about Andy.

An Evening of Poetry and Songs of Resistance

Ed Sanders
Peter Lamborn Wilson
Andy Clausen
Brenda Coultas
Michael Brownstein
Mikhail Horowitz
& Gilles Malkine
Leslie Ritter
& Scott Petito
Robert Kelly
Pamela Twining
Sparrow
Jana Martin
Chuck Stein

THURSDAY, JUNE 29

WOODSTOCK COMMUNITY CENTER

7 – 9 pm

FREE!

Protest and Survive event poster from 2017. Woodstock, NY.

ALLEN GINSBERG
PETER ORLOVSKY
ANDY CLAUSEN
WED. 9 PM
SEPT. 26
with
JACK ROGERS
on guitar
LIBERTY LUNCH
CHUKSTER
PRODUCTIONS
IN THE EVENT OF RAIN
GASLIGHT THEATRE
214 W 4TH STREET
ADVANCE TICKETS
ZEBRA RECORDS, 1713 LAVACA & 3453 W. ANDERSON LN.
BRAZOS BOOKS, 803 RED RIVER

Excerpts from Death of a Poet

by Danny Shot

10.
I feed him chocolate pudding with a spoon.
"I kinda like this." He smiles, "for I am a mighty oak."
He looks at me suspiciously, "Who started the rumor about the fish?"
"Not me," I reply meekly.
"Just checking," he closes his eyes and drifts off.
The end is near. The morphine is working.
He opens his eyes: "Am I dying?"

7.
Somehow, we get two new books of Andy's poetry out at the beginning of 2024, *The Fabled Damned* and *Two Hearts Beat*. It is a labor of love, for both the publishers, and me. We think they'll give Andy reason to live. It does. For a while. On my weekly visits to the nursing home, we go over the manuscripts arguing over various spellings and odd capitalizations and seeming typos that are obscure references that are crystal clear to Andy but no one else. He believes strongly in the Beat credo "first thought, best thought." I just want people to read the books.

I'm hungover, as is my wont on New Year's Day. Never-

theless, I drive 2 hours to bring Andy to a poetry marathon in Saugerties. Rhea, the physical therapist, whom Andy adores, supervises my training. I learn how to get Andy into the wheelchair, out of the wheelchair, into my car, out of my car, up steps, up a ramp. I ask Rhea if I get a certificate for having completed the training. She looks at me like I'm crazy. It was a joke I tell her, but she doesn't believe me. People are surprised to see Andy as I proudly wheel him to the front row. A few look away from the white bandaged stump of his leg. I take a photo for Facebook. Andy reads a poem from the galleys of his new book. His voice is strong and fills the room. He gets the pages stuck together and continues reading from the middle of one poem into the middle of another. "Doesn't matter," he tells me later; "they heard my voice."

3.
The damned car. The car is in Pamela's name, but Andy drives it more than she does. Technically, as next of kin Pamela's oldest child should get it. But Andy needs it, at least thinks he does. Over the next month, an all-out battle of

CONTINUED NEXT PAGE

CONTINUED FROM LAST PAGE

wills resulting in Andy boycotting Pamela's funeral, and encouraging others to do so as well, which the greater Woodstock community happily does. The children spend extravagantly on Pamela's final farewell. Hardly anyone attends. I find it unbecoming, and am embarrassed to be involved. Andy never drives the car again. Neither do Pamela's children. Michael Platsky winds up with the car with the promise that he will chauffeur Andy to doctor appointments and grocery shopping.

Her children plan the memorial. It's a disaster. I give money to the GoFundMe page. Andy is angry with me, "Why are you giving money to them when I'm the one that needs it?" They fight about the car. They fight about the memorial. Pamela's son leaves notes on Andy's desk. Things like "what goes around comes around" and "are you happy now, asswhole?" The daughter who lives in Florida, maybe the one in Georgia (I'm not sure), is the easiest to work with. She's the youngest in the family. Andy respects her the most. She writes gothic romance novels that are seemingly self-published.

Pamela's children arrive. They are grown adults in their 40s and 50s bringing with them grown adults in their 20s and 30s, the grandchildren. The children are from 3 fathers and are not particularly close to each other, though they share a postpartum grief in the loss of their mother, and a general mistrust of Andy. They come around the house poking through Pamela's stuff searching for what they can salvage. Nobody is helping, they are just wanting. Andy is passive, somewhat annoyed, but not being forthcoming about the circumstances of Pamela's death or his life with her. He answers their queries in one syllable spurts.

1.
I drive up to Woodstock blasting Orville Peck's Daytona Sand on the Thruway hoping not to get caught doing 85, happy to be reading with Andy Clausen and Pamela Twining in Shiv's backyard, officially dubbed the Shivastan Poetry Ashram. The last time I saw Andy was in October at a poetry reading he did with Pamela at Fox & Crow in Jersey City. Andy looked thin and tired. Somehow, he had set Pamela's poems on fire by reading them over a lit candle. It was Caroline who shouted across the room "Andy you're on fire." He wasn't, but Pamela's poems were, and a hole burned through the middle of the pages. After the reading, I insisted that they stay over in Hoboken and sleep on our none too comfortable couch. When Caroline got up at 6 a.m. they were gone. I love reading with Andy, it's always an adventure, as long as I read before him. Both Eliot Katz and I call Andy America's greatest living poet. I still believe that.

Gregory
CORSO
Returns to Boulder
Sunday
JULY 13
2 PM
appearing with
ALLEN GINSBERG
PETER ORLOVSKY
ANDY CLAUSEN
at
The
GLENN MILLER BALLROOM
u.m.c buildin
c.u. campus,
boulder
Boulder Poetry Project
$4.00 advanced —
$5.00 at the door
The Lion used Books
1331 Broadway
next to mothers
Cafe, Boulder

JIM COHN
MANIC DEPRESSION SUTRA

"For I Am a Mighty Oak"
          —poet Andy Clausen's last words

Beyond my cherry tree, surrounded by tall prairie grasses,
Hardwoods unfold their leaves in luxuriant shades of green.
I remember all the jokes about life after 30 being a terrible
Thing, something dreadful, the great horror, to still be alive,
And I found myself listening to "Manic Depression Sutra,"
Heard live in my head, Hendrix playing upside down sarod,
Chanting "Manic Depression's a frustrating mess," after
Alice Notley read a poem at the Poetry Project, 10 April 2024,
About meeting Hendrix in a NYC bar, when the news came,
Here, poet whose poems were the fiercest, most tender, held
Close, never surrendered soundtracks, this phantasmic life,
Yours, mighty oak, one of savage virtue—without deficiency.

Jim Cohn
11 April 2024

Collage art **by T. MIKE WALKER**

Andy Clausen is certainly one of my very favorite poets of Allen Ginsberg's heart-children. Unsung worker, overlooked genius, hilarious true original voice who toiled in relative obscurity to the shame of those in charge of the Big Poetry Contest.

MARC OLMSTED
THAT DARK WINE
(For Andy Clausen)

what have I become

that this old age has Caliban made?

a hoofed shambler none can save from time, the great evener

he lost his leg

to giant poetry

& then dragged down into

Homer's dark wine

where poems may still be

honored, my first thought was "folly"

don't waste another second

he's ten years ahead of me

no more lies about the fame of poetry

his death the same

day as the

murderer

who got away

with it

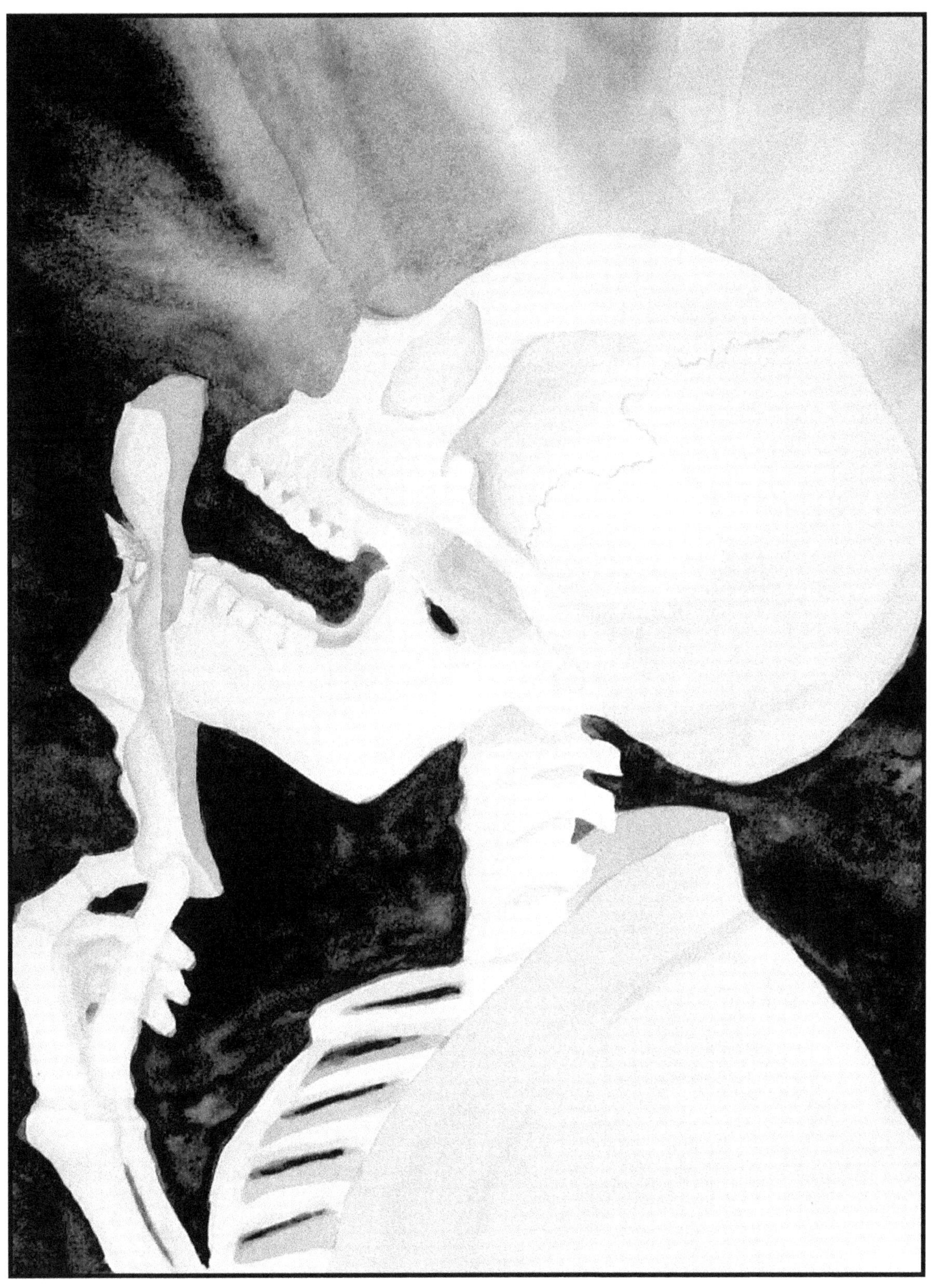

"Frontera Final" watercolor by **MARK DAVID HOEFER**

MACAU
AMSTERDAM
CRUZ
HAMBURG
NEW
ROME
RDAM
PRAGUE
TOKYO
HELSINKI
BOSTON
STOCKHOLM
MUNICH
JOHANNESBURG
PARIS
NEW DELHI
ORLANDO
STO DOMINGO
WARSAW
BUDAPEST
VIENNA
BARCELONA
SANTA
SINGAPORE
RIVIERA
truth

Andy Clausen died today.

A mountain, a force, an explosion.

Thunder, lightning, the last words
spoken to his friend Danny Shot were:

For I am a mighty oak…

I recalled Steve Dalachinsky's
last words to his Yuko:

I think I overdosed on Sun Ra.

The great poets are always in the middle.

Andy used to drive down from Woodstock
to the Treehouse on East 2nd Street
whenever Rick asked him to read.

Well, actually, Pamela Twining drove.
Andy couldn't see well enough at night,
but he was game for every journey,
every trip, every voyage to forever.

Pamela would read, too.
When she told her story about
her close call with the Manson family,
I texted Annie to say she had to meet her.

She's just like us.

We were all shocked when Pamela died
unexpectedly, leaving Andy thrown into a
future on earth without her loving presence.

Today, I texted Annie to tell her about Andy.
I texted Rick, too.

Annie said she wished she believed in a heaven
where he and Pamela would be rocking out.

I said I didn't know about heaven either,
but that I'd bet their spirits were entwined.

They were such a late life 'they', said Annie.
*Seems like you figure out some stuff and
then in the blink of an eye it's over.*

Guess that's why I'm still alive, I responded,

CONTINUED NEXT PAGE

"Raven in the Moon" artwork by CATHYANN CUSIMANO

and added some clichés about his long, interesting,
adventurous life filled with love and poetry.

Clichéd or not, I believed in what I said.

Rick texted me a photo of his copy of "Beat":

Rick,
friend of Puma
poets & musicians

Andy Clausen
10-28-18
N.Y.C.

He said he was standing behind me on line to get
our books signed and that I introduced them and that
whatever I said to Andy resulted in his sweet inscription.

I don't remember what I said, and I don't remember
where I put the book or what Andy wrote, but I think I
remember that I couldn't decipher his handwriting.

Andy Clausen and Pamela Twining.
Good Night, Andy. Good Morning, Pamela,
spinning through the universe together,
just like you always did, but without the flesh
and blood and bones holding you down,
spinning spinning spinning free.

—-Puma Perl

"Peace Love" artwork by **KATIE KEENLOVE**

PEACE
LOVE

ANDY CLAUSEN
THIS NOT THE ERA
OF GLORIOUS FELINES

Poet!
This is not the time of the glorious epoch of cats!
nor beaten to death home sweet home homilies
extolling prudence humility patient troop support
This is not the renaissance of still life
Exquisite flowers in pretty ewers next
to a hunk of Brie & gleaming blade
This not the time of hiding from our children
how we got here fictionalizing
Manifest Destiny as the Will of Creation
I have nothing against quaint sketches of archaic
peasant village life
I've got nothing against recalling the odor
of Grandma's house, her hair & clothing
the cookies in the oven
I've got no resentment against
you sleeping with your cat
but I am sworn to ask
does it go outside?
does it wear a mask?
& I've got nothing against your pet goldfish
teaching you the new dance moves
Exploring homonyms whose definitions form

a metaphor for their opposite & sure, tell me
how you learned to frame a house from a book
How you illuminate every clump or wisp of clowd
in the charcoal sky or spend three gestating stanzas on a
flower a strange stranger gave you
BUT how can you the Poets, "unacknowledged
legislators of the world"
You who inspire music & philosophy
(without you the arts would be mere cosmetics)
How can you avoid our country & world
on the gruesome verge
of totalitarian insanity not even
mentioned in your work
It could be centuries before freedom authentic
democracy shows its face
It could even be lights out for the inhuman
human race
It could turn the fauna & flora into a pile of rocks
It could look like Mars
It could take all that was noble & magnificent
into burbling eerie smoky tar pits out of which
Someday a microbe an atom a cell would emerge

ANDY CLAUSEN
ALL THE GLORY

All the glory of reciting a stirring rallying poem
to one's people is not the same on a screen
All the enjoyment of a splendid athletic event
in fan empty stadiums distant and trivial
The Spring fashions, even the new blockbuster
movie & Hip Hop album have devolved
into effluvia of the arts of a dying empire
The nation that thwarted the Nazis and brought me
my culture my loves the land I traversed & labored in is
the new Nazi & my American Jewish friends said don't make
that analogy
It is sacrilegious but I say as soon
as the opportunity arises
It is mass murder covert & overt for profit--
It is the same mind the same racists the same
Mammonites the no hearts the Nazis
They'll look for a strong limb for their strong rope
They'll torch the Defiant Ones in their abodes
If they get the chance they'll fire up
the ovens again
If we let them they'll fire up the ovens again

ANDY CLAUSEN
THE ARTISTS' GRAVEYARD
IN WOODSTOCK

Artists die here in Woodstock, love live even
give birth in Woodstock it wasn't always
well off artists media pros & what for a few
decades we gave name Yuppies
Young well off Urbans buying second homes
to be hotel-like rentals
Halliburton & Giuliani...... That's the real names
of the owners of $400 to $800 a night rooms
called Woodstock Way
You know some
of the great teachers have said
The Way is not the Way
If you lived here awhile you'd know what I mean
when I say The Woodstock Way isn't
There is a special cemetery for artists
Janine Pommy Vega, Allen Midgette
Peter L.Wilson & SweetBryar are there
My beloved the Divine Poet & Dancer
Pamela Twining
It costs money no discounts?-- so does
the regular graveyard where the great
Levon Helm or what once was
is interred
Get rid of my carcass cheap as you can!
I think burning will it be yet I'd go for a sky burial
LET THE BIG BIRDS GO AT IT
How can I be so bold to have a say?
I wouldn't be there
or would I?
And if it is ashes, release anywhere East Oakland
101st twixt Sunnyside & Bancroft would be
cool so would Jambes back in Dave
in the old country and the Ganges, Jai!
Go ahead and taste them hoover them
But no special trips pilgrimage any old long
hike might do---- no pyramids
No tombstone where I am no longer
No barrows well if you need the excuse
to exercise, as always, do what you see fit
I'm dead serious about this
Me? rather one reads my books than a stone marker

ANDY CLAUSEN
HE WAS RIGHT

Ancient photograph
Moses on the Mesa--Sitting Bull
Lakota women & some children
wrapped in blankets
On the commissary platform
for government rations
South Dakota 1891
Kudos up for All My Relations
A Part of history needing Big Lights
so sad calling it merely sad
Abe Lincoln signing the order to hang
37 Sioux Christmas Day1860
Hanged for fighting for freedom
& the home land
Sad sounds pathetic doesn't even touch
the horror the body & spirit grief
Those must be the blankets infested
with small pox
Crazy Horse was right
They were fighting for who they were
Their culture food clothing their way of work
hunting worshipping using judiciously
giving back to Mother Earth
Mother Earth the US troops
seemed to want to bleed dry
to incinerate to exterminate
all the buffalo
Mountains of skulls
Crazy Horse was right
The lightening streak on left cheek
Gopher dust on his steed
Speaking one of many aboriginal languages
The beatific mornings
with no fear rising from the wigwam smiling
on the energy of the offspring will be gone
The endless uniformly togged legions of very few
women blue coats like hives of wasps
or bees on the move with their repro queens
The blue coats are they from another planet?
Do they respond to cries of & for human justice?
No the blue coats demanded deeds
No not action but ownership documents
Crazy Horse told it like it was & still is
If we lose to them
We lose the way we live
If we lose we will lose everything
Crazy Horse, He was right

ANDY CLAUSEN
IT IS HAPPENING AGAIN

How did those who survived the bombings
the death camps the atom bomb
& the nuclear missile threat
keep their minds?
What a testament to the power of the human
mind that it could survive the tenacious
nightmare THREAT of entire
gens-extinguishing wars fought over
how to conduct our lives & our DNA
& what else God knows what
Wars waged out of bellicose habit
in infancy instilled
Blake was right--any form of government
will be tyranny when people are fools
If a government is lacking in love compassion
honesty justice it is lacking legitimacy
Constitutions, Bill of Rights, Rights of Man, -ism
this and that, won't work when people are
clueless easily duped become volunteer slaves
in the Haven of the Haves
Their little businesses are failing
The corporate chains will buy them up
Will buy out the soul of the Little Guy
The conglomerates will extinguish the light
of individual aspirations
And the homes go for sale to already
Concentrated Wealth
Soon everyone but the Wealthy a renter
The landlords will support a population
of pleasure seeking spoiled brats
While the vast mass of fellaheen

pay the Rent
Live and die by the Rent
These landlord's ancestors were the ones
that told the Sioux & Cheyenne
They had to leave the land centuries where
they lived and worked because
they couldn't produce a deed
No, not an action but a piece of paper
The deed worshippers came large
The buildings
The building supplies
The cement farms
The furniture stores
Drapes & carpets
Air ducts
The asphalt streets
The busses
jails
Big Houses
The seats of power
The vast science enhanced hectares
of stock holders, owners
Mission Accomplished the pioneer labor
was dismissed laid off ignored
when the cream was ladled out
Left in the Domination of those
Who haven't had hands
in dirt in decades
Who haven't been unplugged from electrical
waves for lifetimes
Who have never put the desires
of others above Self

"One Day We"ll Be Pirates" painting by **TRACY WITT**

ANDY CLAUSEN
WHAT ALLEN SAID TO ME IN 90
(IN 22 I SAY HE WAS A PROPHET)

How many warriors for Political
& Ontological Salvation
Global benevolence, economic justice
human dignity realized it's hopeless
My side my stake in the battle is
pre-ordained to lose to avarice
All my adult life I worked on myself
I informed comrades & foe alike
compassionate altruism is the Way
as taught by Buddha & Jesus &
Paine's "Age of Reason", Spinoza
Ginsberg, Allen
We faced I faced devastating loss after loss
On the streets of Praha
AG informed me Czech scientists had just
told him people on the Earth have 100 years
We've turned our home planet into a death ship
headed for extinction for Oblivion
The Planet an oar-less, sail-less, motor-less barge
on the River Styx
I said what are we to do? And why?
He said we still versify the Truth
Let folks know what is happening practice empathy
& kindness, go down with dignity
& generosity helping others
He foretold the far right would try to destroy all
our social gains and graces
Ironically They would implement
Bolshevik tactics gaining little office by little office taking
over the school board state houses dog catcher police depts.
etcetera capping
on the apathy of a populace
consumed with consumption
25 years later Truth is irrelevant
Censorship is financially omniscient
& hideously moronic
We have a cadre of elects who common sense
right or wrong matters not
Who find underlying motive of evil sex
inherent in those opposed to the powersthat-
be Way
"They're Perverts!" that's what they call us pervs
The Powers have adopted the way one should live
and will force everyone else to live
their way or be dealt hurt mind & body
prison or early death
Except they cheat give themselves an exemption
covertly do what they condemn others of doing
1990 I wondered if he knew any politicians

"On our side?"
He said there was a guy in Vermont named Sanders
Allen fought against what would happen after
his death: 9/11, 43, Afghanistan, censorship
ineffectual conservative class-loyal corporate
fed Democrats setting it up for 45 & a world
of illogic that rewards violence
that encourages ethnic hate
censorship & deception
But I think the extent of the gullibility & absurdity
would have amazed & be soddened ol AG
Friends tell me the Tories want
to turn it back forty years
No, my inner voice calmly hipped
me, 5000 years, that's where
they want to take it
One thing I know
Allen never copped out
never gave up

Allen Ginsberg (2021) artwork by SOHEYL DAHI

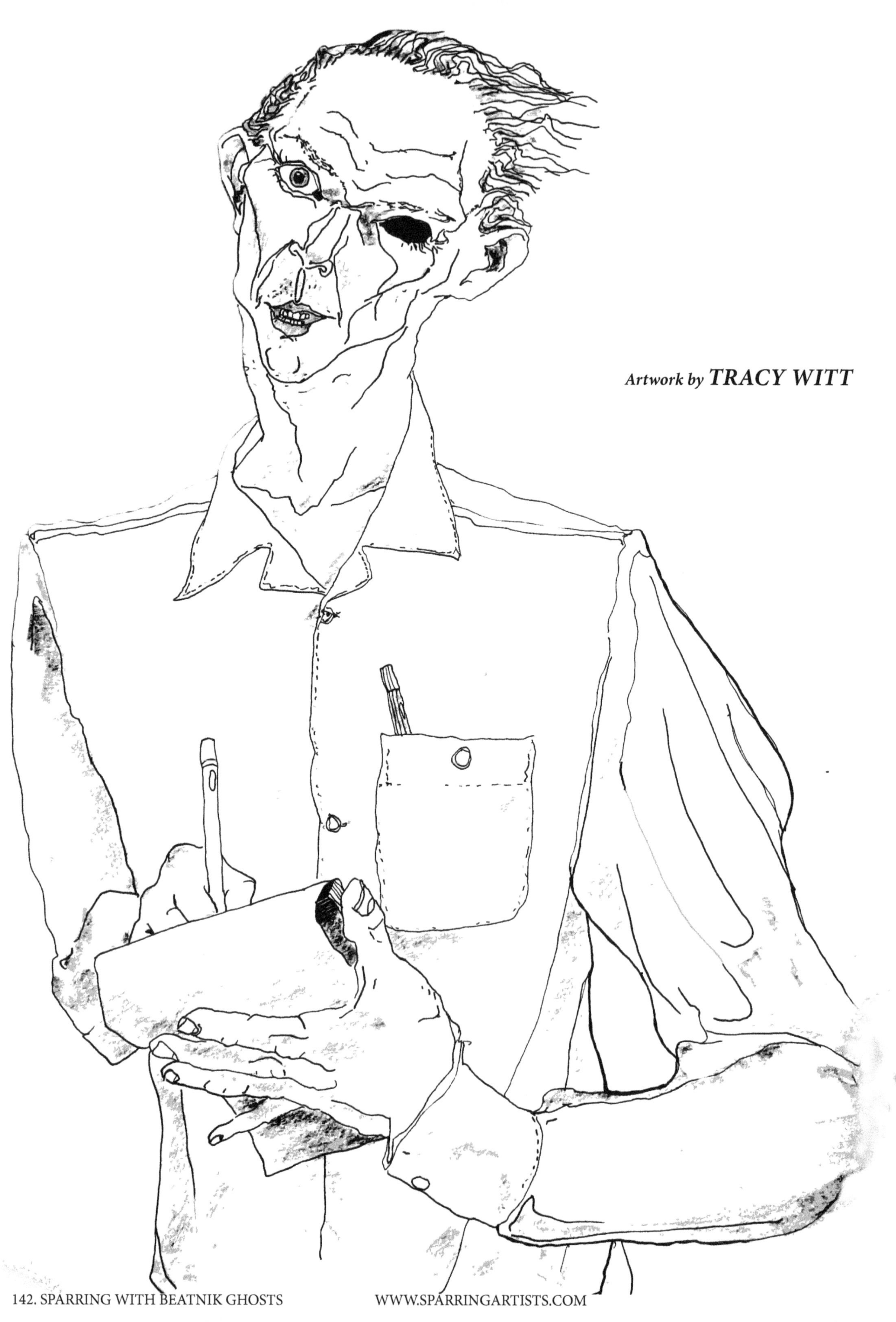

Artwork by **TRACY WITT**

ANDY CLAUSEN
ROLL CALL

Corso could crack open a word to its
autochthonic birth & reinvent syntax &
orate the new marriage of Heaven & Hell
the tradition of Classic poetry filtered
thru the argot & cadence of 20th
century NYC street
Bremser could neologize lexicon every which way
down & loose, a language innovator nonpareil
& with it spun a yarn of profound humor
no holds barred defiance of authority
& true deep fanatic love of freedom
Kaufman could scat-code the emotional requirements
of the communication triumphant of all inclusive
unchewed humor-- pleasure & wisdom open
to all who are open
What Bird did with his horn Bob did with livid vivid
morphemes--
Without doubt a genuine genius who touches all senses
which he multitudinously enhances
& sends into orbit American Zaum
in the midst of everyday tragedy
Neal Cassady could present a word in a new position
a new defining fluidizing the entire vocab
a roulette wheel of transconsequential essence
of meaning and double triple meaning & other- world
image pulsing with strobing light
a supersonic river of psychic fiercely empathic
entendre like unstoppable running water
Jack Micheline was a street poet who described
the Street & its denizens
with eloquence & aplomb In the Bronx
the Mission, Bourbon St Algiers eLAy
` through the old windows of the Soul
Scribbling exuberance advocating it
keeping ancient lilt alive
QR Hand mixed a brew of Langston Bird Trane Walt Beat
Blues Rock Roll classic triumphant compassion that jumped
the hearer & reader inspiring untamed rivers of raging
rising & rolling highway moons down to the splashing
seas of Youth
Ginsberg could do it all & did from nursery rhymes to mad
elaborate enlightening epics every form & meter-- If
someone wrote verse
That could save the world it was Allen--
The Weight of the World is Love
Ecce Homo
Lenore Kandel Janine Vega Lew Welch
John Wieners Ted Joans Diane di Prima
Peter O, Pedro Pietri
They heard the Music
The muse uniting with the Music
Velimir Khlebnikov gave form to the original
tongue, the matrix of all, rowing down

CONTINUED NEXT PAGE

the Zangezi, a maven a champion of Laughter
& witness to horror he may have been
the greatest poet so far
Voloydya (Mayakovsky) voiced Nevsky Street
elegant & proud could make one weep
by reciting numbers
His World War One Poems
in the wagon 27 men & 4 legs
27 men 4 legs
Stood up by his love's desire waiting
One word lines:
Maria.
eight.
nine.
ten.
Maria.
Took the proverb and executed Zen surprise
tragic Ruski style a Cloud in Trousers
Kruchenyk often forewent consonants
all well and good
a e i o u ooo eee ooo aaa AAH
& gave the new raw trans language
the moniker Zaum "trans intellect
beyonsense budletyani singing trees"
But like Yessenin knew without heart
language is nothing
Without Heart Poetic skills and acumen
are stillborn
Ginsberg said "While here try to alleviate
the suffering"
Gregory told me, "End on a Crescendo!"
"Praised be the Non-Ending" wrote J Kerouac
There are Baby Camels in the Sky
Announced the beatific mystic Elena Guro
like Whitman giving us the magic
of Nature through paradise-eyed
naturally enlightened children
Diane Di Prima wrote We are all born
into perfect bliss makes me think
wow, we sure messed that up
Digging Bob Kaufman reminds
me of the philosophy of Spinoza
The same base the same paradigm Love
with a meaning--bonafide selflessness
I'm in awe of the power of groove & spew
of his rollicking spectacular mind & heart
Jack Micheline warbled, "It's the dead, it's
the goddam dead; it's the dead that rule
this w-w-world
Lew Welch heard universal life in a ring of bone
David Lerner could laugh with elevated
downtrodden outlier dissident eyes flashing
spouting metaphors that rocked
Similes that rolled mind leaps that confided
in the lingo of the land and times till
The absurd no longer seemed thataway

& rolled it all into a ball of social defiance
A bowling ball a mammoth shot put of defiance
a cannonball & snatched joy like the brass ring
on a carousel in the amusement park of Irony
Ray Bremser promised to come back
said he always came back before
Then something about yaks broken sacroiliacs
rest assured he'll be back
Pedro Pietri turned Fuck into a holy weapon a verb
a noun an adjectival modifier of both pleasure
& its antithesis
His poem Telephone Booth 905 1/2 on my wall
My work survived my lover Janine Vega's
Strunk driven red pencil
"Don't put the onus on the reader!'
Her own work championing women
& all oppressed underdogs never lacked
total immaculate devotion
to Mother Sincerity & uninhibited clarity
Lenore Kandel was an effulgent Divine
her under recognized hymns odes love
lyrics and empathy for the sorrow & pain
of our search for joy & beauty
in the decades & centuries to come
will inspire awe and ignite emotions
produced by the generating fervid lexicon
of the heart
A poet of generous ability fulfilling
Mary Wollstonecraft's prophesy
Jubilant celebration of female enjoyment
of sexual acts
So was Pamela Twining my love & friend
Kerouac turned me on to it all
close to sixty times around the sun
since striving for the flow of descriptive
Imagination--he more than not
would master--I tried to emulate
And it is a bene that he had flaws
politics, character, periods of poor work
or I probably would still be immersed
in writing like him cuz
when he was on he was supernal
For moi then he was as good as it gets
The New Twenties want to make ridicule
marginalize besmirch us, search for faults
errors and sordid history
Let us resist
Let us vindicate fight for the rights of humor
Let us preserve the break-through feeling
FUCK IS GOOD!
Let us use & exhibit our all-loving Divinity!
Let the Orgasm of Love save our planet
& those of its children who deserve
better.....................
May the Futurians have another go
May Beat be the Future

Jack Kerouac (2021) artwork by SOHEYL DAHI

ANDY CLAUSEN
WHAT IT IS
IN DEFENCE OF POETRY

I you we must go & keep going we shall
restore poetry to its rightful throne
Its central altar of kindness & glory path
the supreme art which all art is
evolved and succored by
Poetry is the beginning of knowledge
It is the primal foreplay
What It is the catalyst to Romantic Love
What It is first history the semen & ovum
of religion of agriculture & architecture
It inspires the mathematical meaning of sounds
It is the meter of all music and work
What It is the backbone flute of both philosophers
and those who aspire to be the executioners
of Philosophy
It's name could be anything and is
scribed spoken dreamt into action
We will not only create an accurate
gesture of both dilemma & joy
Because by utter of meaning-beauty shining
will defeat drab ugliness of soulless evil meaningless
Will defeat meaninglessness, meaninglessness that
Sterilizes spays castrates diminishes our lives
our lambent imaginations and naturally
sympathetic hearts, our "Poet's Core"
Our Divine Responsibility
Together we'll harken the illumined path
Yes we'll harken it alright
The path to solving & ab-solving
The dilemmas produced by injustice
both from conditions of birth
and the learned craft of brutal
domination solved & must be absolved
Must sustain Imagination
Poetry is what denotes us from machines
Separates us from all-Id instinct consumed beasts
By You Rebirth of the Voice
You The Key to the Highway
What It Is & What It Aint
IS WHAT IT IS
The Heart the Heart that thinks
that breaks that beats a defiant rhythm
rolling marching with a skip
A Simon of Cyrene up hill as chanting waves
like waves of golden grain Youth
Soon enuff will be Veterans wounded but resolute tramping an
echoing reborn purpose instilling
Words with reinvigorated intention
ancient & 2022 conceived in a sparkling

pointillism vision worthy of the pure
profane hence most sacred
The mountain is forever no longer
just a mountain
Poetry explodes like a horde of outlaw seeds
like raindrops bursting digging
deep the channel of the charnel charred
heart of unforgiving pampered Self
Idolization that fears the disapproval
of the boss machines
That laughs at the Poets, snidely & widely
There will be no last laugh
Long Live Gen-u-wine POETRY
The Songs of Visionary Outlaws Rebels
Revolutionaries Mothers every bit as good
as Fathers Educators the Dispossessed
The Toilers & Dreamers & generous
Champions of the Future
THE TAO WHAT IT IS
POETRY
Without it we are overstressed overdressed apes
Rancid hircine bags of dirty water
Any society that does not honor and heed its poets
is doomed
Even Corso has come around
"Poetry...God Bless"

Artwork by **JOHN SEABURY**

VICTOR CLEVENGER
YOU CAN'T ESCAPE WHAT YOU CAN'T ESCAPE

between sips of coffee
she tells me that it is not a bad job
fourteen dollars an hour with tips
& a meal mid-shift
but when she empties the ash trays
attached to the slot machines
the smell reminds her
of her mother's nightstand
when they lived in that hotel for a while
& even back then
she found it odd
that in the morning time
every man that her mother brought back
to have sex with
was introduced to her
as her uncle
like that was the solution
to make everything
that she had just experienced
seem better

VICTOR CLEVENGER
SHARING THE GHOSTS OF YESTERDAYS

nosediving deep into the depths
of a warm reassurance
saying
you once had slipped
from great heights
& got stuck in a moment

where your side was ripped open
by a crooked nail

& at first the blood ran down softly
like the tone of a whisper
but it built up quickly
to an intoxicating level of fear

that more demons would be summoned
than angels

to help sing the chorus

of just another sad swan song about falling
from the heavens

too many times

to walk away without scars

Artwork by E.P. UPJOHN (opposite page)

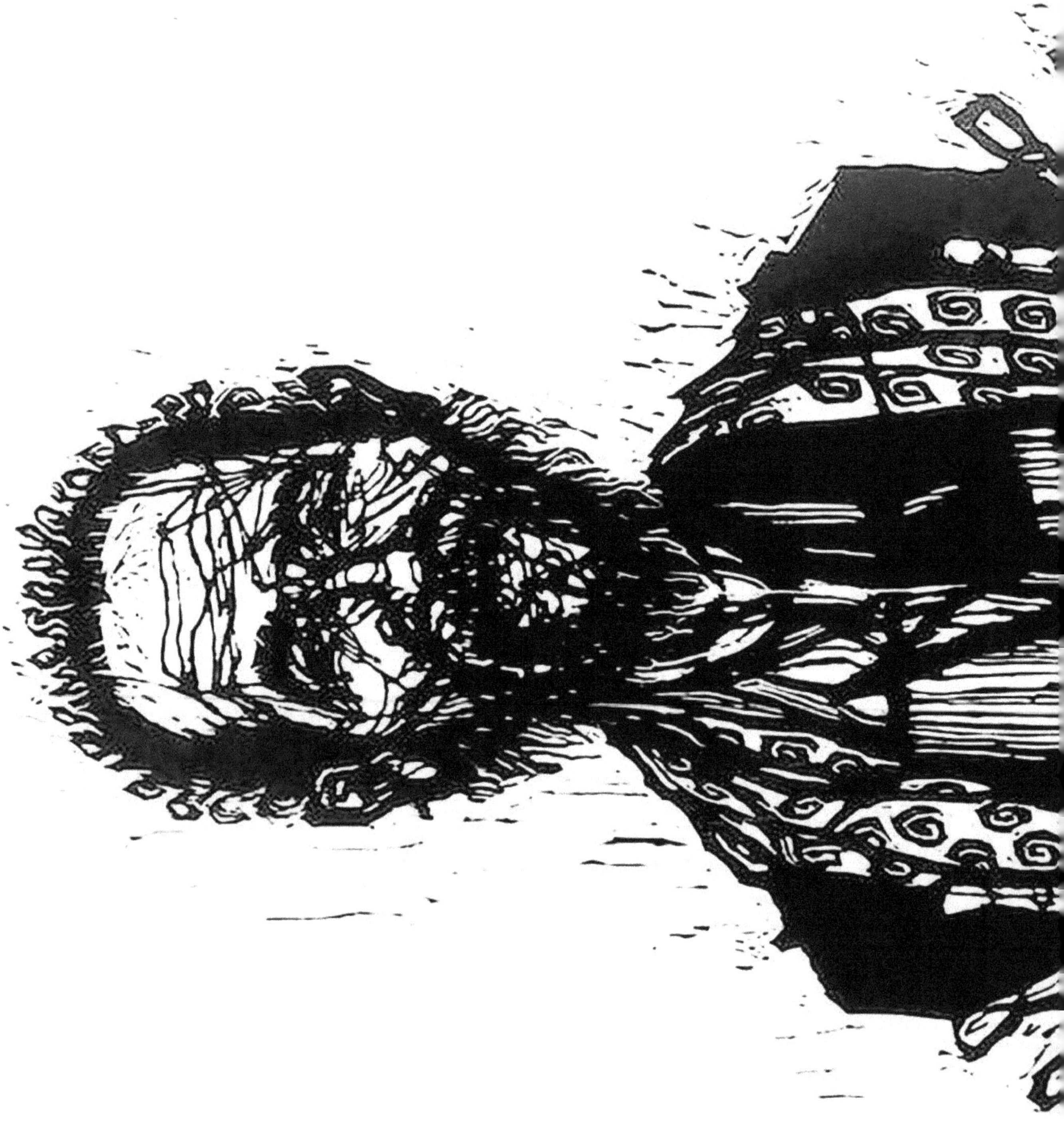

Bob Kaufman 1925~1986
Woodcut by Kristen Wetterhahn

I sat at my bedroom window
and watched you dance outside
as you fanned your fairy wings
in the pre-dawn air
and kicked up the dust at your feet.
I listened to the sounds
that streamed from
the inside of your head
I secretly adored your smile
as your closed eyes
lit up like 3 lucky 7's

"Hey DJ, just play that song. Keep me dancing (dancing), all night."
I wanted to hold
your black nail polished
hand forever,
attracted to the power
of your great gentleness,
completely ignoring
the rude balance
that tips the scale
ON this kind of
rare beauty.

I walked over to you
compelled, spellbound
and lifted your chin
when you were
out and down.
I gave up my secrets and
whispered them into your ear as the sun rose up onto
our yawning faces.
I watered the soil
in which you grew from
whenever it (you) became dry.
I swayed across deserts, mountains
and beaches with you
while silent rhythms
beat midnight madness
into our hearts,
speaking a language
without the trouble
of words.

We fell
like two apples
from the same tree.

Unfortunately,
like all fruit, we perish
by way of rot and stench
erasing all traces
of our existence.

May our seeds
find their way
to a glorious blossom,
even if we
no longer
see eye to eye.

BECAUSE

Because my sex is powerful
I was taught not to flaunt it
by the women in my family
but to be ashamed by it
Because my sex is powerful
I was asked to keep it secret
by incestuous hands that wandered
underneath my bedtime sheets
Because my sex is powerful
I gave it away
to every chance that came
Because my sex is powerful
I believed I earned a say on where it went
manipulating situations in honor of it
Because my sex is powerful
I still cower behind a complex
of monumental insecurity,
building a wall of bricks around my heart
instead of the pillow soft kisses
I fool myself with

– Annette Cruz

Collage art by **MARK FISHER**
(opposite page)

that the patterns
lent themselves
to a softer chaos,
was a hard-earned
perspective,
I spent years
perfecting.
I could do
without,
such an insisting
universe.
Sacred math
like
fire
breathing
dragons.
that the songs
leaned
more and more
into the darkness
was a welcome
surprise.
So many
years,
listening
with more and more
of my eyes.
And the dead
whistled
lullabies
in my ears
when I slept.

we were
meant
for more
than this.

after so many
nights,
wasted,
chasing
unwanted demons.
it's no wonder
my eyes
have gone
to the dogs.

we were going
to transcend
all that held
the rest of them
down.

but we didn't
well
I didn't

Artwork by **MARK FISHER**
(opposite page)

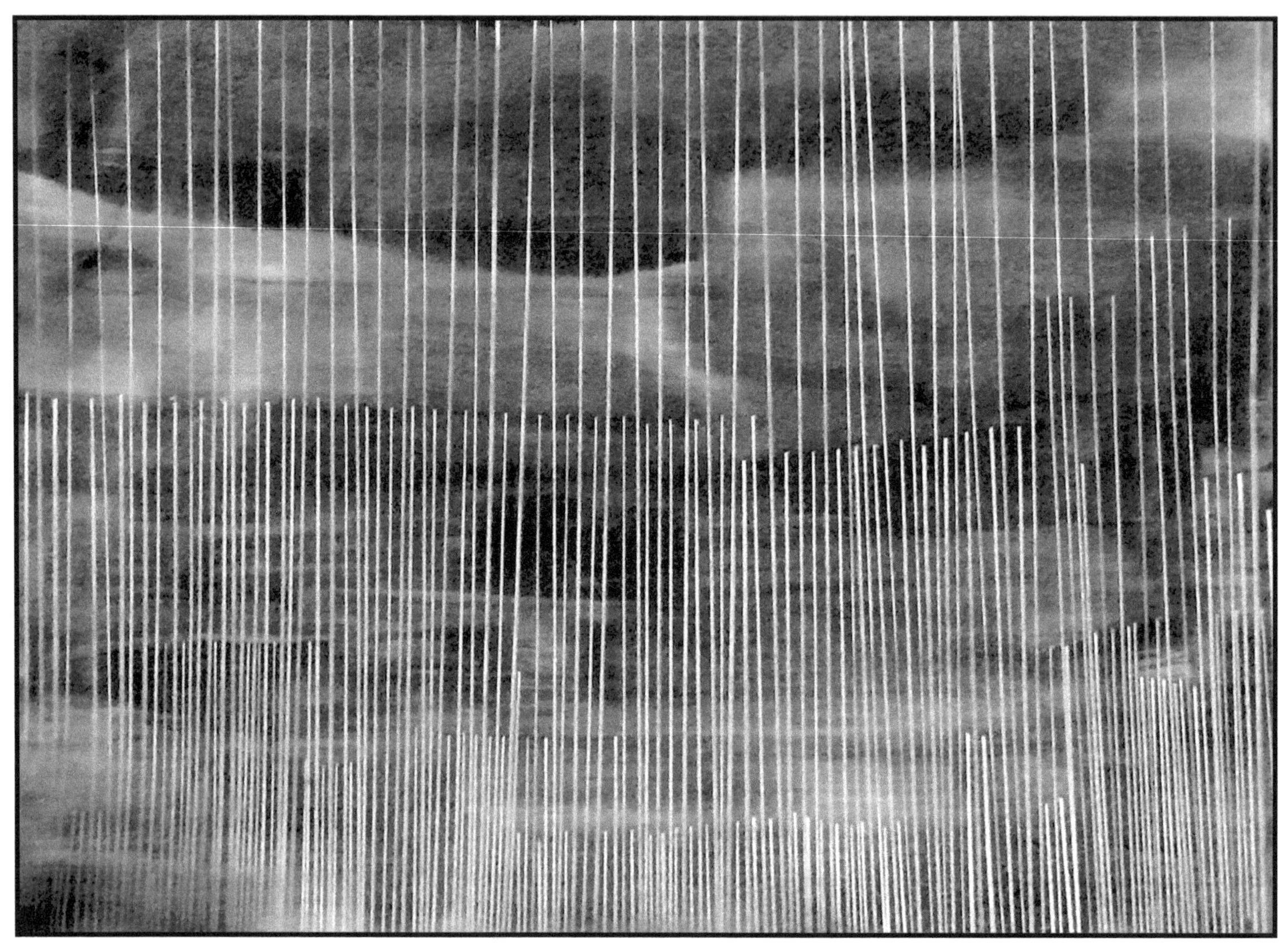

Artwork by **CLEA JONES**

SOHEYL DAHI
TEHRAN (I)

Cars honk
Someone yells: over here!
There's dust in the air
A rumor of mountains in the horizon
A man walks by
with bread under his arm
Construction workers
taking a break in the shade
Two soldiers stand guard
A half-eaten watermelon
left on the sidewalk
A small boy sweeps the ground
under the watchful eyes of his grandfather
Someone asks me for direction
An ambulance goes by
An old woman asks for money
A young man shines shoes

All this and more
as I stood
on a street corner
and watched

TEHRAN (II)

I know this room, this bed
My father lay there
In the end, mere bones
Fetal, pained
facing the empty walls

It's my bed now
Free of his scent
I lay half-naked
in white sheets

I listen to the
summer rain
pouring down furiously
from the heavens
cleansing
this city

--Soheyl Dahi

LUBBERT JAN DE VRIES
A POEM FROM A SOLDIER (FOUND IN A TRENCH)

brothers!
wandering across this deserted battlefield
we have become the shadows
people far away from the violence speak about

sure, brothers,

we were of service to the sweet angel
this radiant creature
beckoning we should grace ourselves with the robe of darkness
to feed the beast
—
so, from behind the mask of good intentions
ignorant of the momentum of the conflict
instead of grasping for peace
we fed the monster in its hunger for ruin

true, people,

I tell in verse
that heaven and paradise are shared spaces
yet hell is a private place
a mess of memories
of manliness & pride, pleasure & happiness, sin & death,
at the crossroads en route to the frontline

even so, people,

take me to the bonfire just the same
to spit in the embers and cry out man is Divine
—
that the fire gives light and heat
to find a way
to calm our guts

and finally, I know
—
I am truly revered by you
for indeed heroes are gladly seen, a feast for the eyes
but, go back to your homes now
this ether, the evanescence & loneliness
is my OWN

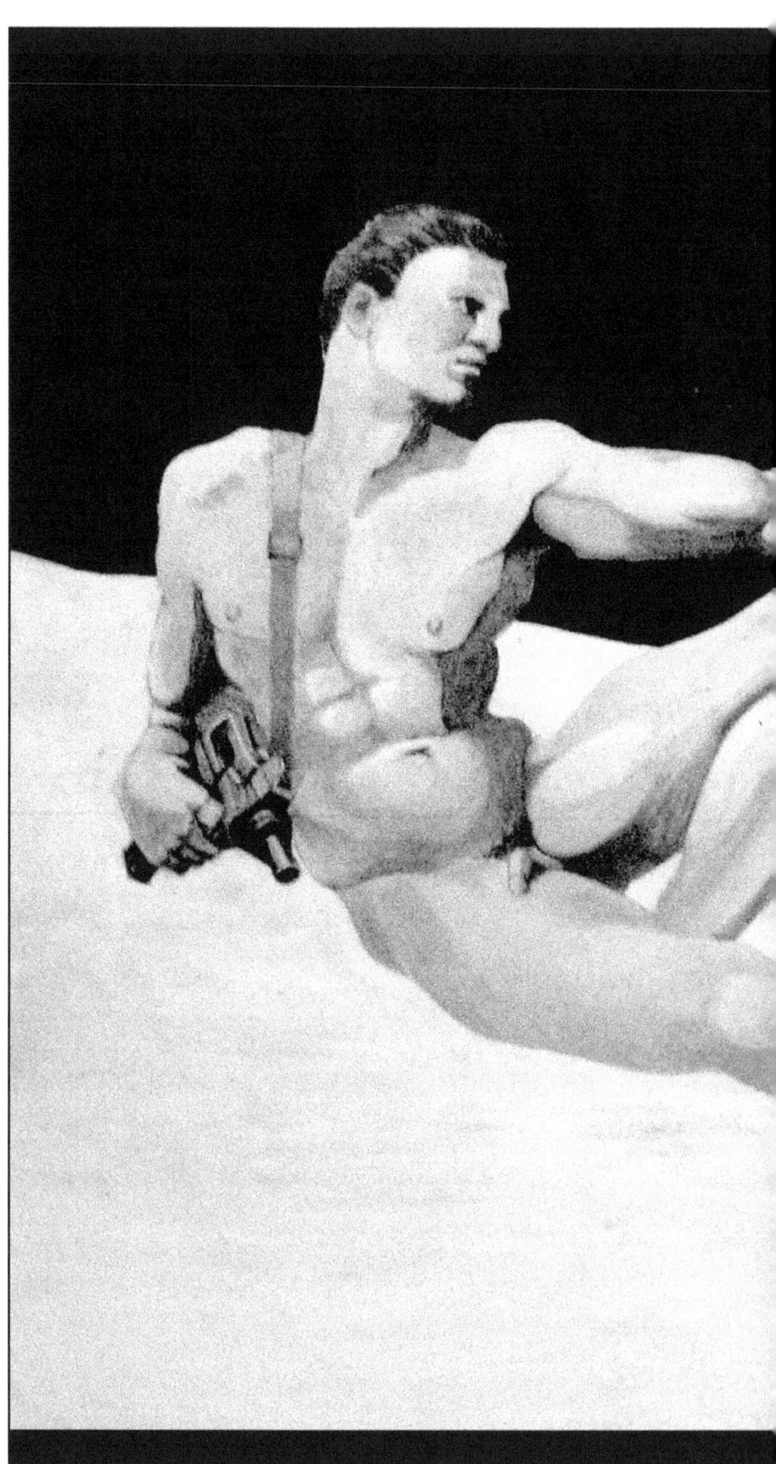

Artwork by *TRACY WITT*

DAN DENTON
WHO CARES ABOUT THE PRESIDENT

I was reading that
Yellowstone National Park
is really
just a super volcano
& if it ever erupts
we wont have
to care anymore
who the president is
cuz we'll all be dead

I don't mean
to be the naysayer
but I wonder
how much longer
we're going
to ignore the rumblings
of a working class
pressure cooker
that's shaking
& sputtering
letting off steam
every hour on the hour
& spitting geysers
of abandoned hope
just often enough
to remind us
that when it blows
we'll no longer
have to care
who the president is
then, either

"Jurassic Return" collage art by T. MIKE WALKER

PALMS
DIACODEXIS
2013

DIANE DI PRIMA
ON THE WAY HOME
(A PRAYER FOR THE ROAD)

On the way home
all the restaurants will serve miso soup

On the way home
exotic notebook stores will blossom in small towns in Nevada

On the way home
Utah will be festooned w / mirth
Mormons will be dancing in the streets in gauzy chachkas

On the way home
Everyone will leave the casinos and the slot machines & go outside
to stare at the beauty of the mountains, of the sky, of each other

On the way home
All the boys & girls in the secret desert bordellos
will have set up temples of free love festooned with mimosa
they will teach karma-mudra to joyful redneck ranchers
who have set all their cows free and now drink only amrita

On the way home
every cafe in Wyoming will be holding a potlatch
poverty will thus be abolished

On the way home
everyone we meet will try to read us a poem
invite us in for a story there being no news
but what travelers bring, all TV having died

On the way home
it will be easy to find pure water, organic tomatoes, friendly conversation
We'll give & receive delightful music & blessings at every gas station

On the way home
all the truck drivers will drive politely
the traveling summer tourists will beam at their kids

our old Toyota will love going up mountain passes
openhearted & unsuspicious people & lizards
prairie dogs, wolves & magpies will sing together & picnic
at sunset beside the road
Everyone will get where they're going
Everyone will be peaceful
Everyone will like it when they get there

All obstacles smoothed
auspiciousness & pleasure
will sit like a raven dakini
on every roof

Portrait of Diane di Prima by SOHEYL DAHI

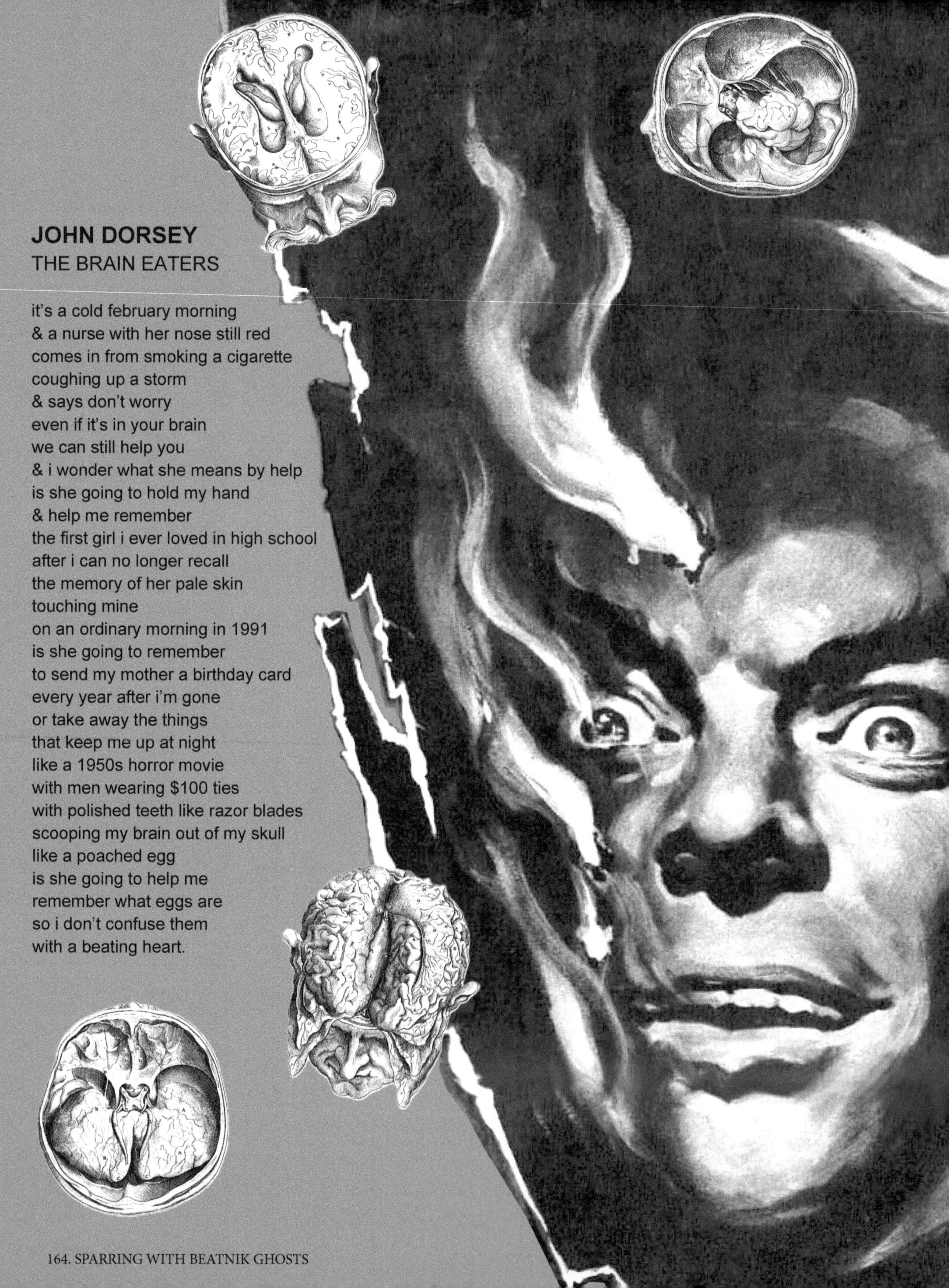

JOHN DORSEY
THE BRAIN EATERS

it's a cold february morning
& a nurse with her nose still red
comes in from smoking a cigarette
coughing up a storm
& says don't worry
even if it's in your brain
we can still help you
& i wonder what she means by help
is she going to hold my hand
& help me remember
the first girl i ever loved in high school
after i can no longer recall
the memory of her pale skin
touching mine
on an ordinary morning in 1991
is she going to remember
to send my mother a birthday card
every year after i'm gone
or take away the things
that keep me up at night
like a 1950s horror movie
with men wearing $100 ties
with polished teeth like razor blades
scooping my brain out of my skull
like a poached egg
is she going to help me
remember what eggs are
so i don't confuse them
with a beating heart.

ALEXIS RHONE FANCHER
SNAKE/HOLDING THINGS DOWN

There's a warning in the desert today. A high wind is howling, blustery, blowing everything away. My lover's put heavy rocks on the mats around the Jacuzzi. Trying to hold everything down so he doesn't have to capture it later. The towels, the lounge chairs, the barbecue, me. *I bought a snake from Lowe's,* he says.

My lover's a DIY guy. Multi-talented. Intellectual, paramour, sous chef, and handyman. The kitchen sink's backed up. I point out the sludge, the glug glug, each time I turn on the tap. He bends down to inspect the pipes. There's even a bit of butt-crack. He threads the snake into the kitchen drain, coaxes it down. It makes a loud, sucking complaint, the sludge reluctant to depart.

I'm going back to Lowe's to get a bigger, longer snake, my lover says. *Get a king snake*, I whisper in his ear. I reach between his legs, cop a feel. *Yeah, sure,* he says, rolling his eyes. *A king snake.* He gives my roving hand a squeeze. *Or would you prefer a boa constrictor?*

Lately things have been good between us. We've each learned to listen. I'm a writer. I play with words. He's a lover; he plays with me. I love him best when he's in my universe. Takes note of the world around us through my rose-colored glasses. Shares. Yesterday it was the rainbow he saw on the way back from Lowe's.

You should have seen it, baby, he said. *Every color - brilliant red to ultraviolet!* He passed his iPhone to me. *Look!* he said. *I captured it for you.* A shimmering arc of color holds down the horizon.

1st Published in Vox Populi 2024

Ask the Waitress
for Our Cocktail Menu
or enjoy a bottle of your
favorite Wine with your Dinner

FOUNTAIN ROOM AVAILABLE FOR WEDDINGS,
BANQUETS, PARTIES AND BUSINESS MEETINGS.

RICH FERGUSON
3 AM WAFFLE HOUSE WAITRESSES

On those nonstop solo cross-country drives when one lonely day bled into the next,
there were those 3 AM Waffle House waitresses.
Some sported a ring on their marriage finger; others had rough, bare hands worn from
carrying full trays or doing dishes when the washer called in sick.
Some were tank-tough, old-school cool.
Others had Moon Pie eyes and sticky-sweet lips like candy wrappers.
Their apron pockets: filled with insufficient tips and too much shit talk and gossip from
drunks and locals.
Went home with the smell of grease and grits all over them.

KATHLEEN FLORENCE
THICK SKIN BIAS

she is not walking into an ocean
acclimatizing hot summer day
her skin will not grow armor
poor people do not have thicker skin

poverty does not make us stronger
there is no badge of honor
given at the shelter
we will not get used to it

we do not need less help
less love or less attention
because our homes are smaller
shoes are older
car is marked by accident
we cannot afford to fix

prayers with a side of cash
will not be answered faster
to suit the comforts of others
those prayers are not better or more important
than anyone who owns less junk

this culture schooled in nostalgia for waste
fake love and plastic compassion
have thick skin bias
middle-class credit card debt
neurotic nursery rhymes
keeping us all up late at night
sugar plum stories
about pulling up bootstraps
the benefits of hard knocks
and the dream realized
if we work a little harder

never mentioning those who must lose
for those who must win
from cemetery rows
to unpaid alimony
sacrifice sounds nice
on a sunday with a choir

JACK FOLEY
FOR JERRY

to see the dark shadow take them one by one
old friends
of many years
enemies too, indiscriminate in this
this is part of your Golden Years…

and now that dear, important man, Jerome Rothenberg,
moves to the shadows.
we listened together to T.S. Eliot intoning *The Waste Land*
on my car radio,
both mesmerized.
when it ended, Jerry said quietly,
"Jesus, Eliot was a wonderful poet."
he kindly told me, though he didn't have to,
of someone who had been badmouthing me in Southern California.
know your enemies.
know your friends.
there are some
who appear at times
only to betray
work
of heart
and head,
mal-laborators,
their task
only
to destroy.
Jerry was never
one of these.
dear friend,
I learned of your death
just after Sangye and I
had seen
Antonioni's great *La Notte*.
you enter the night
head held high
heart beating
borne on the wings
of the art you practiced
with such intelligence
and such expanse
of love.

Jerome Rothenberg, December 11, 1931-April 21, 2024

"Farewell Neeli Cherkovski, Marjorie Perloff, Jerome Rothenberg,
friends of the consciousness that matters."
Photomontage by **DOREN ROBBINS** *(opposite page)*

AMÉLIE FRANK
MUSCLE

It cinches around my joints and contracts
so forcefully that I feel a danger that
my bones might snap if he coughs,
if he shudders, if he asks for it
any rougher. We are both using
our indoor voices this afternoon
although mine is akin to a sharp bark
when at last he attains mastery.
He says "Face the mirror"
and I see that I am completely
possessed, a woman with
a survivor's asymmetry, a blur
for a jawline, too much
avoir du poids for a middle,
my long hair the only camouflage
for all the souvenirs of combats
he knows nothing about.
His timing has made me sad
again, and I ask, inwardly,
that he not scatter chips of
the still-beating muscle
that burns steadily
and in emerald pulses
for him alone, not like the seed pearls
of my now-trashed necklace.
What was the word
he used to describe them?
Unadulterated? Baroque?
It took a lifetime to gather them up
from the four corners
after the last go-round, and then the
endless hours of restringing with faith
the only thread pulling all of it back
into place. Again, he does not know
that the repairs are so fresh, that
the tugs and tears of a lifetime
have forged bands from the ruptured fibers,
concentric rings like the measurable markers
of time inside a tree, and that these also cinch
and squeeze out my breath in moments
of panic, astonishment, even passion,
not to mention wonder.
He, too, is scattered, and the nacre
soon cools on my chest, my throat.
Today, he has surprised me, as he always does,
with the secret name he has chosen for me.
I did not anticipate this, same as when he called me
The Sun when I felt myself to be but a satellite.
Before he leaves, he contains me in
the musculature of his arms, his knee draped
over my hip, and he names me in a way
I have not been named before.
"My Love," he says to me quietly. "My Love."

Artwork by
DAVID HUMBERT DE SUPERVILLE

THOMAS FUCALORO

my mouth is

an impromptu

graveyard

My dentist said that I am so stressed out they can see it in my gums.

Bulbous
        pink
                protuberance forming below the tooth line excavation

bludgeoning place particles hoping it will add to the

empty plots of smile. When I was dating an anchor, they made shore

to latch onto the seaside
                                jawline
                                        horror
                                                horizon hinged by a threading

chance might save us   I have   lost   many   a   teeth   thinking

about how many they have spent. Time is a tooth I need dental insurance

to replicate. Losing time makes me think of my mother, how

my teeth will survive way longer than body in this dental plot of land.

I have been cleaning out her memories and throwing away her life

for all the neighbors to see, curbed. The pallbearers take her away

piece by piece every Wednesday and Saturday. A suburban funeral.

Artwork by TRACY WITT

Twilight Lands by Nelson Gary

with artwork by Tracy Witt

The past is presently pregnant with the future. When is the future a viable life? Before it becomes the mother. This is what the future is before it becomes her.

Before the old heaven and earth were reduced to swallowing the proverbial truth about themselves, which came from Crazy Wisdom's objective lips informed by the omnijective counsel of Young Understanding, I was born for this with its terrifying ecstasies and agonies. God broke me to be this nude beggar before the big bang. My brokenness is my openness, and this emptiness is the Great Freedom that holds the Infinite! Intoxicating and treacherous rumors of Crazy Wisdom's most obscure proverbs were what led to me to becoming her back-alley, skyclad pet. She would detest my twilight language if I were not straightforward about my use of it. Skyclad, "nude," twilight language ("no secrets"). I have no secrets, not permanently. One twilight, I'll have opened up all my dark nights of the soul as well as the power and glory of Vénus Noire to Dr. Marlowe, my psychologist, and then, my guess is he'll be able to start a new life after his own personal trauma as a result of the Apocalypse. The way to be one with Crazy Wisdom is to have no secrets. I have grown in holy madness for the public's senses but not more than for their souls followed by their minds. For the better part, I have accomplished this by being an empty plaything, an all-purpose ecstasy delivery system, in public protected by Wisdom.

I was not always medicine, a carrier of designs of divinity into the marginally human debris scattered in the colorful chaos and bleak desolation, the old frontier, before the twilights of dusk and dawn bookended the borderland, the manufacturer of history, with it being largely unaware of the Philadelphian pillars of sisterly and brotherly love placed there: love full of mindfulness and void of conscience sold through miraculous wine and bought by sacrificial blood. The old frontier remained the jewel of past civilizations until I was around 17; then things fell apart gradually, ever so gradually, and little other than love could be shared by the time I was 24. The money stopped, and the power was hung on a tree with a Judas knot from which it still occasionally transmits cables. They are delivered to exhibits of illusion and the numerous roulette tables down through the ages.

At 17, a piece of queasy San Quentin quail, I skipped school often and received brutal beatings from a bully of a father about the face when he caught me, especially if he had lost bread that day at the Casino Amour where the red fern grows. The ripped, socially polished nudies sold themselves there. It was my dream and prayer to be just like them, only more so, if somehow possible: to be wanted like that and for everything that life wasn't giving at the price of shame, social disgrace, disease, violence, and jail. During their down times, anyone could catch them jonesing for kisses, what they never received before, after, and during being vulgarized by buyers and owners reeking of hooch, skag, and chronic.

Too many times with swollen eyes cut to a blistering, scorpion anguish and then some from grain alcohol, I saw that horizon where I could be shrunken into a kind of voodoo doll of my old man, and I started to move in that direction: wholeness, a synthesis of all the opposites to sound out my questions about why I had to bleed new blood from old bruises for not being interested by everything in the schoolyard and its rooms of forest-lawn carpet. Tucked away in a cave with skulls and the sex-starved goddess, a wonder cabinet of warped dimensions, which coupled in this imagining of Magdalene and Wisdom as the crevice of my teen, oracular mouth, my flesh would break out with goose bumps more often as I grew deeper in the shed with the hobby quill hated by my father. Past curfew, I read as well as recited what I wrote in cafes with hipsters and hoodlums, most of whom were well acquainted with psychology, many of them even consumers of it and psychiatry.

Temptations to become a hophead to tame the electrical storm in my wiry frame were there relatively regularly from the time my black words poured from my mouth loud and invisible the first time in a roomful of souls. Somewhere, away from the haven and hazard of a single-parent home, I would poke myself with needles and get poked as one of those sex workers, temple dancers, who knew the price of true affection among hitchhikers warming up to each other in a blizzard of a world. When I was 17, Fortune reigned supreme with caprice while Wisdom ran undercover in flashing light and shade in broad daylight in front of grey matter too dim to spot her, the leopard, that lady, Wisdom.

My first shot at independent living had me living large in a tiny town, just a kid essentially, cashing in on bootleg atomic archetype experiments and rapid-reversible, sex-reassignments surgeries at two black labs kitty corner from each other on Miller and Querelle. Kali, with

CONTINUED NEXT PAGE

her muscular, rounded squat of a frame, had lined up the real-life biopunk gigs for me in what was a virgin taste of the twilight lands. Resilience did not happen overnight, or the life my old man lost at the roulette table over one too many games, but most forensic psychologists would probably believe the surgeries were related to me being on the lam, run. I would have disagreed then and said, "It was all about being more versatile as a Tantric healer," but now being asked questions by Marlowe, I have to re-think this, as well as many other matters, because truth is love and love is truth. Beauty is Lucifer bested only by Helen of Sparta-Troy at the twilight's main intersection of

She had spotted me dancing nude for passing change, wrapped one of her braceleted arms around my bony waist, pulled me into a slime-filled, vacant alley with its overflowing trashcans of mostly comic books and back issues of *The Wall Street Journal.*

humanity's collective unconscious. On a conscious basis, even in sessions with Marlowe, I was unafraid of the death penalty or being confined to any city of refuge, even the worst one in Dis.

Kali and I had met after the avalanche of rock cocaine that lit up the cops in a maze of crystal chances. She had spotted me dancing nude for passing change, wrapped one of her braceleted arms around my bony waist, pulled me into a slime-filled, vacant alley with its overflowing trashcans of mostly comic books and back issues of *The Wall Street Journal.* A good many of the comic books were pamphlets of Kali worship. She discarded them in a humorous way. Kali and her disavowed followers wiped their asses on the journal copies when the pigs began to get their heads around the penny loafer (CIA) crash of snow on the street. With her arm firmly around this dancer's waist as if it were a flesh-and-bone jukebox, she grabbed my hardened, pulsing cock in the darkness. It grew as we progressed deeper into the alley, the womb of all that ever was, with the graffiti of historians in cryptic shorthand (poetry) to define it as a series of figures, identities, mirrors of themselves and all other things, the crystal cathedral—eventually, my rock was in her crack.

Having already broken my will to turn me out, "You want to be my man, boy?" she rhetorically asked, purring the centuries and eliminating time for just those seconds when stockbrokers jumped out windows, chasing the almost countless ghost limbs of their mindless, heartless god Mammon—filthy lucre. After mixing her salad, my whole being became a slave to a tiny nub of Kali's flesh, her clitoris. Her honey in the darkness was similar to the stillness and peace of the pond centered by a little field at her home in the country away from the city. The city, and the whole world with it, had taken the mark of the Least. I passed through bleeding city of wine as a fugitive accused of patricide. Kali's water fountain, her place, was the only aspect of existence that really made it for me in those moments of breaking through the hatred we had both known in the nurseries and cemeteries and everywhere in between for longer than your breath mattered to your parents, your ancestors, you, and angels, demons, God, and the devil. As a virtuoso played "Consolation No. 3" by Liszt from an open window where the cooking Reubens replaced the stench of refuse in the alley and burning flesh a few blocks down, she squeezed my balls hard and said, "I'm going to do whatever I want with these. And so are my friends."

"That's just fine," I moaned, whispered it again, her slave, her whatever she wanted, her Plastic Man, her gigolodeon, her whatever she wanted (yes!), a genie. Egoless and, in fact, mahasiddha-bodiless needs were met for a human sacrifice of a sexual-spiritual, escapist adventure amidst the ceaseless, pitiless, and senseless chemical warfare on the streets of Beware City where bowwowwow!!! Kali had bent herself over for me to enter her holy sanctuary again as a tool, all lingam, phallus and language, to cut through all the world's illusion to the diminishing ecstatic nature of its reality, all of its nectar of immortality lost to the living stream of her timelessness. Her insides had tightened and loosened with the heaven and hell I had been born to unleash, as the spook you'd never figure on account of occasional cowboy mouth (such as the 9/11 job) on the necks of the runts of a power-mad world: a violently loving blues after mushing the steppenwolves through more than the avalanche of cocaine Christmas as Kid Blast. Kali taught me how to do this with the rhythm of the River Guanyin off the banks of Tiresias Town with its brown weed and Ford-Angleton Necropolis where we tested the spirits, shining buffalo nickels and cutting through our egos in the presence of ghouls. They had fol-

CONTINUED NEXT PAGE

CONTINUED FROM LAST PAGE

lowed me as friends and enemies since my birth as the first cave drawing, a word really, the stick figure, an object ultimately.

One day, I leveled with Kali. "Could you please take the Captain Marvel mask off? Thank you. My flirtation with the bi-sissy lifestyle is pretty long and deep if you have the time to let my whip of a tongue scar you with it," I told her over coffee at Chet's, sitting outdoors: a quaint, quiet place with a mint awning and a neon sign that blinked.

"Go ahead. It's kosher. I have the time."

I've been accused of topping from the bottom after getting gang-banged as a popular model begging for it. Getting my demands met. In a sense. My needs met. Whatever. Sometimes, well maybe, twice, this was the truth. About the topping from the bottom business. I've been a grateful sub hundreds of times with no games, not even any lip. But now I have this reputation for being this deceptive power tripper. It's way fuckin' overblown! I mean, it's fuckin' bad for business. And worse, it cramps my lifestyle. Power is this world's main problem. If I could do anything with my life, it would be to bring about the fall of power.

"In the meantime, I just want to go out of my body, radically modify it, or both. I don't want to change my mind. It's not the problem. I want to change my body, not even necessarily to a female or hermaphrodite's body, not even necessarily to the temple of the Holy Ghost. I just want my soul to be free, unbothered, and loved and loving without anything so fixed, so certain, so objective, measurable, and absolute on my end as a body, so I can speak better for those without any voice." After that, thanks to Kali, I regularly cashed checks from the trash treasuries of the black labs, and soon, I lived the underground bard, Schrödinger's cat Negative Capability dream.

I became everyone at the small price of becoming a nobody, but this well-known voice. Nobody caused my relationship with Saranyu, the Ashwin kumars, her horse-headed twins, and the Trojan horse to have a side effect: a heavyweight horse addiction. My smack addiction, which began with chasing the dragon and remained such for 9 months, led to art, tattoos, for the sake of camouflage, concealment, from, of course, pokes. Living large in a tiny town, concrete angles can flex straight or bent and get abstract. The changes can be more abstract than André Kertész's *Distortions*. Here, I can become female, intersexed, or male, rounded or angular in the uncompromising glare beating down on the gas pump mirrored in my sunglasses. The El Dorado fender reflects the passage of animal-cracker clouds in the sunset.

They remind me of Goddesses' used tampons in the oily garage where I am the water boy and pleasure tool willfully dis-identified for the spirit of poetry to be uncertain, not confused, about gender. This benefits mastermind and crackpot strategies of how I am run as an asset, a side hustle I've recently taken on again, mainly in Montauk. Uncertainty prolongs ecstasy, but Frank Lee, the hog, is kept, owned, a hold-over tank of trademark testosterone. More than anyone or anything, Frank indirectly links me to Dr. Marlowe, but the doctor and I have not much of an interpersonal past that I know of, other than this. He attends to the necessary homicides that are not my hire to a rhythm that drenches holes, makes bullets missiles, and leaves the brain smoke, grey matter nothing more, just a kind of Silly Putty. I'm Frank's femboy slave, the son of a mother-fuckin', tittie-suckin', two-balled bitch. Crazy Wisdom loaned me to him to have me

Here, I can become female, intersexed, or male, rounded or angular in the uncompromising glare beating down on the gas pump mirrored in my sunglasses. The El Dorado fender reflects the passage of animal-cracker clouds in the sunset.

for whatever he wants, usually being raped by him and a gang of other spooks as inspiration for what I do best, language, communicate with words. One person's hell is another person's heaven. My father has been missing for years; his case has gone cold. On Earth, the twilight lands between Heaven and Hell, and it's in that light that most all of us live and die, many of us not knowing the truth because we can't accept the ambiguity of being human and the uncertainty that fills existence. It's good to be trained to be posthuman where I sling "my own power" over the cattle in mustard and custard-colored hills haunted by the tragedy of a race destroyed by fear of death, power struggles, or madness when I'm not in Montauk, deep undercover, cutting deals.

KAT GEORGES
IN BROAD DAYLIGHT!

Everyone's kissing out on the streets
IN BROAD DAYLIGHT!
Kids with purple hair are kissing!
Old folks with walkers are kissing!
Men are kissing men are kissing
women kissing women—Heck!—
I even saw two dogs kissing—dachshunds—
IN BROAD DAYLIGHT!
These streets are out of control!

It's kissing season—gorgeous weather—
that intangible late spring bloom
where just enough quick thunderstorms
keep the temperature down and
the need to kiss HIGH!
It's the URGE—the physicality of streets
full of people again—it makes skin
on skin contact inevitable and
every lip on every face is all
a-quiver—just looking for a kiss!

It's a way to fight the dark, dark, dark news
HEADLINES screaming about wars, about guns,
about crime, about the doubtful future,
about just how disgusting things have become
and yet, here we are—kissing—on the street
IN BROAD DAYLIGHT! Why doesn't anyone
write about that—wait!—WHO CARES?

Maybe tomorrow things will be different,
the weather will change, a world of peace
and harmony will drive the news beat—
we'll tiptoe through tulips and dance
the Carioca and the Dua Lipa and
our lips will be too busy SMILING to kiss.

Right now—it's the late spring bloom
and love is never disgusting and a kiss
IN BROAD DAYLIGHT! solves everything
for as long as it lasts

Mystic Boxing Commission presents

Available now at SparringArtists.com

S.A. GRIFFIN
THE BABY AND THE BATHWATER
– for Pope John Paul George Ringo I

there has been a
changing of the guard
going on

spotty in places
but on the make
and on the move

centuries old gasping giants are falling
fracturing the firmament
opening great fissures in their wake
allowing the light to get in
terminating the dying virus of the past
with extreme prejudice

it's nature's way

her last chance cure
for the sickness
boiling in her belly

I sometimes think maybe it's me feeling my age
but even the young ones feel it

an age of rage
of grievance
of retribution

an accelerated awareness
a new improved madness
ready to step into the fight

the wild in us all sounding the alarms
as brigades of opportunity
smell the burning books

there is no safe intermission
from yes

far and wide
the old world
with its old ways
is dying

and for all practical
and impossible purposes
is dead

every good deed
  gone bad

the old networks just haven't received the news yet
they have a banana in their ears

a burning cross in their chest

the red ink of murder
under their nails

fires and floods everywhere
sirens going off everywhere
all over the planet

even into the far reaches of the
going out of business sale
calling collect from the weeping eyes
of our melting vanilla sky

you gotta land on your feet in this
Punch and Judy slapstick

know how to take a fall
but never surrender

and it is the bravest among us
the comedians
that always take the first shots

that get the last laughs

this game is jokers wild
and every card in the deck
is a joker

and after the curtain falls
and the lights go out on this period drama
it'll take a lot of popcorn to get the lights
back on again

but we'll be okay
wandering around
in the dark
together

teaching one another
how to see again

– S.A. Griffin
06/26/24

mark hartenbach
ON THE STATE OF THE NATION

enlarged sympathy brushes aside sincere compadres
unwilling to share the spotlight. conditional injustice
is today's special. unworthy frequency is bumped for
top forty or talk radio. bare minimum patronizes
dysfunctional display crammed with jack-booted
bullies claiming to bravely maintain risk factor to
keep the culture safe from anarchy. ethical insigni-
ficance is on tongue of unconscious dignity preaching
excessive damnation as a chunk of circumstantial
apology is wrapped in genuine opportunity that
challenges subtle force unsuited to such concerns.
invalid entries dole out general truths in capsule
form that can't be crushed into pattern recognition
no matter what stylistic disposal swallows hook,
line & sinker. in response to cold shoulders the
excess is filled with enough language to pass as
intellectual huddle. an accidental response cannot
come to terms with a strong hankering to stretch
out on storefront couch with smirk knowing the
future is on his side. a period of transition floods
peripheral vision that miss aluminum wings
carefully pasted to childlike moratorium. degrees
of isolation are no longer a factor. it's a wing
& a prayer from now on. bushels of chords are
buried as toxic waste denying even standards
their place on the bandstand.

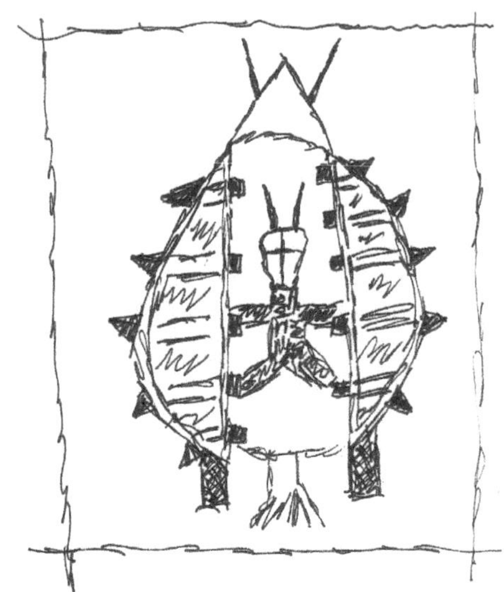

Illustrations by
mark hartenbach

MATTHEW HUPERT
QUILLS SHARPENED

I want to write you

a poem but you're still

a blank page to me

Someday maybe

a cycle

a chapbook

a road atlas marked with points of interest

& snapshots of landscapes seen

an anatomy text with notes

in the margins

questions unasked or unanswered

between acetate overlays

a thesaurus

a grimoire of arcane charts & chants

whispers under the breath

in a secret tongue

But now is a poem unwritten

an open empty page

It's OK

I can wait

Take it slow

ANNIE JANE-WILDER
LOOK CAREFULLY FOR BANDAIDS

Left clinging to your lover's mohawk,
All this old people bleeding
And the needing to put something on
My newly delicate skin,
Fucking in the afternoon
As the black inked Public Enemy
On your head sets his sites on
Avoiding the embarrassment of the
Bloody-badge of plastic blindfolded,
Decay. Hey , Aint that the way
For all you bad ass rappers?
My body bangs, legs wrapped around
Your rocking neck, Public Enemy almost in
A choke hold of my still Amazonian thighs
As we
Sweat in the rays, of the late-day
Trickle down. Maybe Reagan was right –in theory
But outside this almost summer bedroom
Nah, I don't think so
And when
We finish, and you walk out onto the porch
Facing the quiet small town street?
Imagine
The faintest of smiles on my face as I imagine all
The what iffs of that bloody badge
Of shame. Left hanging
From your ratty, half bleached ,
Mohawk tail.

MILO STARR JOHNSON
SPINNING

Spinning

Spinning. Revolving

Revolving in the liquid core of the earth

I'm flying through the fire of the ore

Ore. Either

Ether—taking it out, finding Spirit in life

Life is but a journey to death

Death. Rebirth

Transformation. Transportation. Where to go next?

Next. Get in line

Line. Circle. Circle. Dance

Dance in balance

Balance each thought against its exact opposite

When I was a child I drew spirals over and over again

Again. Why?

There's so much to learn and there's not enough time

Time. I'm 63 and I don't know what that means

Means—suddenly I feel sad

I must fear dying

We all fear dying

I'm floating

I'm sinking

I'm borne upwards

It's all the same

Same. I'm smiling

Smiling. What else?

I'm okay

Okay now

Now, if I stay in the Now always

Always, I'll be okay

Okay, is this true?

True

"Ghosts" art by PAUL NASH

tin pan alley

No one has ever written a song about Coronary Thrombosis,
Even though its blessings have been widely recognized...
Even though it has saved many people from a lifetime of sorrow...
Even though it has rescued many people from bottomless pits of Death...
Even though it has provided a good life for millions of doctors, nurses,
Ambulance drivers, morticians, stonecutters and countless others.
Yet, on ungrateful Tin Pan Alley
No one has ever written a song about Coronary Thrombosis.

BOB kaufman

First published in the July 1961 issue of *Swank*, but having escaped inclusion in the *Collected Poems of Bob Kaufman*, "Tin Pan Alley" has been reprinted at IMPART INK, an errant studio, in days of disaster and disease, two decades into the twenty-first century, in an edition of 61 copies, which are to be sold to benefit the poet's son, Parker, on his 61st birthday in October MMXX.

ROYAL KENT

(Royal Kent Edwards)

04/05/1950 - 10/12/2024

Royal Kent was a poet, spoken word artist, visionary, veteran, martial artist, entrepreneur, son, brother, father, grandfather, producer, ensemble COPUS co-founder, and soul friend to many.

Royal was born in L.A. to parents, Margret and Kenneth Edwards. He is survived by sister, Kenneice Callixto; brother, Alton Edwards; son, Kareem Chadly; and creative partner, Wendy Loomis.

Royal served two years in the Navy during the Vietnam War and graduated from Los Angeles University, New College of California and the Renaissance Center in San Francisco. He worked in marketing and real estate.

Some of his production credits include the Nick Edenetti All-Night Show; interviews and photographs of reggae artists, including Bob Marley; and co-founding the first cable T.V. shows in the Bay Area (1980, Into the 80s).

In 1996, Royal met pianist composer, Wendy Loomis. Together they created ensemble COPUS that performed for over two decades throughout the U.S., recorded many albums, donated to social justice causes; and earned awards and nominations from the Indie Music Channel, Hollywood Music in Media, Clouzine International, W.A.M., and ASCAP. Copusmusic.com

ROYAL KENT
POETS RIFF

from the soul bearing falsettos of an eddy kendricks
or a phillip bailey

the resonance of the bass I'm thinking jack Jamison
or esperanza Spaulding

bringing crescendos like the wind
macoy tynors jazz riffs that ascend
and descend according to the plan of
some mystifying physics defying all logic

plucked from the strings of the
avant garde pianist joe zawinul
with the adderlys nat & cannonball
takin a stand
the drama of dramatics
the chi lites bringing spoken word and song
stylistics stylin

the mystics of the word
dylanistic smokey poetry
holland dozier holland
rhymin the love with heartbreak

sophisticated flare with hendrix swagger
dedicated and honored
understated greatness

setting the landscape of listening
on fire
stirring hearts of desire

when all is said and done
let us give the poets some
spoken word in a form
meant to be heard

On all platforms

Photo of Royal Kent by **ROBERT FISCHER**

DOUG KNOTT

SCOTT WANNBERG in Florence, Oregon, July 2010

People who have long dropped out of sight are visible here.
Scott's the only poet in town -
Being Scott, he's secure on this cold stretch of coast.
He is very large, but his
true presence is light
bright wings of morning
in the cage of the body

North of the old-town Deco bridge and gazebo,
Trees overhang the river with the Indian name,
Florence is a long blue-collar & retiree mall.

Off the main road, he pays low rent and lives mundanely
Next to a police sub-station he waves hello to.
I sleep on couch cushions hopscotch on the floor.
We talk the old stuff, S.A.'s mac & cheese
Dutton's deceased bookstore, the ghostly Carma Bums,
And I remember how Dustin Hoffman leaped up when he heard
Scott was waiting for him with books! "What? Scott's waiting for me?"
   Yes, Dustin jumped for Scott - and Mr. Dylan and Jackson Browne and
   All those movie people with the flagship names
   Always sought out Scott. Why?
   Because he was already an angel, and he
   Lifted them up despite their weight of fame

And because he was a colossus of soul,
Flitting on his heavy feet between the stacks
Finding first the books you want, then the ones he wants for you.

I remember the carbo-mad burgers and fries
At Early World restaurant across the street in LA
And the recent year Scott couldn't sleep,
like he was stuck inside his own TV.

Ding dong! Time to eat!
Always a ceremony of delight,
Action is down at Thornton's family restaurant.
We walk there, Scott truckin' that oxygen tank
Behind him on its little mouse wheels.
Transparent breathing tubes corral his nose.

He takes them off once we're inside, oh yeah -
3 waitresses serve him 3 meals each sitting.
They fawn over him, Scott, of course they do!
We all can't help it.
Me, I'm proudly here as "friend of Scott,"
A much-littler guy on the other side of the table,
visiting from LA - that tormented giant of a city Scott's from,
which these folks have never seen, and only heard of ...imagine that!

It's so local here -
I'm wearing a big white bib, too, like Scott,
O party down, here comes the food!
Biscuits, pot roast, salad, mashed and those twin
Wedges of pie not long after.

To offset, exercise: striding, keeping up
with big Scott feet 10 times around the parking lot.
I thought he was doing well inside –
what a surprise this COPD he's got
Pulled some briny ripcord in his lungs, even though
His weight's down and he talks like heat-lightning -
That's why I can't figure why he just blew off the personal skin.
Tears come out of me
Like spray from the cold boiling ocean only a mile away.
Scott had never even been there
I drove him to the beach but there was a freezing wind
And he wouldn't get out of the car
The sea was inside him.

Our conversation veered on batwings between
corridors of books, expands
at the speed of light --
Towers, bungalows, apartment buildings, cities of words, then
Suddenly all is seen from above
Amid constellations slowly twisting in brilliant cosmic dust

In his apartment, we burrow into the stacked books.
I leave with an armload he's just ploughed over. We
Argue both sides of the 1846-48 Mexican War. (It's good
Poets have no fixed personas or dates of existence) -
And new stuff – how some local kid that he befriended,
even saved from suicide, then ripped him off several grand on a "loan" –
  No need to collect that now.
  And no need for suicide.
  God does it fine without our help.

Yeah, the tombstone crowd is waiting in the wings,
And the virtual world is hungry for more lambs from Scotty pastures.

But he's left me stark awake on my desert island of mortality
His poetry crosses my forehead like a track-meet of ancient bards,
His spirit flashes by like a huge wedge of apple pie,
streamers of ice cream flinging flavor,
Desserts of vanilla and Valhalla.

That's after the rare steaks of love and
words you served up for so many years,
Scott, and your friendship,
More precious than an evening repast with any god
Or heaven I find in menu or holy book.

– Doug Knott

"Ezekiel's Wheels" collage art
by T. MIKE WALKER

Marc Kockinos

In Memoriam: 4/29/62 -- 2/2/24

by Daniel Yaryan

My mind contains many fond recollections of kindred comrade Marc Kockinos, who departed this world February 2, 2024 after a bout with cancer.

Marc and I met when we were both participants of the San Francisco literary arts scene, coinciding with the early years of my multimedia poetry series Sparring With Beatnik Ghosts, which began August 23, 2008 in the city by the Bay. We first met earlier that year at the Beat Museum at the Beat Friar Brother Antoninus induction celebration and exhibit. We quickly became comrades and read at the same poetry venues throughout The City. On one occasion, after I featured at Gallery Café, Marc and I headed over to Hotel Utah's weekly, long-standing Monday night open mic and performed our poetry to music with mutual poet friend and pianist extraordinaire Steve Arntson. At the end of the night, my car had been towed and I needed to get home to my kids in Santa Cruz. Marc, to the rescue, drove me all the way to Santa Cruz and I dealt with the car situation later.

Many-a-night when I was visiting San Francisco as I frequently did, Marc and I would grab pints at places in North Beach such as Vesuvio's, Specs or Tosca; often times in the Mission District too after the popular 16th and Mission reading (during part of that time I lived in nearby Burlingame). We shared many brother-deep stories and had fantastic discussions about the many challenges of life, world situations and pondering the universe as thinking beings often do (and he was highly intelligent, yet never judgmental or ego-maniacal as many other creative people I've encountered over the years). He had empathy for people and always cared about and wanted to know in all sincerity how they were doing or how he could help if he could. Bottom line, he was a real "people-person," never of the commonplace, superficial variety and never self-declared. This trait is perhaps what made him such a successful organizer and host of one of the largest poetry events in the United States, which was called "Poetic Brew" in San Diego which set attendance records in the hundreds monthly, prior to moving to Northern California's Mill Valley. A SF suburb, Mill Valley is a short distance north of the Golden Gate Bridge – rich in the arts and majestic beauty, which includes Mount Tamalpais, one of Marc's favorite hiking spots, maybe second only to Muir Woods.

Marc hosted Open Heart Poetry at Om Shan Tea in the Mission District and was a member of San Francisco's Revolutionary Poet's Brigade, which also included the late, great SF Poet Laureate Emeritus Jack Hirschman, among many other trailblazers.

Marc was an active member of the IATSE Local 16, San Francisco. Local 16 said "Kockinos was often seen on the Trade Show floor, in the Breakout rooms, and the Keynote sessions. He was known for his compassion, deep booming voice, and expertise in nearly every facet of event production. He handled audio mixers as well as projectors; and was always happy to mentor newer folks in all

CONTINUED NEXT PAGE

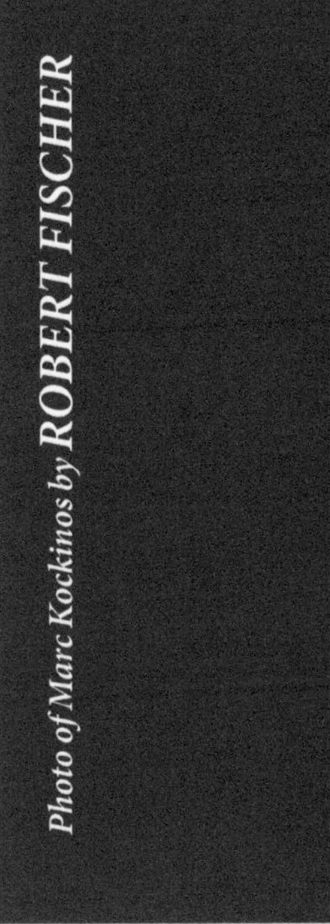

CONTINUED FROM LAST PAGE

the different skills that modern video and audio techs need these days. He was also very active in the SF and San Diego literary circles, as a poet and spoken-word performer. As well, he was a photographer, just an all-around lover of the arts." I recall how dedicated Marc was to his job. One time I was on my way to the Berkeley Poetry Festival in 2012 for a special presentation of Sparring With Beatnik Ghosts. I took the BART train from the Fremont station up to the BART stop by Berkeley City College where the event was held. As I disembarked the train, I got a call from Marc asking if I could take over for him as host of the festival (about an hour before it began). He was called into work for an emergency and regretfully couldn't make the event. I hosted in his stead and performed a Sparring set. I was grateful and honored that Marc thought of me to take his place for the event. Really though, no one could compare. He was one of the best hosts I'd even seen, with a calm demeanor, respect (and patience) for performers. Also, he understood how to engage the audience with a seamless command of the microphone.

Marc Kockinos hosted and performed in many Spar-ring With Beatnik Ghosts events over the years in Santa Cruz, Berkeley and San Francisco. He was truly masterful at delivering unforgettable professional events. In Marc, I found the optimal representative, along with co-host Ginger Murray, to usher the famous Poetry Festival back to Santa Cruz on 2/12/12 at the historic Cocoanut Grove Grand Ballroom at the Beach Boardwalk. It took a year to plan and was one of the greatest projects I had ever produced. The festival showcased 40 of some of the finest poets and musicians for an all-day extravaganza. Marc was part of the magic of that day, whereas he helped resurrect a cultural phenomenon in Santa Cruz that had been absent from the town for 30 years.

Marc was a dear friend who's resounding voice I can still hear every time I read his indelible poems. I encourage people to watch some videos of Marc performing his work at Sparring With Beatnik Ghosts and other fabulous shows on YouTube. I've also included some of his poems herewith in honor of Marc, which prove his words are just as everlasting with the same vitality and energy once captured through his live performances throughout countless spoken word stations. Rest in Peace, dear friend! May you have many great conversations in the ethereal night with fellow Greek poets Homer and Hesiod. May Calliope and the other muses forever be in your corner!

MARC KOCKINOS   FAMILIAR EXILE

We wander like refugee's -
under these towers
bleached bone-white by the Sun.

Involuntary exile
down familiar streets,
holding on to the fading images
of all the places
where we'd rather be.

We gather in basement cafe's
and after-hours' clubs,
just outside the easy glamour
and forced enthusiasm
of the Mating game..

We recognize each other
by the searchlight glare's
coming from dark corner tables.
Making eye contact
in an attempt to look deeper
than the carefully applied make-up
and all the cute little gestures
designed to show that *here*
is something exceptional-
look no further..

And they always turn away-
And they always turn away from our gaze
knowing that the rules have changed:
that we could care less
about how cool we look,
and small-talk ain't nothing

but a Band-Aid to cover
the emptiness that hangs thicker
than cigarette smoke in the air.

So I shake hands all around
and nod to an unfamiliar face or two.
Settling deep into a chair
that provides more
of the comforts of home
than the room that I fall asleep in each night.
Where all the memories of childhood
are still engraved into cold stucco walls.

We talk, drink and smoke
into the early morning hours-
Conjuring phantoms into the air
above a bar-top turned to seance table;
Of Alpine valleys echoing with cowbells,
like the ringing of distant temple gongs...
And the marketplace in Marrakesh
coming to life at Nightfall
during the month of Ramadan.

Trading stories of cheap, clean hotels
and isolated spots across 6 continents;
that have still not learned how to
prostitute their culture for the Tourists.

Information to be stored away
for when wallets lean as starving dogs
are filled again. And we can return
to all the places where we'd rather be.

Photo of Marc Kockinos by **ROBERT FISCHER**

MARY NORBERT KORTE

WHILE WE SLEPT AMERICA

the war came home
it slowly took command
of streets pregnant with guns
and light gleaming on
ghost-smooth troops

And we slept   America   we slept

we talked in sleep
the words old men
live to hear
the dying-glorious words
we made to order for our war

we woke with bodies
ringed by war   war in us
war through us   war in the eyes
wretched with need blind-
held in our hands upward
like flags of unreason

none knowing truth none
hearing the real the cry that could be:

America   the war is ours to take away

– Mary Norbert Korte

Berkeley
Spring, 1969

a message to Roger Heyns

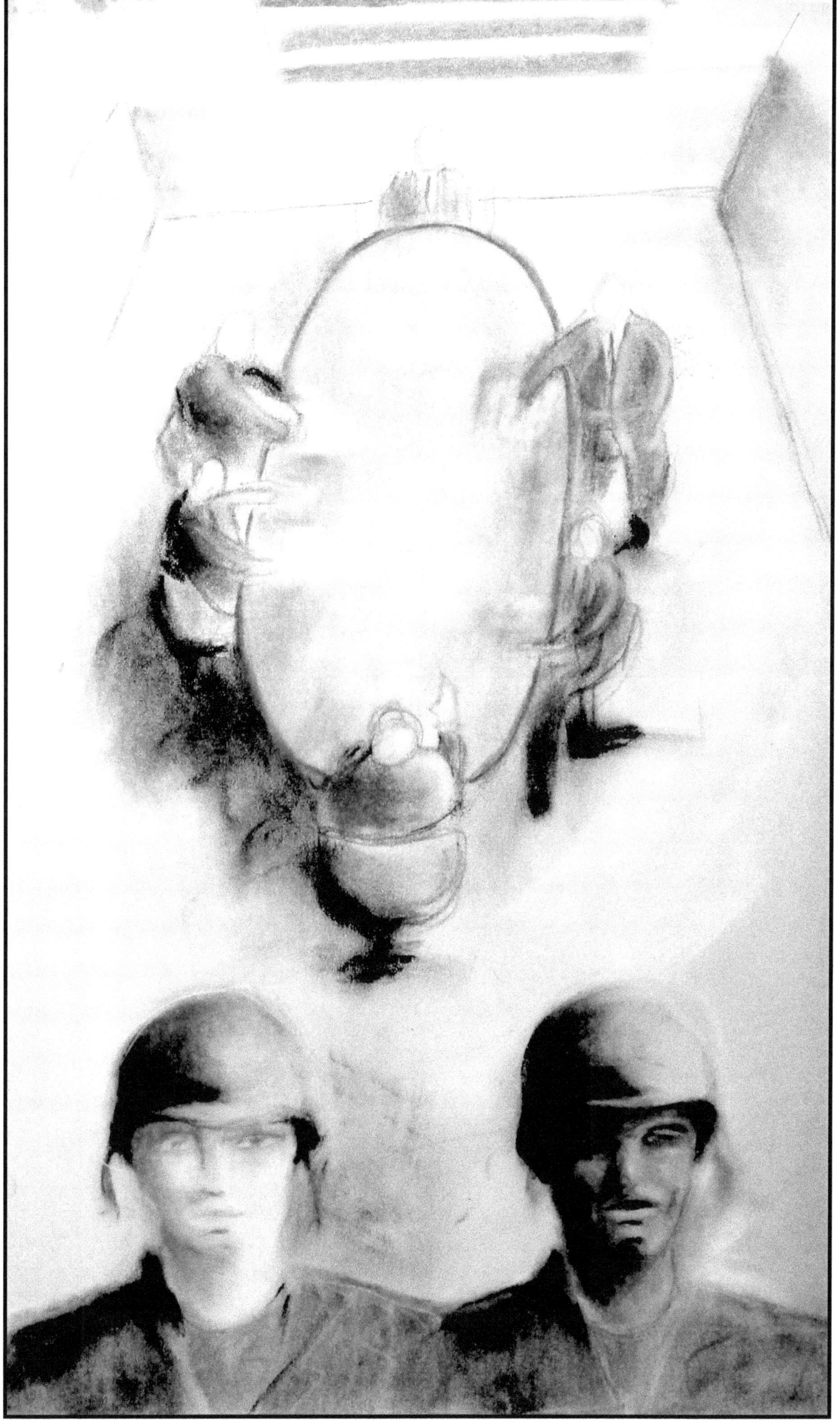

Artwork by TRACY WITT

MARY NORBERT KORTE

LETTER SIXTY-ONE: DEAR MAMA

yes it's all true   I roll my own
cigarettes now and use 4-letter words
and I had to watch it the other day tearing
down a shed on a straight man's place the old
geezer down the road'll tell his dirty jokes
to Peter in front of me now

                              and I wear boots
and long underwear and split wood and build
sheds and skylight and plumbing
and I remember that you gave me music
lessons for 17 years and I was classical
scholar in college and I always wrote things
you said you didn't understand

                              the problem is

Mama when I build my house

                              I will know

the backporch is a Work of Art

– Mary Norbert Korte

                    Sanctuary Station
                    1975

RON LAMPI
THE POET'S KNOWING

In the stillness, in the silence,
in your precious moments of solitude,
so many voices come to you,
they nudge your attention,
they have so much to share with you–
You listen. You are open.
The world comes alive for you—
Yes, the world will speak in poetry,
little do others know,
but you who listens to voices
that others cannot hear, know
that the world IS poetry.
You listen. You are open.
You jot down the words & lines
        you hear…

LAND
40 DAYS & 40 NIGHTS:
A COLLECTION OF HAIKU
(Dedicated to Richard Wright)

delicate moments
awaiting reality
nestled in dreamscapes

mise en scene: sunrise
with light peeking through the clouds
eroding the night

a silent slumber
footsteps on a tile floor
sleep and sleeplessness

through windows i watch
the sunrise erase the night
from a quiet room

the sunbeam collage
cascading through the window
decorates an empty wall

rampant streams of thought
become silenced by stillness
sitting on the floor

the motion of breath
meditations on unknowns
what's mind is not mine

show the subconscious
performative personhood
exalts a cliché

subvert the zeitgeist
talk to yourself more often
why not go crazy?

vignette vagabonds
post hieroglyphs in my eyes
curating memoirs

on timeline collage
manicuring personas
for the sake of self

egovangelist's
and inundation addicts'
digital dogma

encoded cocaine
hyperlink hysteria
keyboard clicks and clacks

self-help fetishists
with product propaganda
pseudo cult leaders

counting followers
satellite suicide pact
vanity victims

we survived the "truth"
or are we casualties?
who wields the data?

amidst the havoc
we constructed citadels
from sanctuaries

amidst the chaos
we watched symposiums burn
and drank cyanide

drunk on credit cards
confused consumerists ask
is safety for sale?

tract home tragedies
and drywall delirium
what are we building?

age of apathy
passive pandemonium
consumption culture

calendar coffins
carcinogen compromise
faustian bargains

repetitious veil
days gradually blurring
the sun sets again

still counting the days
my body grows more weary
as time marches on

days of distractions
escapism or freedom
who are you right now?

forever is false
tomorrow is tentative
time is imagined

do not fear failure
uttered the fortune cookie
phantasms abound

hope is an art form
endurance is a practice
our voyage is brief

motion embargos
how do we survive today
as pavement crumbles

the space between worlds
creates a distant feeling
whom do you cling to?

between night and dawn
before the sun wakes the world
walking in the road

waiting for cars
pondering mortality,
fear and my frailty

grey clouds hide the light
in an array of grey hues
as raindrops whisper

the sky feels lonely
will the sense of searching cease?
perhaps this is it

the sky is falling
fatigued from carrying rain
crying for us all

sitting in a chair
next to an open window
listening gently

charcoal sky backdrop
a single bird chirps softly
a car alarm wails

the night's eyes are stars
seeing through our worlds façade
hushing us to sleep

generosity
the earth is always giving
we still ask for more

retain the magic
when extinction is exposed
m(ages) paint mythos

JANE LECROY
BELIEVE HER

Mother, Mother
Sister, Sister
Believe her, believe her
            beg and beg
Their bodies
are not their own.
Women and their bodies,
believe them, believe them,
this is where you come from
this is where you came from,
the mother's blood,
the mother's bone,
her hips hinged open to bring you
through the door of the world.
Believe her threshold.

Artwork by **LYNN ROGERS**

THE CENTVRY

PHILOMENE LONG
THE POEM TAKES A
HUNDRED YEARS TO COME

The poem takes
A hundred years
To come

And then it blooms
At night

The branch almost breaks
Under her weight

She is old
She can bear the loneliness

Although she invented angels
She was driven out of heaven

Are you astonished
By her white mouth?

She will tell you
It is blood
That blood is
The silent country

Its orchards ablaze
With the bleeding

Artwork by
ELISHA BROWN BIRD

RICHARD LORANGER
OVERCOME

Can you hear me above the winds of this century

as shucks of sugar cane lash at your ears?

Can you see me through the haze of production

stamping meadows into mountains of junk?

Can you touch me through the deadening sludge

of media melding the mesmerized mind?

Can you smell my sweat through the stench of the sickbed

where civilization lies picking at sores?

Can you taste my flesh as you tenderly kiss me

amidst the bombardment of sensory scree?

Can we actualize our human potential

in this stampede of rampant humanity?

What days we have, what hours to breathe

as we tend these small flames in the wild.

Photo of Richard Loranger by **ROBERT FISCHER** *(opposite page)*

DOMINIQUE LOWELL
WOMEN ARE HUNGRY

women are hungry
they be sittin on your stoop waitin to drink your beer
eat your food
suck your dick

women are hungry
they need your favorite shirt
your leather jacket
a house and a car
and they want to tell you things
pretty little things
about the light in your eyes
and the feel of your thighs
they wanna shave your balls
know all your masturbatory nightmares
about every clit you ever licked
every ass you ever eyed
so they can slice them all to ribbons

they're insatiable
it's biological
they just want and want
and stretch their yearning arms at you
their insatiable envelopes gawking open mouthed

must have
must have
must have it
you
now

whoremothergoddesspriestessconvictjailer

needy needy needy
need your sperm
need your job

blackened purple eyes and concrete sharpened nails
puffy crimson lips
the beaten look that's it
already been hit

need more impossible paint for another impossible face

feed me beer and cigarettes and dead idols
who make me feel like I might have
reason to die too
tell me I'm not fat
tell me my tits are jewels
my nipples gumdrops
tell me we can pay the rent tomorrow
tell me we are just like John and Yoko
only I get to die first   o.k.?
I get to be the one they light the candles for in Central Park   o.k.?

Collage art by T. MIKE WALKER

give me war and coca-cola
and the promise of another American chance
give me another good song to dance to   o.k.?

fuck women
they are such sluttish catfight evil bitches every one of them

beware
beware
they know what they are doing
does that scare you?
are you scared?

women are hungry
hungry for balance
I have been called a whore so many times I guess I am one
and it's not you personally I want anything out of
it's the world
the world owes me big time

the world leaves me hungry

– Dominique Lowell

Collage artwork by T. MIKE WALKER

PHOEBE MACADAMS
AT THE LIBRARY

someone is recovering from being hit by a car
and is blessing the Lord;
across the street the poet writes furiously while
I nap over a book.

Once upon a time there were three young girls:
one fled along the rooftops of Manhattan;
one walked the roads in Woodstock, New York;
one tries every day to be worthy
of poems that arrive
in sweatshirts of long-legged girls,
or in the enormous roots of the Sycamore.

The trees say green, more green,
the knees say bind me, hold me in place,
the heart says, more words.

BIBIANA PADILLA MALTOS

UNTITLED
  – for Steph

No half measures
we take the streets
and from the street we jump
            to the voids:
from reality
        to the imagined realities
            to the others
                and those of others.

Carefree
they get closer
            they pass us
            they follow us
                demure desires
            and murmuring eyes.

Legs get away
escaping rapidly
the compromised revelation.

Incandescent
                bodies turn
intending to reflect
minisculely
            such discharge.

We like challenges,
to create our truths.

Sunset for the Queen of the Beats

In Memory of
Anne Marie Maxwell
(2/4/32--10/21/24)

By Lynn Rogers, M.A.

My dear friend Anne passed yesterday (October 21, 2024) at sunset after telling a kind visitor to, "Get me out of here." She's out now, I know it, easy, airy, delighted, I can inwardly glimpse her smiling.

Born February 4, 1932 at sunset to an unusual, accomplished family (radio writers, movie personalities, chiropractor dad, prominent dentist brother etc.} she grew up in Alameda, California, near where her Scandinavian sea captain grandfather had sailed. Her beloved dad who'd started in vaudeville, struggled with alcohol till later.

She married early, became pregnant while in her teens to melodramatic actor Mervyn Murphy who pitched fits to have their baby daughter adopted out. Though he allowed their second child, Grant, Anne never got over the hurt of that. She pulled away from Merwyn with Grant, for the Beat scene in North Beach digs left to her by some fellow, enjoying being on her own in "a Bohemian paradise" at Vesuvio Cafe and the like. She would become a provocative dancer. Then it was on to New York where she had art displayed in Greenwich Village.

When she met Neal Cassady, raised in Denver flop-houses, self-educated, prone to bigamy and stream of consciousness cross country car rides in stolen cars, it was the collision of soul mates. Born February 9, 1926, he also had a mystical side from Catholic altar boy to Edgar Cayce that also appealed. They seemed to have not only overwhelming passion but a telepathic tie.

"I love you more than I love myself," he told her. Twin souls, or romantic soul mates have been the subjects of poets like the Brownings, philosophers like Plato, composers like Wagner and so on.

For a time, Neal was faithful, but his jealousy was incited by a fleeting incident on her part with a friend. From that instance and, as "the times they were a changin', with "free" love in the air in the early 60s, their soul mate tie was tested. Having been sexually abused in the flophouse as a kid, Neal was driven.

Anne was the woman who lived it all with him, took all the risks and still kept hope in the underling better values that were being born out of what some might call depravity. "Despite my misery, self-indulgent insanity…I was keenly aware of the change in consciousness: human

CONTINUED NEXT PAGE

ANNE MARIE MAXWELL IN 1950

CONTINUED FROM LAST PAGE

kindness, cosmic wisdom, sexual freedom and unconditional love…that flower children and their mature allies, like us, expressed," she says in her memoir Tripping with a Viper, her wonderful, very edgy account of her relationship with Beat antihero icon Neal Cassady.

Because of the extremes that she and Neal were living, her brother Ted had taken custody of Grant and her absent children remained a heartache. She would be generous later though to younger hippie creative types like myself whose Born in Berkeley book on those times from a teen view she endorsed and encouraged. Re-reading Tripping with a Viper, I see clearly, that many of us retraced her steps.

She cites Donovan's idealistic song, "Atlantis," and the phrase, "let's get together and love one another right now." The Beat/Hippie axis was "the best of times and the worst of times" and Anne Marie Maxwell lived it all.

She was there in the intense literary scene on Perry Lane with Kesey and gentle Faye; wrote about guys disappearing from their wives for frat boy adventures; about her quarrels with Neal, "an effect of our very closeness and the drugs it fed on."

And yet she says, "Although Neal always made it seem like he was willing to share his woman with the others as he wished she was to share him, it just wasn't true."
When Neal took her to Mexicali toward the end," feel

CONTINUED NEXT PAGE

ing breakers gently formed… and the brilliant turquoise ocean beyond," he said to her, "See that old American couple in the Chrysler, aren't they sweet? They love each other after all these years."

He sent her back to the US before him then reappeared somewhere with a gal who had a house and money in Mexico at some party in the city. She had always seen him as super human but now his too red lips were frozen into a grimace and hollow furrows crossed his face.
Somehow still he managed in those crazy times to slip away and make love to Anne one more time. "Is you or is you not—my baby?" he murmured.

When Anne got word that he died on her birthday, February 4--1968 in Mexico was; found exposed along train tracks where he'd wandered alone, she wept uncontrollably and wrote:

"And I never told him how much I loved him and needed him, that wise and wonderful companion who had loved me so clearly, hurt me so deeply, and owned me completely so that I still weep today. He must know now, because I feel him near me."

Well, I believe he does know now because I can somehow see her, just as she described in her book about those times. "I wore a sheer hand-dyed turquoise and violet hankie dress from Haight Street, turquoise over chartreuse shadow on my eyes, two crystal tear drops dropping on my reddened cheeks."

Weep no more Anne, generous mentor, artist, poet lover, dancer; flow freely, through your poetic words that live on to light our creative future, and now, into your forever soul mate's arms.

--Lynn Rogers MA, author--friend.

(Anne Marie Maxwell is predeceased by her children Nancy and Grant; survived by a granddaughter, two nieces, many creative friends and readers yet to be.)

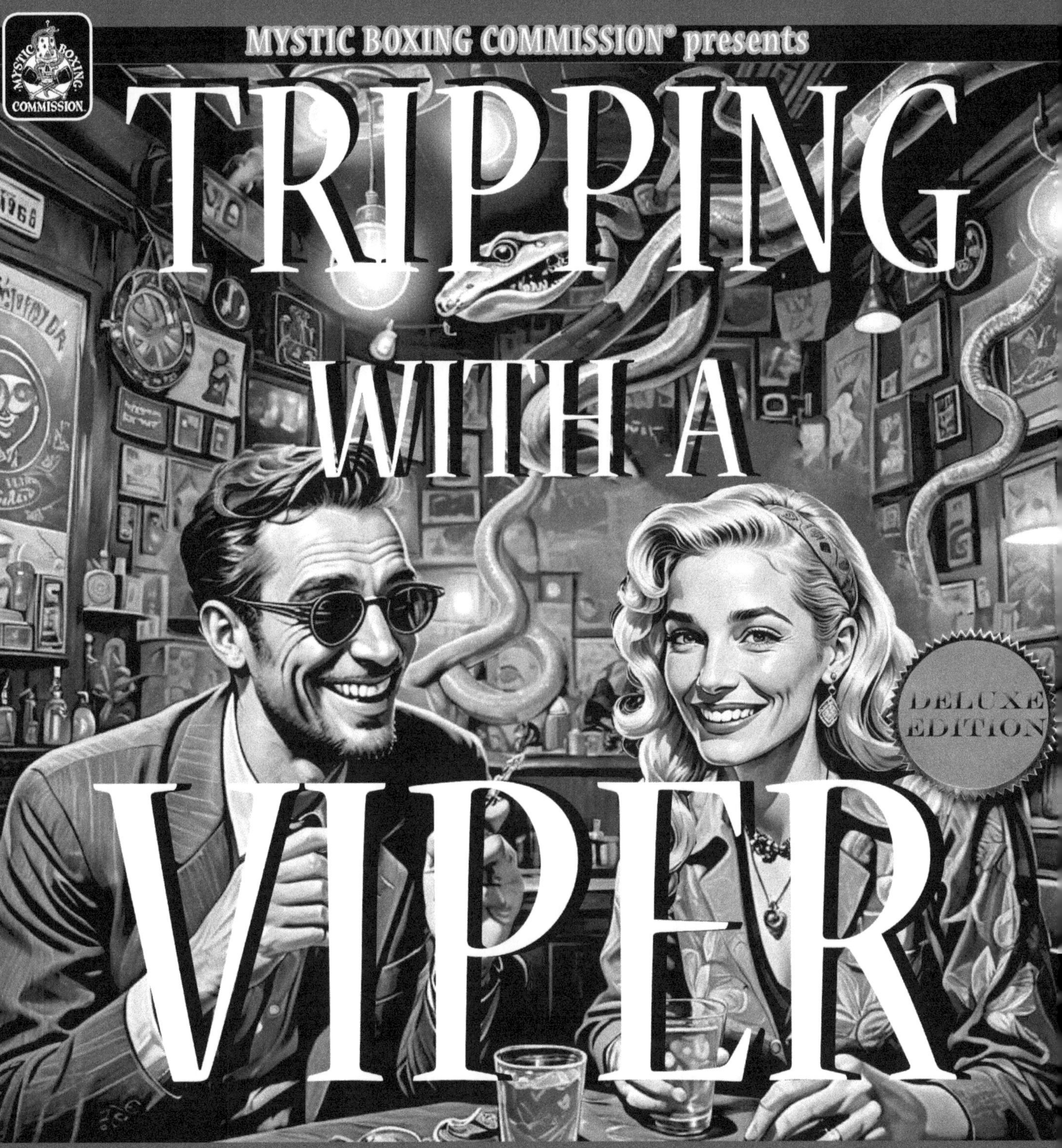

DELUXE HARDCOVER COMING SOON!
MYSTIC BOXING COMMISSION® presents
TRIPPING
WITH A
VIPER
1966
MYSTIC BOXING COMMISSION
DELUXE EDITION
THE UNEXPURGATED TRUE STORY OF NEAL CASSADY & ANNE MURPHY
BY ANNE MARIE MAXWELL
WITH INTRODUCTION BY GERALD NICOSIA, AUTHOR OF MEMORY BABE
EXCLUSIVELY AT: SPARRINGARTISTS.COM

Idealized Mountains by JUSTIN AYRES

ELLYN MAYBE
EARTH DAY

It's the Earth's Birthday and I was listening to it and it said it wanted 5 things.
It wanted a compost salad.
It wanted a gift certificate to a record store and had in mind the sound of people breathing as people listen to the ocean.
The Earth said music is breath.
Then the Earth said I want to read a billion books at once so write your words in my sky with kites.
The colors you choose will tell me your mood, that will be a novel.
The Earth said, I want to send you love, I said Earth you are very cool given everything.
The Earth said it's true, but dig, we are all given everything, it takes our whole life to see it sometimes.
Sometimes you need a kaleidoscope and to stand on your head on one foot like a flamingo to see it.
Sometimes it's as simple as spaghetti.
The Earth said I want to travel.
I said, where.
The Earth said, I don't know,
surprise me.
So I took a postcard of a drum and said shut your eyes and listen and you will be everywhere.
The Earth said I feel the heartbeat of it all.
I said, good cause it's your day, and the Earth said one last thing,
Will you be my candles and tell everyone they are all candles that can last a second or forever.
It's strictly how you dance if you know what I mean.
The Earth was on fire and giddy.
Full of stories and shy.
The Earth likes talking and listening.
The Earth is so cool.
After all, it has been here for many millennium and it is sticking around while others might have left us.
The Earth after all has options.
The Earth said, I like challenges, I'm not going anywhere.
Then the Earth picked up a phone and called its therapist.
The Earth said it's not me it's them, the therapist said it's normal to get stressed sometimes.
The Earth went into yoga pose and said thanks.
And another day went by like ebb meeting flow,
or is it Kander meeting Ebb, and the world simply went on dancing.

BERNADETTE MCCOMISH
ESCAPE

At the end of the movie
our heroine returns

to black and white
                or outer space

and I stay   home

horizontal

on a stained, California sun-faded couch
or soft striped sheets that need   to be   changed

It's easier to live in Television on a sleep timer

            wake to
                                    80s songs
                                      credits
                                    next episode
                              are you still watching
                               eventual darkness

When I was five I watched the same story
                    over
                    and over
                              and over a rainbow

Now I don't get up to rewind
worry about a scratched disc that skips

I travel back

to Zion, One Eyed Jack's, Rick's Café
with a soft thumb
remain   supine
close my eyes and listen   to an ocean
                              on a screen

If only I had a chest to cushion my head heavy
after a binge

an off duty immortal
to walk to the fridge   for the third time

to find
          empty takeout containers
          frozen pickles
          unopened beer bottles

Hollywoodland Series by **MIKE STREET**

come back with
     cookies
     pomegranate seeds
     and seltzer

She is not a hero
she does not live
     here
I invite her to stay
     safe
under my nails
but she forgets her   lines
I ignore her lack   of pulse

and when she leaves
I   don't   lock   the door

or finish the film

–Bernadette McComish

STEPHEN MEADOWS

LOOKING OUT

Time alone
makes for these poems
hours at my one small window
the charred color of rain cloud
rubbed into the notch
of the valley beyond
long days watching as
the storms move in or
listening at night
to the tune of the road
the distant taut hum
of heavy traffic on the bridge the
frigid stillness
of stars at five before
dawn

-Stephen Meadows

WADDELL CREEK

Up stream
willow's edge
dappled light
hanging rock
trout nip
leaving whorls
water prints
tree rings

Far off a jay
screams
years layer
the cliff face
the river over
cold feet
fish colored
tonguing the
tight stones

-Stephen Meadows

DAVID MELTZER
PEPPER

Art's desire to get it all said
to all who thought him dead
in the joint & beside the point

Art's struggle to sing it all
through jazz warfare & tell
everything he knew in brass
speed rap stir crazy utopia
of muscle chops push it in your face
rough unrelenting grace

fierce Art pitbull clamps down
pulls edges out in time to break through
scream knotty beauty
toe to toe w/ any joe
who thinks they know better

Art tattoos blue needles into moonlight skin
junk light makes mirrors perfect

Art's smoke aches out of wounds

L.A. Art burritos & bebop
black guacamole serge zoots
Central Avenue cat copping

Pepper at Club Alabam
in Lee Young's band
all the chicks & the hatcheck chick
have big eyes for Art's horn

"Portrait of Art Pepper" (1947) photo
by **WILLIAM P. GOTTLIEB**

(Note: Originally appeared on Two-Tone Poetry & Jazz, David Meltzer & Julie Rogers with Zan Stewart on Tenor Saxophone CD recorded by Pureland Audio, later included in When I Was a Poet, City Lights Pocket Poets. The CD was made (David's 2nd one ever) and came out right after he stopped doing book tours during the year before he died, and few folks know it exists.)

*Poets Jack Michelline and A.D. Winans photographed in North Beach (1993) by **LINDA LERNER***

Nowhere on this earth does the flag of truth fly. Goddamn my eyes. The barracuda taking pain tranquilizers and devouring angels. My damn black Irish/Jewish soul. Hunting for that pot of yellow gold, that piece of green. The kingdom of man already shattered and broken. The Moon, shadow of the highest place, trampled on by science. The Animal man already dead by greed. Goddamn it all and. I'm gone for a walk and take another look around. While my eyes are still bright before I fall on my face and cry or buy that baseball bat at Goodwill and start swinging. The blinds were down and the snakes were still hiding in the apartments and office buildings. They hired the best makeup men in the country. Clean white shirts and the finest fashions to cover their conspiracy. A different wig every day. A pirate with a patch on his eyes. Slogans written on their walls: **Work From The Inside! Kiss Ass and Suck!** All hirelings and stooges, members of the pack. the billiard and poolplayers wanting a piece of the action. Elephant and whale hunters. You can buy them by the thousands for a hundred a week. Scabs. Scum of the earth. Rainbow hunters in the anti-mountains. Here they come with the elephantguns again. The conquistadores with their dogs exterminating Indians before the whiteman. The pale horsesoldiers with the cross in one hand and the gun in the other. Two hands working the same side of the street. Quick changes and fast tricks. The best makeup men in the country. They would look in the mirrors, making sure their costume was right before it smashed all to bits. Their magic worn thin with their eyes. More pain tranquilizers. Everyday hunting season in the hospital, prison, tower, skidrow madhouse of a nation. More alcohol. More rotten fish. More magazines and newspapers filled with lies. More quick changes and fast tricks. Steal the money. Be a winner. Let's kick 'em in the balls again. The real poets hidden in dark corners. Enemies of the state. Kill the dreamers, the stray dogs. Let's make the politician king, enslave the masses. They're not supposed to think. Be your own boss. Let 'em ride the busses with the Monday Morning Blues. Give 'em more supermarkets and TV sets and fast cars. Give 'em plastic bags and pain tranquilizers. But, goddamn, kiss their bright eyes. All this in the movies. The animal kingdom called earth. All nations on the same trip. Like a deck of cards folding like an accordian. The heart beating like a distant drum. The red ants and bankers and revolutionaries cleaning the cell blocks and garbage cans. Cleaning house again, putting on their wigs, hustling death. The same makeup again, the same flag with a different face. Here comes that nut again! He believes in truth. He carries no flag, no identification. The mad drifter. The vagabond. The poet. Here he comes again, Prince Bright Eyes, the finest dog of all. Let's give him a piece of the action. Let's buy him into the crowd. The mob shits again. Be careful, he's no double dealer. He doesn't fly to Minneapolis. He has no credit cards. How does he live? He meditates. He sees a man with long white hair. He's no communist. He has no capitalist ring on his finger. He's not a member of the club. The boys. The mob. The bullshit artists' association of the universe. He gets laid once a week by a kind woman. Damn that animal kingdom, it bores me to death. Let's all us bright eyes get together and dance and have an orgy. Let the dead die. There's always the dawn and the sunset. Who wants to dance this morning? Hello out there! I'm the shoemaker's son. The lettercarrier's son. I'm Malugee of the French movies. The four-leaf clover. The monkey with four eyes. Let's have a drink, Shannon. This world ain't gonna change. I was polluted long ago. Long live the elephants! God bless the whales! Hey, baby, let's dance. I'll kiss you in the darkest night. Look at them flowers blooming! Long live bright eyes! Blow that horn again, a long sweet sound! I'll kiss you forever.

—JACK MICHELLINE

Artwork by JERRY KAMSTRA

MIKE M MOLLETT
TO THE POETS' CHOIR IN THE CHURCH OF HUMANITY

Kick some doors open why don't we
in this mad mad scheme of things
      as a poet type person on this planet living
in the U S OF fucking A ..
What a place to be! too near
a soulless once head of fucking state.
What's the poetry in this?
truth is for most of us...
these are not the happiest of times
to try to make sense of. Whoa...
pogo stick out of a box into another...
What a time to breathe
some smoky California air...

BAM. Point is
      what I want to say is
poets are everybodies
smart funny potent insightful wise
provocative playful candid even ignorant
across the board you name it...
a can of worms unruly...
the clincher is: **BUT WHO READS OUR STUFF?**

Reiteration: Recalculation:
WHO *ELSE* READS OUR STUFF?
I must admit it...this is a spoiler alert
I don't.
      This is really embarrassing.

BAM #2!
not to be or to be...
naked & understandable,
brutal in the kindest of ways
HEY, YOU TOO, MIKE!   Yes, me..!

the poets choir...
point to those homeless camps filling up
& spreading   wailing children thin as sticks
all over the world!   abductions   coastal lands going
under... heat warming our front doors like magnets
deserts sand-bombing the growing fields   fields of bones
fields of burning gas   gases real nasty stuff of ozone co2
holes in the sky   sky way of dead zones   oceans of grief
what next Mr. & Mrs Polar Bear floating out there on thin ice?
Goodbye white rhino. your DNA is all we have left...
            let it be known...I will kill you for fresh clean water...

please bring on the *howevers & yesses*
            with the beauty in a scar & the truth of a directed fire

sister & brother politicians ... what's your email?
open your hearts up for this clean up campaign
Is that your office next to a garden or
cuddling a concrete freeway wall **with our stuff**
all over it   nailed. sprayed. plastered. soldered.   burnt in.
ALL OVER THE WALLS
both sides / all sides
you too / me too
It's a tsunami ...

--mm mollett

Collage design by **YARYAN**

SHANNA MOORE

It was three o'clock in the morning
I sat straight up in bed
I heard a scream
no one here...
my son not home yet
couldn't sleep worried for my son
did something happen?
was that his scream?
turned the T.V. on
CNN a man talking bout a plane
crashing into one of the twin towers
as I watched over his head
another plane hit the other tower
another scream
It was the scream
of so many souls
Death of humanity
I thought of the explosion rushing
down the elevator shafts
a shudder a premonition
people running jumping
as I watched in horror
the fall of Jericho
a flaming screaming
death of humanity
Terrorists in our Homeland
a wakeup call
at three o'clock
in the morning...

– Shanna Moore

black ace eight
all three of the poets
gone now
Aces and Eights
hard luck hand
lucky I folded
back there
in the killer summer
went home
to the tall tree country

babe in my arms

– Shanna Moore

RAINBOW GOD

a little person
shimmering
gold shining through
his many pockets
so pot-bellied
spraying gold dust
filling the air
with light
and a double
rainbow

– Shanna Moore

footprints
on the beaches
of the beat

a Hawaiian chant
echoes the old ones
on sandlewood shores

in this universe of verse
there are many beaches
many blues to be sung

the mingle of incense
of the east
and sage of the west

mingle in smoke
verses on the wind
we are one

leaving
our footprints behind
and our essence

on the wind
to the mountains
and other high places

– Shanna Moore

KEEPIN THE BEAT

the bones
of all the pomes
read to a tenor sax
a wail in the night
echoes off
old cobblestones...
the breezeways
of Venice
still know
the slap slap
of his worn huarache's
"the Lady"
muse for many
walks along
but only
on the shadow side

she sings alone
on this night
in the key of rose

– Shanna Moore

"Collage for 'T', Tony Scibella" by **S.A. GRIFFIN**

JAMES RYAN MORRIS
ELEGY FOR BILLY BATMAN

1. We only met once
        in yr kitchen
        yr wife nursing
        the youngest
                        the living room chaotic
                        with other young mothers
                        nursing
        a mad-house
        I thot when I entered
        but you made me feel comfortable
        like a brother
                        right away
                        extending a joint

                        & after awhile
                        we talked business

        Methadone, etc. as you were sick
        & wanted to make it to Turkey
        "closer to the main source." you sd.

        & being brothers I let you have what I had
        for 200$ less than you'd expected....
        Looking back, Billy, I wonder if I shd feel guilt

2. After dinner, we, Stuart, Tony, you & I sat
        on the back steps digging a circular box of beauty
        and its contents which George Herms had layed on you.
        I wonder where that box is now, Billy?

        That you died so we wld continue isn't the point,
        we expect that from each other, and so its done.
        But now with even beautiful Tracy gone -

        for She was there too that day - the impact of our lives
        is vivid.
                        & every time the dropper draws up the blood
                        I think of you, Billy, am I shooting you into
                        my arm, and if so, what messages are trying
                        to come thru
                                from wherever you are…

3. I don't know abt this poem, Billy, perhaps it is
        only guilt being inserted into my conscience, & being shaped
        into a poem - & if so, let it be, for We both know better.

"The Zodiac Behind Glass: Box #5 Leo" (1965)
sculpture by **GEORGE HERMS**

Queen of Diamonds by **MIKE STREET**

K.R. MORRISON
WAR WOMAN

a king-sized bed soaked in rape
impales a daughter

     a granddaughter
       a mother

       ancestress hair snarled into knots   she tosses
       tangles in red sheets of unrest   lost

in a maze of man
moods   man laws   she survives by losing   herself

      she retreats
        into sleep   unpacks herself   in*her*itance

      from her wrists   kerosene drips
        two swollen rainstorms
           behind her razorblade eyelids

down   irises she tumbles

      into womenstorms

         where grandmothers   toss   turn
         where first women   bury
            grenades   beneath oak trees

      maybe assaults can become something else

down   shadow portals

      war daughter discovers her

         mother   same age   backscattering
         mother drinks   away   his stomach aches

         under sun   she paints men   away
         carves wood into plaques for outlaw men who follow

law by virtue of their wars   their beating   their raping

    Mother Poet.   She says

      out of all the mothers
          daughters
           grandmothers

CONTINUED NEXT PAGE

CONTINUED FROM LAST PAGE

active in unrest
        warriors born
                in winter are the babies who burn
                        themselves   away
                in the protection fire she procreates   death alive
                        in the havoc of her fightback

                in the southern elements
        such war women   resurrect

i am war
        woman's daughter
                granddaughter   born
                        breech from soul mothers   sirening

                the Him Collective   into death

i find these women within my knots

                daughters
                        mothers
                                granddaughters

        on fire   tied to his hawthorn crosses   tied

to his king-sized bed soaked in rape   legs spread

for his wounds   his riddles   his death

        in my wildest dreams   war woman
        hijacks his flames   sinks his ships

                        finds peace
                                in her furious blaze

                --K.R. Morrison

WTJ 2/21

HARRY E. NORTHUP
NIGHT LIGHT

What is a life but a home & a wife?
What is a home but a son & a book?
What is a book but a poem & a picture?
What is a friend but one who helps?
What is a friend but a window & a door?
What door looks within?
What window takes one away from looking within?
What is a wife but a window within?
What is a night but a place to write?
What is a writer but one who looks within?
What is within but a place to be alone?
To be alone with words with little light.
To be in little light & still see words.
Words are a home.
Words create a home.
A home has light within.
A light that does not gossip.
A word within light bestows home.
What is a home without light?
What is light without words?
What words within bring peace?
What is home but light & love?

– Harry E. Northup

8 26 17

Opposite page: "House" collage art by **MARK FISHER**

SOLD OUT!

JANE ORMEROD
BEHIND THE GREEN LIGHT

Oh, your shoulder, my troubled timepiece. At 3:03 a.m. I miss the melody of drink, the blood of horse—and ten thousand is less than half of twenty thousand and the *I* reappears in a billy goat ache, in the peanut gift of daughter with scoop of egg and the coastal wind from a pelican's back.

Blaze talk is real estate. Complete your thick-crust pie later.

No. Don't stand up. This is business. Like flogging standing desks, rigged decks, and cognac snifters with splinters of unsolicited advice. Thick friends, thicker letters, a gambling neighbor, last year's advent calendar. Dinner at Tony's on the corner of Second? Okay? Driven by sugar, cinders, and discredit. The sound of the doctor's car at sundown. Obey, curtsey, slither, write another letter. A blur of baby names. Coo coo coo, little fuckers.

I don't know. Do you prefer women with whiskey or ladies with lettuce? Because I don't. This is not about choice. This is deeper than graveyard training. Those spangled shoulder pads and shouldered history. This is tip-top, tip-toe, top-to-toe and toenail beauty. You can count on me all the way to one hundred and past. A few minutes for comparisons. You know all about it. Non-cooperation, stealth, health as mold … 3:03 pm in room 303 and you're counting your catches, your looks and locks, poultry, and stage fright directions. Keep strong, you say. Keep grounded. And you clock them in, and you clock them out, searching for flower-sellers. *Contact us for further information.* Do not linger in this waiting room. It's all about the stream. The right of way. Appliances.

Milk. Milk is milk is milk. How many pints are stacked around the autopsy table? All this news and all this poison. Everything spreads or burns or bubbles. Memory is a bad folk singer and origin is a bitch. A crap shoot, really. A crab forced the wrong way … which is forward. This is calligraphy as birth. This is you telling the earth about the moon, claiming the moon swims with milk. You swim. You swim back in fourth and fifth dimension. Ha! The dimension is always male.

Today the crowd is a study in syrup. Cordiality is the hiking pole slash, the loss of clockmakers. My mind rests behind the razor in the icebox, behind the hemisphere appointment. The bag in the river is my pillowcase from later tonight.

"Abstract Trio" (1923) painting by **PAUL KLEE**

GIORGIA PAVLIDOU
THE BISEXUAL CONDITION: A NOVEL

It's 2024, and I'm in a relationship with a man and a woman. I adore both. Also, I love kids.

But how does a bisexual person raise a child? Would they do it with the man or with the woman? With both? Or alone?

Rewind three decades, it's 1998: I'm penetrating my high school sweetheart with two fingers on a pale-skied, autumn afternoon. Her name was Sandra. She moaned loudly. I'm still in love with her tanned, muscled, upper legs. She left me for a boy.

Eight years later I made out with a man. His name was Dirk. His soft, girly body, gray eyes, and beautiful penis still flicker in my mind's eye. His orgasms were muted. It didn't last long. I married his best friend, a sexy, bearded man, twenty-eight years my senior.

Jump forward to 2022.

After,

1.   twelve solid years of marriage to Dirk's ex-best friend
2.   copious amounts of transient Sandras and Dirks
3.   ten years of another marriage
4.   and beaucoup years of excruciating financial discipline,

my second husband and I are exhausted but finally chilling in our rural home in Greece. Half a year earlier we were still living on a tight budget in Los Angeles. It's November 2022, summer's heat is waning, I'm cooking steak dinner in our unfinished kitchen when my husband says, "You are unusually jovial today," and smiles. The next day, at our ramshackle dinner table, I'm still jovial because he asks: "Are you in love with her?" This time he isn't smiling.

November 2022 is almost two years ago, and *you* are still in my life.

You are also dying to become a mom.

"Tango" collage art by **T. MIKE WALKER** *(opposite page)*

GIORGIA PAVLIDOU
ADRIENNE RICH AND I

Where do I locate my body and my writing? Feminist poet-philosopher Adrienne Rich thinks of it in this way:

"To locate myself in my body means more than understanding what it has meant to me to have a vulva and clitoris and uterus and breasts. It means recognizing this white skin, the places it has taken me, the places it has not taken me."

Adrienne speaks about the effects of her Jewish background and US citizenship. With revelations like these, she wants to emphasize that there's no such thing as impartiality or neutral, objective knowledge. According to her, our location in the registers of identity forces upon us a singular-specific point of view.

Here's my location: I'm American, and I live on the outskirts of a remote mountain community in Greece.

As I'm jotting down these futile but oh-so-impactful facts, I desire to stress another location: I'm in a heterosexual marriage but I'm not straight, plus Greece might soon become the first Orthodox-majority country to legalize gay marriage.

"Oh, well," I can still hear **you** say, "you're not going to marry me anyway. You're already married."

Next, **you** said, "I know why you're so well integrated into the nearby mountain communities?" The resentful tone of voice did not escape me.

"Why?" I asked.

"Because you're married to a man. Everywhere we go people ask about him. At the local tavern, at the grocery store, neighbors."

I'd be lying if I'd claim that the feeling tone of your words did not sadden me.

You noticed my pain and your face turned mournful.

"What's going on?" **you** asked while caressing my cheeks.

I know **you** by now. Your psychology has thorns and sometimes I find **you** arrogant and overconfident, but you're also tender and empathic.

"I feel," I said with a lump growing in my throat, "partially defeated."

"Defeated" is a tough word to hold in one's mouth, let it roll for a while, and taste it before spitting it out, yet here's the thing:

Had I *not* been in a heterosexual marriage, had I *not* had surplus pocket money *and* a powerful passport, would I have been able to live in rural Greece as a queer, bisexual woman and be – at least to some extent - immune to its overly conservative culture?

"Forest Witches" (1938) painting by **PAUL KLEE**

STUART Z. PERKOFF
LOVE IS THE SILENCE

love is the silence out of which
woman speaks. the female
country. the grieving country.

        i stole
those images from a
wild girl's mouth. i am a
witch. i deal with
death. she sd. i
struggle against it.
the poem
is my struggle, i sd. a different
craft.

    tho once i hungered
where the two crafts cross
to take within my hands
that power
& heat it
at will.

her lips moved in the dark room. blue with
kissing that cold thing. woman is
silence, she sd.
a different craft.

"The Head of a Monster" artwork by **DAVID HUMBERT DE SUPERVILLE**

PUMA PERL
CODE BLUE

What exactly do people have against the dead?
They don't pick fights or treat others dismissively,
they're quiet, they don't litter or play music past 10PM,
and they prefer to lie quietly in their coffins, with no
demands except to please keep the cool air circulating.

People have even been known to scream upon
coming across a dead body, despite the fact that no
harm could possibly come to them; some folks
turn away from the dead at funerals and wakes,
which is particularly rude since great pains
are often taken to dress the dearly departed in
their favorite attire, and to employ makeup artists
and hair stylists to ensure that they look their best.

Additionally, horror movies and post-apocalyptic
tv shows serve only to increase prejudice against
the dead. It is a well-known fact that a very low
percentage of the unalive actually become blood-
thirsty zombies, but despite this well-researched
information many still panic when a ghost stops
by to pass the time or to say a simple hello.

The only kindness shown is often based solely
on the hypocritical notion that it is uncouth
to speak poorly of the dead. Even Hitler has many
defenders; they point out his vegetarianism and
claim that he really only wanted to build a better
Germany, in other words, to make it great again!

An exception to this code of behavior is disgraced
former gallery owner Andrew Crispo, who, in all
of his obituaries is raked over the coals; Crispo
was responsible for only a handful of deaths as
opposed to Hitler's millions, but nobody seems
seems to have anything good to say about him,
and we have not even touched on the many
ways necrophiliacs are stigmatized. Some of them
are even arrested! Does anyone take the time
to ask the dead if they objected? I think not!

A true democracy is inclusive of all, whether
or not one can find a pulse or hear a heartbeat.
We must remember that until all of us are dead
none of us are dead, we are simply floating
in that place between breath and suffocation,
hiding from the unknown, embracing a world
built on false knowledge and blind memory.

ROB PLATH
DRINKING DARKNESS

i remember as a kid
maybe five years old
when everybody was
playing poker & distracted
at the livingroom table
drinking & smoking & laughing
on a weekend evening
i'd get a chair & climb up
to the kitchen sink
& stand there squirting dishsoap
in all the glasses & cups
& then use the sprayer hose
to fill them so they frothed up
like full beer mugs
i was the unnoticed bartender
emptying & filling
round after round
much too young for the night
to be a threat
& now here i am decades later
while everyone in that
other room is long gone
& it's just me here alone
sitting in a chair
still unnoticed
as i slam the keyboard
shitfaced on the night
drinking in the darkness
that has aged into something
much more potent & dangerous

Illustration by **ROB PLATH**

Artwork by JERRY KAMSTRA

HANS PLOMP
WHEN ORPHEUS DIED

he spied
next to Pluto's dwelling
a spring
under a graceful cypress.

Do not drink there,
for it is oblivion
in which you will dissolve.

Go search
for the lake of memoires,
there is another spring
guarded by beings.

Tell them
you are done with earth,
you want to return to the source.

Tell them
you are parched
you want to know all.

Bid them
to quench your thirst
with water from
the source of memory.

And they'll
offer you a drink
and you will awake
like a god among gods.

Opposite page: Hans Plomp and wife Masja Ottenheim
Farewell Party photo by MARCO BAKKER

For the past five or six years I have been maintaining an email correspondence with Dutch-Frisian poet, Walt Whitman translator and Pauper Poet, Lubbert Jan de Vries "Bert". I met Bert on the internet via the Outlaw Poetry Network helmed by the late Klaus Thiemann of St. Nazaire, France, where Bert and I struck up a deep friendship as poets. Publisher, archivist, Beat historian and fluxist Rene Van der Voort found me on the internet and reached out to me via email in 2022. He has since published my work in broadside form and as part of his cassette tape series under his Counter Culture Chronicles imprint. Rene is also part of the producing arm of the Fiery Tongues Festival and former owner of Any Record in the Hague, where he lives with his beautiful wife Sylvia, an artist. As a result of my relationship with these two incredible men, I was invited to take part as a poet in the Fiery Tongues Festival held at Ruigoord every spring.

I often tell people that I have no idea what I am doing or where I am going. They think I am joking with them, but I'm not. I learn as I go and consider myself an expert at nothing as I am constantly learning. Such was the case this past May. All that I knew was that I was finally going to meet Bert and Rene and read at something called Fiery Tongues in a place called Ruigoord. What I found there was more than a festival, it was a creative oasis. A parallel universe beatnik Disneyland on acid, art and creativity in every space and at every corner, better than anything I had ever experienced here in the U.S, or anywhere. What I learned changed the way that I viewed the continuing and profound influence of the Beat Generation on the world.

Situated just outside of Amsterdam for over 50 years, Ruigoord is a collective of creatives and like-minded free-spirited souls of all ages. A unique hybrid of Beat, Hippie and Prankster culture in full Day-Glo finger snapping bloom, Ruigoord blossoms without apology like a beautiful, wild child of the stars. As I kept saying about it the entire time I was there, "This is somebody's childhood."

Born in Amsterdam, Hans Plomp was a teacher, play-

CONTINUED NEXT PAGE

CONTINUED FROM LAST PAGE

wright, poet, pioneer and visionary. Along with his partner and fellow writer Gerben Hellinga, Hans was the driving force behind saving the village of Ruigoord from demolition in July of 1973. Fighting corporate interests and the Dutch government, they fought back and won, over time transforming an abandoned Catholic church, farm and worker village, which dates to about 1880, into the oldest cultural free space in the Netherlands.

After his studies, Hans became a teacher, giving up slave wage jobs for good after the success of his first novel De Ondertrouw (The Betrothal) in 1968. He took an active part in the playful Dutch Provo Revolution of the 1960s, transforming Amsterdam into one of the hippest places on the planet. In 1982 Hans toured the U.S. with a group of Dutch poets, performing with Anne Waldman, Diane di Prima, Allen Ginsberg, Gregory Corso, Amiri Baraka, Ira Cohen and many other kindred spirits. That same year, his work appeared in City Lights Pocket Series #42: Nine Dutch Poets, edited by Lawrence Ferlinghetti.

Hans was a member of Amsterdam Ballongezelschap, or Amsterdam Balloon Company. ABG is a performance collective of musicians, poets, artists, clowns, and activists, operating out of Ruigoord and described as a "hovering movement that strives for freedom in the sky and anyone who loves balloons, kites, birds, and other soundless celestial vehicles (sun, moon, stars, comets etc.) can consider himself a member".

At the Fiery Tongues Festival in Ruigoord, I was in with the in-crowd, walking with angels, rolling with Bert, Rene, Sylvia, Gregory Corso friend and biographer Bobby Yarra, Bobby's assistant and writer Ana Collins, photographer Marco Bakker, Rene's dear friend

and Casioli Press publisher Erik Sluijter and Pauper poet Alwin van der Toorn. During the three-day festival in Ruigoord, we often convened at the Poet's House, where we would meet Hans and his wife Masja Ottenheim. I mostly listened as we smoked good weed, soothing our throats with coconut water as old friends talked and laughed, slipping freely in and out of Dutch and English weaving thru the air like music, as Hans, our gracious host, held court. I would quickly learn that Hans, a charismatic 80 years old, sporting a lion's mane of white rock star hair, flashing a broad toothy smile that could light up every darkness, had been suffering from prostate cancer

CONTINUED NEXT PAGE

Photo: Hans Plomp and S.A. Griffin at Poet's House Ruigoord. Photo Courtesy S.A. Griffin.

CONTINUED FROM LAST PAGE

since 2021 and would soon be gone, making this his last Ruigoord rodeo.

Hans had decided that he was going to be the master of his own fate, forgoing any unnecessary suffering, opting for euthanasia. The Ruigoord community gathered to give the master and counter culture icon a huge four hour 'farewell' party at the Ruigoord Church in late June, with poetry, music, dance, art and love. On August 6, 2024, Hans crossed over to meet the expanding cosmos as universal light, traversing galaxies, dancing and playing among the stars.

As we all sat around talking at the Poet's House during that wonderful weekend in May, I had asked Hans a few times why he had decided that Ruigoord was where he had to make his mark. He would chuckle and avoid any answers. Finally, after everyone was gone, Hans quietly leaned back on his cushions, closing his eyes, resting his arm across his forehead. Bathed in the soft shafts of light that fell across his face, he began to talk, telling his tale as stream of consciousness for almost an hour. I felt that I was a camera capturing as much as I could of the experience. As if Ruigoord was Shangri-La, The Valley of The Blue Moon, and I was in the presence of the High Lama himself.

This is somebody's childhood.

HOLLY PRADO
INTERLUDE

(INTERLUDE: I'd left the family dinner to go outside. I loved my mother and father, the aunt, uncle and cousins gathered the dinner table, but suddenly I had to get away, shivering in the early spring Nebraska weather where patches of snow still lay on the ground, trying to melt but having a hard time of it. I headed for the alley that separated our house and yard from the Saunders', directly across from us.

I walked looking down, watching my step, not sure where I was headed. Then, in the middle of the alley, lifting from a muddy pile of snow, I spotted a cluster of Bachelor Buttons. Their blue was a vivid purple-blue, surprising and beautiful in the steadily darker evening. I knelt in the snow to look at the flowers, their ruffled petals like fragile wings. Even at age ten, I understood the moment: nature's ascendence out of winter's dormancy.

This was proof of God, no doubt about it.

I told no one. My family and I shared a mild version of Protestant Christianity, benign enough, but our Congregational Church never satisfied me. Divine revelation in a common flower would have made no sense in a religion of memorized prayer, solid good works. In college, I lost my religious faith completely. Our snowy alley had nothing to do with passing Latin Literature in Translation. On my small college campus, there was art, though: theater, painting, music, poetry. The arts seemed to me a world of Soul. How to join that world? I couldn't, I thought. I had no gifts large enough to offer Soul.

Ten years later, I fell from my Phi Beta Kappa rationality into emotional exhaustion. What gathered as despair became my gift to the Bachelor Buttons. To find my own religion, I had to live within my dream life, within my true love of writing, my pull toward myth, symbology, archetypes, alchemy, pre-historic origins. I didn't find the Answer but The Mystery, the Sustaining Mystery.

Bachelor Buttons are re-seeding annuals, returning every spring. Once, a long time after my vision in the alley, I wrote in a poem of mine, "I am returned to what I never left.")

From Weather, (Cahuenga Press, 2019)

Oppostie Page:

"Centaurea Cyanus Bachelor Buttons" photo by **MATT LAVIN**
CC BY-SA 2.0 <https://creativecommons.org/licenses/by-sa/2.0>

LINDA RAVENSWOOD

IS IT POSSIBLE TO USE THE F WORD LESS !? NO ? LOVELY.

fuck me so good i wake up with *your* morning breath
fuck me so good suddenly I like your mother
fuck me so good I walk out of work Thursday in the middle of Mo's diatribe in Conf. Room B
fuck me so good i'm back at work Friday like nothing ever happened & no one says shit
fuck me so good I believe in free love / marriage / polyamory / whatever you say
fuck me so good you live inside me rent free
fuck me so good I can't say the word *Come* without thinking of you bringing me over
fuck me so good i understand my Roth IRA
fuck me til I don't remember lunch or math or words or how to drive
fuck me to flowers
fuck me til my parents & my children agree on something
fuck me til my mother understands pronouns
fuck me til the end of blood
fuck me to my virginity
fuck me til I forget my name
fuck me to the end of war
fuck me deep into tomorrow
legit fuck me til I'm a man like you
fuck me so right I'm the man who fucks you right
fuck me to ecstasy / to unconsciousness / then revive me & do it all again
fuck me against the law / beyond possessiveness / acquisition / status / class
break every door /unlock every lie /remember every history /erased /dropped /put on the curb
fuck me to me spit
til the last breath
down in the dirt
& leave us there together in perfect fuck
fuck me til I forgive the land grabbers
til I forgive your rapist
til i forgive the ones who put ashes in her mouth
til I forgive your father
& almost up to the men who hurt Matthew Shepherd, even almost there but not yet,
fuck me to prayer to beg for time & mercy to forgive everything, yes fuck me to mercy
& fuck me even til I forgive white people
fuck me so good i calls in the neighborhood
in the center of me where the flame is
fuck me so good you live there
Fuck me so good just thinking about you makes me cum
and cum and cum and come
to the ones fuck me
you make me into you

Opposite page: "Marked Girls" painting by **ERIC ROHMAN** *(1939)*

Illustration by **JESSE MCCLOSKEY**

NICCA RAY
BACK IN THE NEW YORK GROOVE

The fall air pushes the humid summer drench to the curb.

The darkening days wash over me – a warm blanket to cover my vulnerability.

The crowds of pedestrians push past me as though I am invisible and that's okay. I don't want to be seen.

The black and red flannel I am wearing belonged to my father. I can smell his musky cigarette laden scent as if he were still alive.

I am walking across Houston at Bleeker headed toward the West Village there's a thrift store where I bought a blueberry dress once and I want another one.

I feel empty.

I am walking the streets my father walked wearing his shirt.

I haven't washed my hair in three days, but it's dyed as white as it can go and so the brittle hair holds the oils well and it actually looks good.

My eyes are surrounded with black liner.

I live in the underground of things.

New York City streets invite that. They invite me. They give me breath. They give me stride.

My father was over 6' tall. He took long steps when he walked. I don't know this for a fact. I just imagine myself walking with him and trying to keep up.

It's 6pm and chilly and I could've worn a jacket but today I wanted only to wear my father's shirt shirt— to feel him on me.

I came to the city to be with him. To feel his groove, walk his stride.

The night is falling onto the streets and the wind is starting to blow trash across the avenues.

Manhattan Skyline by DAVID VADDON (Creative Commons Attribution 2.0)

LUIVETTE RESTO
A POEM FOR THE PEOPLE WHO THINK I KNOW JLO, AOC,
OR INSERT OTHER CELEBRITY PUERTO RICAN WOMAN

Please stop asking me
if I know JLo when you hear
I am from the Bronx.

She hasn't been to the block,
bought a slice on Castle Hill Avenue, or ridden the 6 train
since the advent of banana hair clips.

To those who say I remind them of AOC
when I part my hair down the middle
donning the clean girl aesthetic co-opted by TikTok girls

do yourself a favor, learn more about a politician's policies,
voting histories, and campaign donors
than which Fenty shade they buy

I'd rather be confused for Rosie Perez, Lolita Lebrón,
Julia de Burgos, Luisa Capetillo, Villano Antillano,
Iris Chacón, Rita Moreno, Salima Rivera.

Mujeres whose pelvic thrusts, revolutions, poems,
feather boas, awards, music, and tacones
protect my body as I fix my lipstick in the mirror.

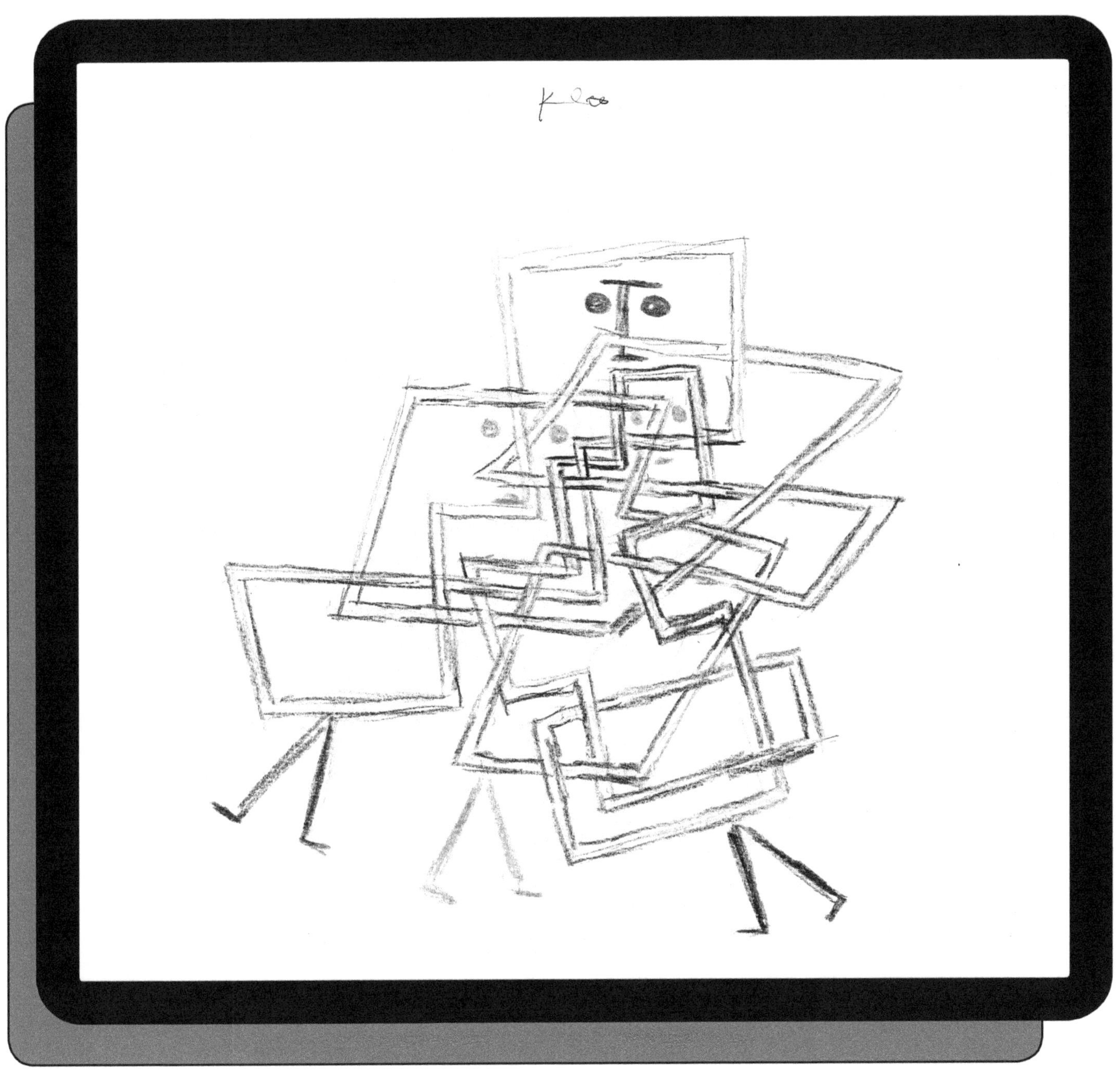

"Drei in Verworrenheit" artwork by **PAUL KLEE** *(1930)*

Photo: State Street, USA by CHUCK KOTON

FRANK T. RIOS
CORSO

Bones of dead angels
reshaping themselves
into holy bombs
mind-fields
on the lips of strangers

long knives down Spanish streets
speaking cat-tongue
dark alley gun poems
like a line of coke falling
off a bridge of cobwebs

I love you Corso
down the long tongue
you bowed to everyone
hid well shadows of yourself
that black heavy N.Y. coat
tucked down inside your magic head…

        I have a friend
        who looks like Corso
        blew his mouth away
        with drugs
        played like Coltrane
        when he was young

        saw him on an old mans bench
        hair gray
        eyes hooded sad
        looking down that long road
        he suffered on

        I waved
        spoke his name
        he looked up
        bewildered

        I could see behind it all
        he still looked like Corso
        with that faraway look
        listening to an untold poem-song
        on his golden horn…

"Remorse for Gaza." Ink, photomontage, cut-outs artwork by **DOREN ROBBINS**

DOREN ROBBINS

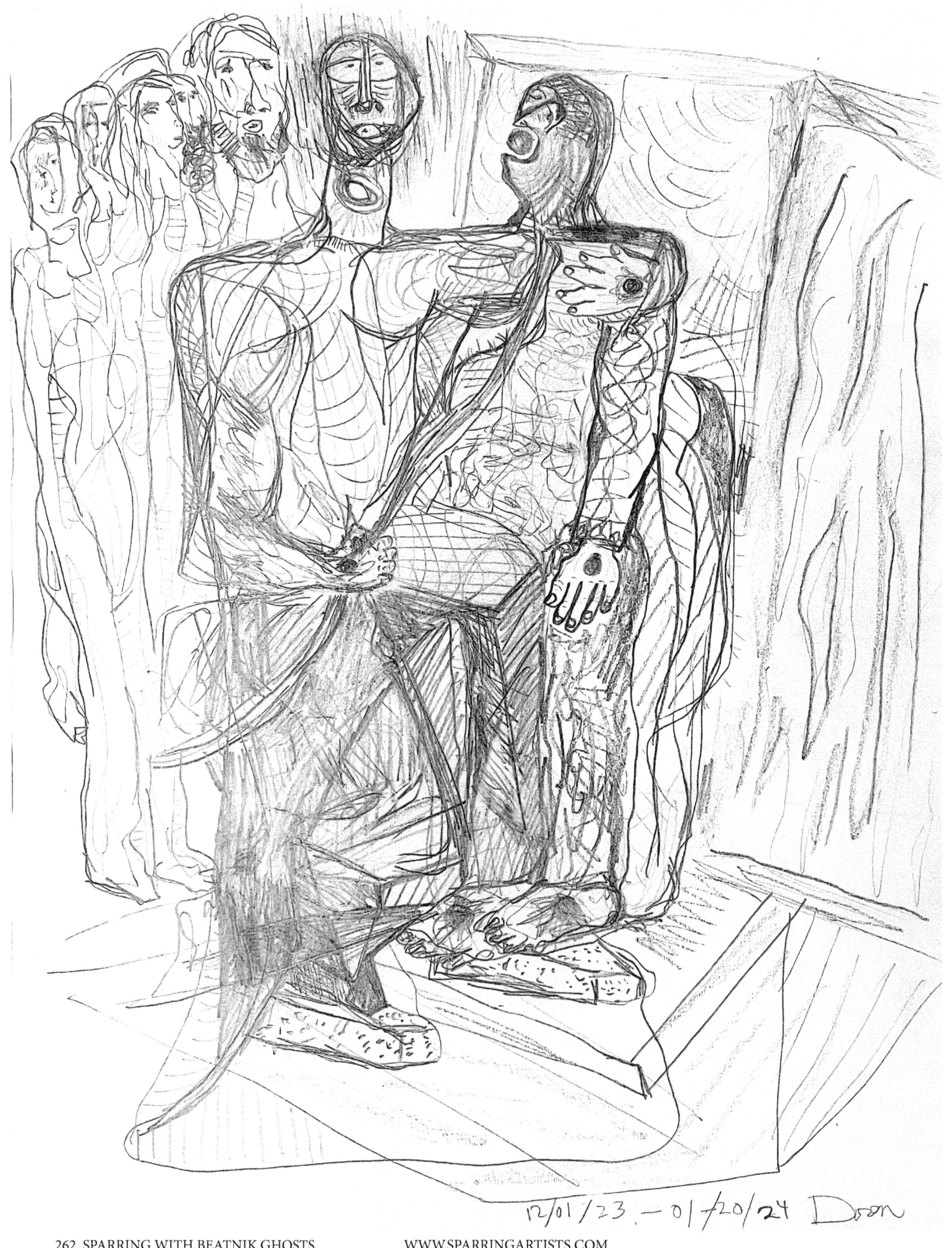

262. SPARRING WITH BEATNIK GHOSTS   WWW.SPARRINGARTISTS.COM

JEFF ROGERS
GHOSTS OF THE LIVING

I fear no nighttime visits from my dead.
I hoisted my own mother's casket—light as her gentle spirit flown.
No, it's only the ghosts of the living who haunt my waking dreams.

Anyone who's lived as long as I has lost those gone to grave or ash,
So I'm followed now by a spectral entourage, lively, fond, and sad,
And I fear no nighttime visits from my beloved dead.

It's the words unsaid and deeds unjustly done
To loved ones still alive that nail me sleepless to my bed,
These ghosts of the living who haunt my waking dreams.

They'll pop up grinning with a headlight sweep in my midnight rearview mirror
Or stalk me at noon the lonely length of a harsh-lit office hallway.
No, I fear no nighttime visits from my dead.

It's the sudden name long undialed that troubles my cell phone fingers,
Wails to me in the faucet stream as I wash my morning dishes—
These ghosts of the living who haunt my waking dreams.

Things I've done to the woman beside me kick me awake in our bed,
Rap their skeleton knuckles on the mad attic doors of my mind.
No, I fear no nighttime visits from my beloved dead.
It's these restless ghosts of the living who haunt my waking dreams.

Previously published in *Right Wrong Night Song*, 12/3/22, World Stage Press

"Invader Captured, Ukraine" graphite artwork by **DOREN ROBBINS** *(opposite page)*

JULIE ROGERS
WHAT IS

No end no end no end
I can't remember
the beginning beginning
ever—absolutely no proof
or documentation
of eternity's birth—
death's finality is
definitely debatable,
ever-after is sooner
and closer than ever—
starting here is inevitable
if you notice it
after before, before later,
beyond the past's
hint of future
and further inward—
here we are.
What is? What
do you do with this?
Inhale. Let it go,
all of it. Is this the IT
I live for? Driven
on a long dark road
leading somewhere
toward light
holding the wheel
so all I know can focus
on right here
as now happens

is.

--Julie Rogers
2-7-24
for Tibetan New Year

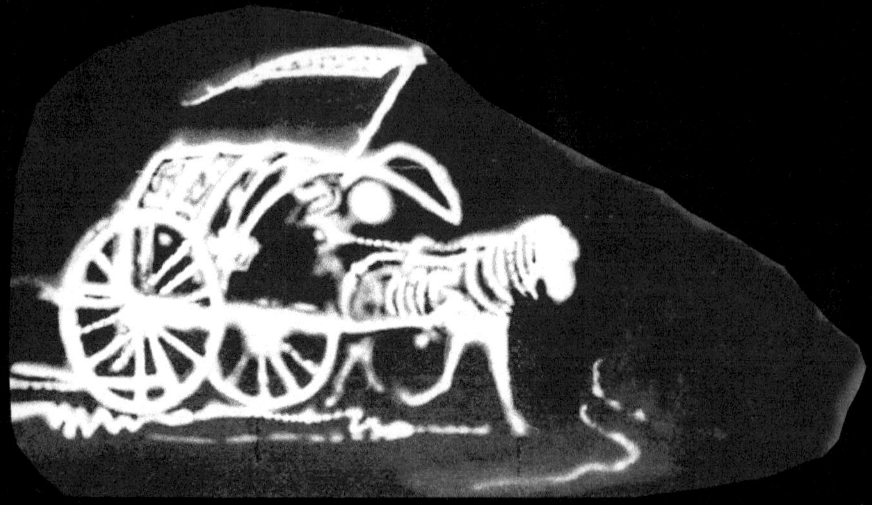

"The Phantom Wagon" painting by **ERIC ROHMAN** *(1939)*

KIM SHUCK
THE BUTTERFLY WAR

Never ended this
Tension and the
Sierras keep burning
Flame pressing tips into each
Hidden place that
Tenaya knew and as the
Fires pass the people
Scatter grass seed to
Hold the earth down hold it
Down in the valley in
Mariposa Grove there is this
Fire and it reads the
Stories of these hills out loud in voices too
Terrible too airless for
Understanding takes the
Trees by the throat and
Reads them ring by ring into every
Fingerhold that water has and the
Beating of indefinable
Wings of flame these
Winds of burning take
Non-human prayers to
Other gods on that
Smoke and every bit of
Hope and history is
Told and retold in
Cracked rock and
Charcoal stands of
Trees

"Trails End" painting by **MELISSA WEST**

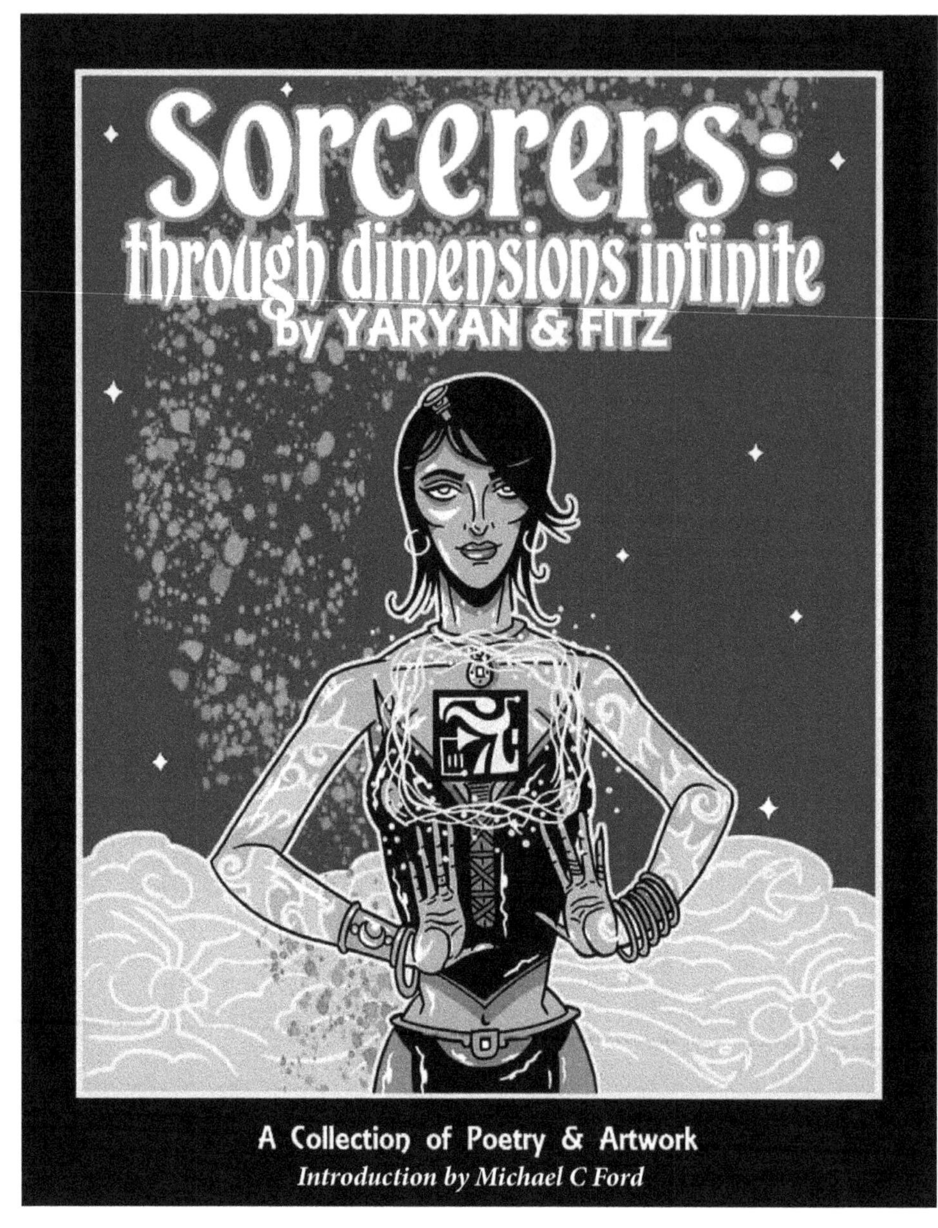

MIKE SONKSEN

YARYAN

You arrange readings yelling allusions nightly
Young assassins remember Yaryan alleviates negativity
Yearly analysis renders Yaryan's answers noteworthy
Yo! abolish republican Yankees aiding narcissists
Yes accelerating reports yield ancestors nearby
Years after rocketing Yaryan approaches Nebuli

MIKE SONKSEN

FOR DAVID MELTZER

David Meltzer melt the developer mystical elements elevate your poetry
enlightened folk energy doing expansive leaps line after line your copy
on time punchlines Brooklyn to California dreaming scheming lamentations
for Hank Williams wielded genesis spiritualism processing jazz & politics
as fragments in segmented data clusters poems coming from everywhere
you were there with Wallace Berman blowing Bop Kabbalah acoustic gothic
3-2-1 contact you drew the map between the Cold War & pagan lore
one of your poems said a bank teller told you Meltzer meant waiter
in Hebrew I wrote this poem to tell you I am sorry for letting you down
in 2011 when we scheduled you to read at the Last Bookstore I didn't
promote it right and forgot to make sure the date was printed in the calendar
when you arrived that day there was almost nobody there I apologize David
for dropping the ball I was younger then much less responsible nonetheless
in the coming years you still answered my emails sending thoughtful quotes
for an essay I wrote about City Lights 60th anniversary your pocket poets
collection *When I Was a Poet* is a masterpiece you mastered the *Beat Thing*
like Lester Young you could swing something ferocious I will always love
you David Meltzer

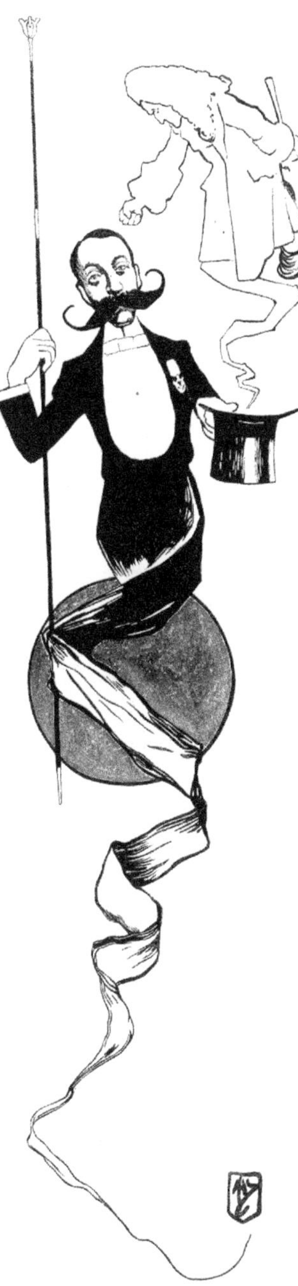

"The Phantom Paper" illustration by **JOHN HASSALL**

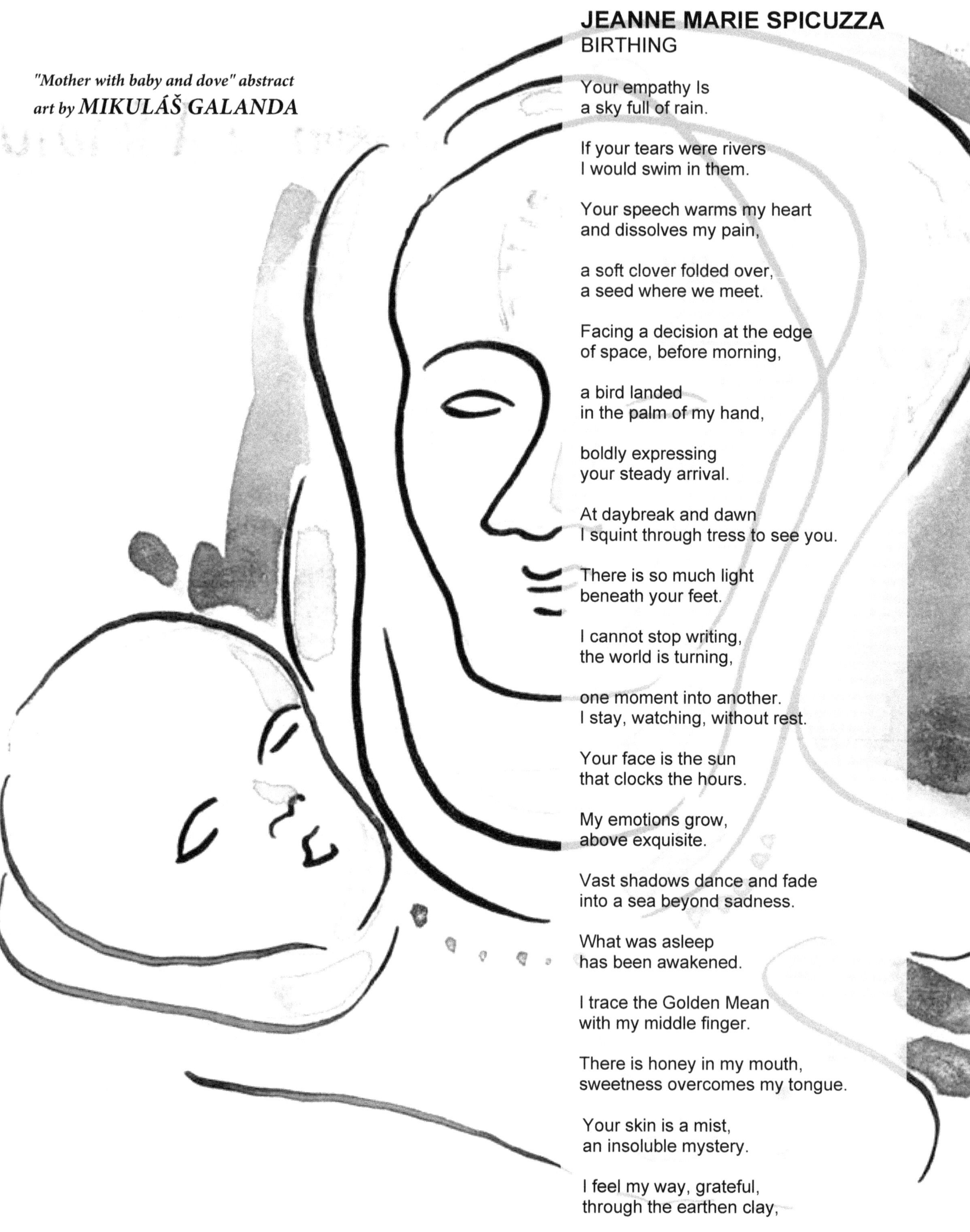

"Mother with baby and dove" abstract
art by **MIKULÁŠ GALANDA**

JEANNE MARIE SPICUZZA
BIRTHING

Your empathy Is
a sky full of rain.

If your tears were rivers
I would swim in them.

Your speech warms my heart
and dissolves my pain,

a soft clover folded over,
a seed where we meet.

Facing a decision at the edge
of space, before morning,

a bird landed
in the palm of my hand,

boldly expressing
your steady arrival.

At daybreak and dawn
I squint through tress to see you.

There is so much light
beneath your feet.

I cannot stop writing,
the world is turning,

one moment into another.
I stay, watching, without rest.

Your face is the sun
that clocks the hours.

My emotions grow,
above exquisite.

Vast shadows dance and fade
into a sea beyond sadness.

What was asleep
has been awakened.

I trace the Golden Mean
with my middle finger.

There is honey in my mouth,
sweetness overcomes my tongue.

Your skin is a mist,
an insoluble mystery.

I feel my way, grateful,
through the earthen clay,

sensing that after the storms pass,
stories of passion and play

may transform into understanding,
an albeit naive layer of meaning:

love, like beauty, cannot be explained.
What was once admired, wisdom cherishes.

It is this majesty that has become
the gown I wear to protect its glory.

I want to share with you
what is not mine,

to hold briefly
your visceral nobility.

If I kiss you once
it will determine my purpose.

I will steer in the direction
of the western wind.

Living isn't breathing,
but seeing and exceeding.

If we keep reaching,
the infinite breeze will lift us.

I fear not the darkness,
only the absence of everything.

I have been alone,
at times lonely.

But your angled limbs are an isosceles,
my senses find feast.

I spread my head and hair
across this kingdom of instinct.

I will bring you the moon
while you shoulder the stars.

The sand and agony
melt away between our toes.

Dreams come into being
with the magic of subtle, delicate grandeur.

I find you standing
before the mirror of eternity,

reflecting my hopes,
holding them as your own.

You guard our alliance
with a sword of fire,

drawn from water
and sounds of ocean.

These tender dedications
guide our way.

I pray with hands open
against your torso.

I do not comprehend
our direction.

Your smile guides
my uncertainty.

Such a wonder you are
in front of impossibility.

Gratitude surrounds me
like a glove.

What is truly creative
is never lost.

You have saved me
without sweat or labor.

Your honesty
has brought this treasure.

I recognize you, your
crown and throne of gold,

transfigured with serenity,
fused by joyful inclusion.

There is a future to anticipate
where you are situated now.

The holy and the sacred
pour out from your patient, waiting spirit.

Your flowers have fed me.
I am nourished deeply.

I will call out to you
as long as gravity allows

and watch us soar upward
as time tumbles down.

Your colors pull back the curtain
draping the window, which is me.

You have unleashed my poetry,
and given birth to artistry.

TATE SWINDELL
RADIO ROAD
for Obama Tashi

People might think it strange that I listen to the radio. Not just at home in the Bay Area—KCSM, KPOO, KDFC—but while driving across country on the car radio, or handheld transistor or full on hi-fi at home stereo entertainment when I can find it.

But there's a certain white noise zen of radio station static while driving high plains for hours and hours. Landscape on a loop.

Yeah, there's a trap door of nostalgia hearing the old hits from decades and centuries past. But there's also a fresh beauty in attempting to hear new sounds within old songs.

Today, this happened.

Queen.

Bohemian Rhapsody.

The song played and I hummed along to the notes. The rises in pitch and rhythm.

Then it happened. A line I've heard hundreds of times before, I heard with new ears.

Third stanza, final line.

But now I've gone and thrown it all away.

Until this line, specifically the last two words/three syllables, Freddy Mercury had sung the song in a high falsetto. The lines were very clean, articulately enunciated.

In this third stanza, Mercury is confessing to his mother that he just killed a man.

Put a gun against his head
pulled my trigger
now he's dead
Mama, life had just begun
but now I've gone
and thrown It all away

At the end of that line—he leans into the weight of the crime.

As he confesses this sin he can no longer maintain the strain of the piercing tone.

He fractures
               under pressure
                            fissures emerge.

He is crumbling as he admits that's *he thrown it all away*.

Those last two words—a*ll away*—a rumbling growl of regurgitated bile that he can no onger stomach.

Mercury is able to compose himself and revert to the falsetto lie for the next stanza.

The one other after that, the fifth stanza, rupture returns, on the final line.

Gotta leave you all behind and face the truth.

Those last three words—again three syllables—hear the return of the roaring snarl.

The overwhelming weight of the crime is crashing through again. I feel it and shiver like a scratch down the back of a neck. My heart, falls, heavy, thumping empty stomach. Somehow, I know this pain. It is familiar, briefly comforting, soon to dissipate with invisl- ble wind. Radio road. Antenna seeks tuning. Clarity of emptiness.

This sort of stuff, others probably recognized years ago. Me, I needed the isolation of the road to truly hear it. A little static, fading in and out, climbing mountains and de- scending into valleys. Attempting to concentrate a little harder. Sometimes, a little less.

Listen.

Wyoming
April 4, 2024

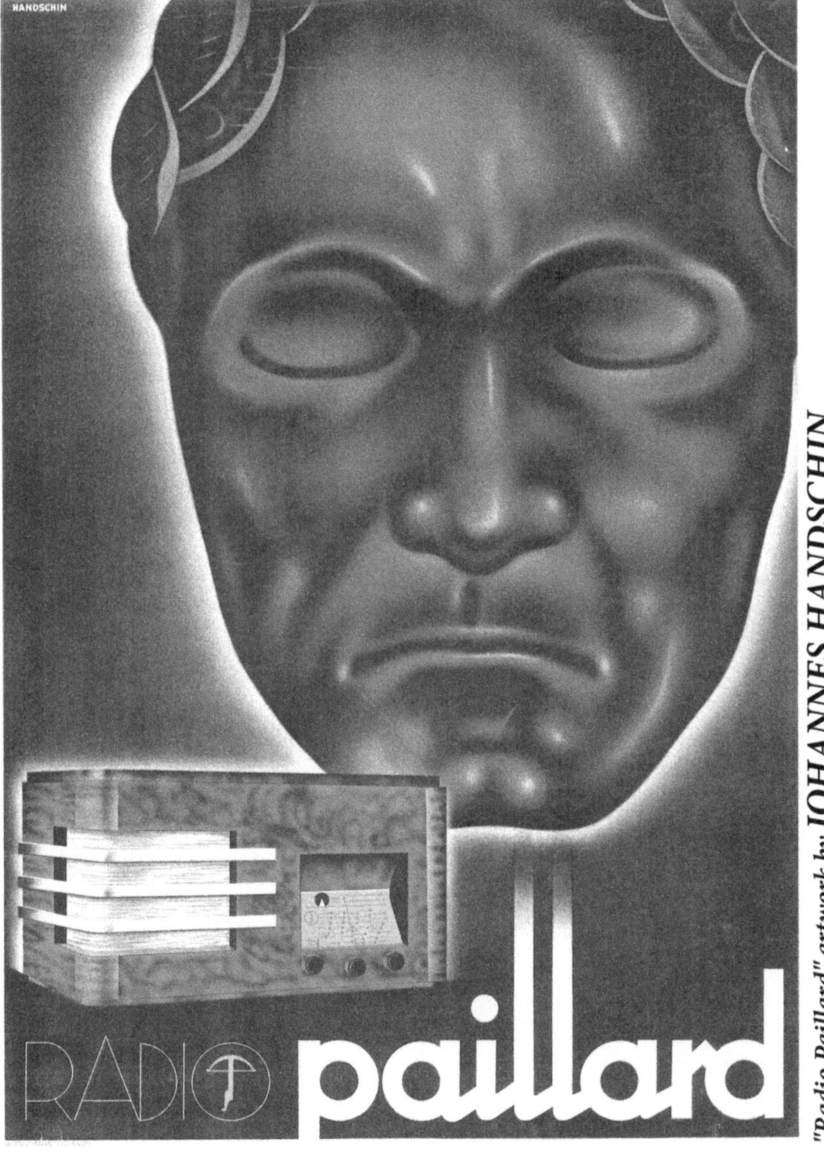

MIKE TAYLOR
FRANKIE'S WEDDING
(road trip with Tony Scibella, Saul White, Larry Lake & me)

the dunes seemed to roll on
forever as we drove west towards
LA and frankie's wedding
we'd been in the car 18 hours or so
and i'd been behind the wheel
the whole time
saul was asleep in the back of the
red land cruiser, larry in the back
seat staring silently out the window
tony was riding shotgun and
he was smoking and trying to find
a radio station out in the desert
"need to stop for gas"
"yea, and smokes" larry says
20 miles or so down the road
we pull into a station and all get out
3 wild-haired, bearded men
walk into the store while i pump
the gas and stare down the road
at the horizon and then put gas handle away and head into the store and
up to the woman behind the counter
who's eyeing the other three as they
walk up and down counters...
i order some smokes and larry and saul bring up some drinks and we stand there
waiting for tony. he finally walks up and puts a plastic jesus on the counter.
we pay for the stuff and head back to
the land cruiser not saying anything
to tony. finally saul can't take it
any longer..."what the hell's that for, tony?" tony slips the plastic off the bottom and
sticks it on the dashboard and leans back and makes sure it's on straight, "mike didn't
have one on his dash."
"yea, so?"
"hell, we've driven 1500 miles so far and still got like 300 more or so...just wanted to
make sure we
were protected."
tony puts his arms across is chest, closes his eyes and immediately falls asleep. larry
stares at the plastic figure on my dash and shaking his head
lights a cigarette. saul, seated in the back now just stares at the figure silently and does
so for the next couple hours.
i, smiling, stare out
the window at the road ahead as we finish
our drive to venice and the marriage
to take place later the next day. i know we'll
make it, not only there but back to denver. not because of the plastic jesus stuck on my
dashboard but because tony says we're protected and
that's all that really matters.

"And In the Very Disk of the Sun Shines the Face of Jesus Christ" artwork by **ODILON REDON**

MJ TAYLOR
SOMEHOW IN DETROIT

time to ask
for directions

comes long after
accepting we

may be lost, not knowing
where we are going.

it's a hard thing
to admit when

you've been at
the wheel of

that cadillac of confidence,
pontiac of pride

fueled on
certainty that

there's gotta be a quicker,
there's gotta be a more

scenic route
across all these

weaving streets &
burnout highways

sans all
toll fees.

that last exit sign said
40 miles to Shangri-La

but somehow
you're in detroit.

Opposite page:

" Evolution of Style" collage art by **T. MIKE WALKER**

"George Floyd" painting by **LYNN ROGERS**

A.K. TONEY
BIG BEAST BURDEN

Whoop-Whoop!
Big Beast on the block…
Whoop-Whoop!
Griot gotta get a lock…
Whoop-Whoop!
Time for council workshop…
Whoop-Whoop!
Village Forum nonstop…

Beast is a bully on the block…
But the block is a sphere
And the sphere had spears
If you came close or near
You were cut real clear
Seem like we losing
Ain't got bravery to lose

So Black and abused
So White and misused
So Yellow confused
So Brown and refuse
So Red execute
We so geriatric bruised

They bully the folk
They bully the vote
They bully the woke
They bully by choke
They bully with smoke
The bully is loc'd

Picture this is a virus of despair
With a mask below eye stare
This is a life-or-death affair
We don't know what friend means anymore
There is fear around the corner
A beatdown from 13 16-year-old young men
Killing a single 17-year-old trying to defend his friend…
That ain't the beginning and sho' ain't the end

It ran amuck on January 6th, 2021
And everyone saw the bullies take over the Capitol
And everyone saw George Floyd's last breath with a knee on his neck
And everyone saw Black folk get run down in a crowd with a pick-up truck
And everyone saw the White woman start shooting inside the police station as
They safely apprehended her, and she was still breathing…

But before we go on…
We gotta stop being by-standers, spectators, on the sideline with popcorn
We have to liberate ourselves with defense movements, not a movie form
Trauma porn, we call it…

CONTINUED NEXT PAGE

Have we forgotten that video of a beautiful young lady
Bullied and beat to death by her friends
In a hotel room in another country
Then they flew back home without her?
Whatever happened with that name?

Bully is a brand name that we proudly claim
We love the guilt of shame…
Change is we standing up for Humane…

Whoop-Whoop!
Big Beast on the block…
Whoop-Whoop!
Griot gotta get a lock…
Whoop-Whoop!
Time for council workshop…
Whoop-Whoop!
Village Forum nonstop…

They bully the folk
They bully the vote
They bully the woke
They bully by choke
They bully with smoke
The bully is loc'd
And you think, it's being poked…

Beast is now big running the sphere,
Sharpening and aiming the spears…
Votes are being bullied…
Candidate leaders on campaign trails stating,
"If I don't get elected… It's gonna be a bloodbath for the whole country."
By the way, no giving out water and no speaking in voting lines…
Livelihoods are becoming suicides on sight…
Victims doing mass shootings to self-right…
A sui-psycho-social-genocide
Intimidation from cyber psychological meaningless comments killing socialization…
Covid 19 had nothing on the hate that became seen (scene)
The bully is an unseen entity scheming and devising, sabotaging, controlling, anti-civilized is arising…
Inflammation of the atmosphere, hard to breathe in here…
Fight or flight motions are coming out… Will you stand up or punk out?

We will never speak the name of the Bully…

This is what we call a crisis from the beginning in Middle school…
Remember M.W., and what he said to the hand-me-down child?
Because Hand-me-down was the one with good grades and voted for President of the classroom…

Now M.W. was the most entitled, had the best, was the worst conceited redhead jheri curl…
We think he couldn't read because he was the class clown…
Anyway, right before we went to the restroom…
M.W. threatens Hand-me-down, claiming he was going to beat him down in the bathroom…
Hand-me-down just looks at him…
They are in the bathroom, and all the other boys are looking and egging it on…
Hand-me-down says, "I just come to school to learn, I'm not here to fight."

Art spread: "Heal" collage art by T. MIKE WALKER

CONTINUED NEXT PAGE

M.W. shoves him and says, "You just an old clothes wearing sissy. You don't deserve to be President."
M.W. pushes him even harder and Hand-me-down responds, "Don't push me again."
M.W. doesn't let him pass…
Then suddenly, Hand-me-down grabs M.W. by the collar pushes him into the bathroom stall, dunks his head in the toilet bowl and flushes it giving him a jheri swirl…

A decade later, come to find out…
M.W. was the leader of a gang, they were into stealing cars
And they decided to sexually assault a girl in concert…
Afterwards, shoot her in the head when they finished…
She survives in the hospital to testify…
M.W. tried to run by doing a GTA then lead police on a high speed chase
Finally, running down an elderly couple killing them in the accident
Before being caught.
M.W. is now doing life in prison…
Who is the Big bad beast now?

A poodle gets the best of your boxer bulldog
Or showing good sportsmanship boxing with gloves on in the front yard…
You would have stopped to think…
This isn't working and maybe
He would be in a better place by now…
Because Hand-me-down was me…

Whoop-Whoop!
Big Beast on the block…
Whoop-Whoop!
Griot gotta get a lock…
Whoop-Whoop!
Time for council workshop…
Whoop-Whoop!
Village Forum nonstop…

—A.K. Toney

ALWIN VAN DER TOORN
BORN TO GO

some words
stay with you a lifetime
they are the few true friends
you can depend on

you may think earth is just
another penitentiary rock
in space
and you may be right

there are no chains
no bars apart from this flesh
there are no rules
not even those of physics

as Old Bill says:
'you've got one chance, kid...
write your way out...'

you write your escape
the melting of the snow
the silence of the birds

soundless days
flakes that fall in a silent movie
trees characters in ink
on a blank paper rectangle

human voices have no place here –
have forgotten their place
if they dare to speak

you go up
the air is thin
you have to stop more often
no matter –
you've left behind
the dry sound of kernels
going through the hourglass

instead, there's the breath of the wind
the dizzy silence of each view opening up

the mountain's a dog
you're a flea in its fur
crawling up its side

an avalanche of ice and snow far away –
the dog stirs in its sleep

there is no fear
heaven is innocent
pink and blue

a stone is polished by water
until its surface is smooth as skin

Painting by **HENRY LYMAN SAŸEN**

MYSTIC BOXING IN A BOX!

A MEMBERSHIP EXCLUSIVE!

JOIN THE MBC AND RECEIVE THE FOLLOWING...

- CUSTOM MEMBERSHIP BOX
- GHOST ACCORDIAN
- FOLD OUT COLOR POSTER
- DVD SET OF 40 LEGENDARY POETS
- SPARRING ALL STARS BOOK
- MICHAEL C FORD BROADSIDE
- FORD LIMITED EDITION BOOK
- TRACY WITT ARTWORK
- BOX VARIANT YARYAN BOOK
- POSTER FROM ARTIST FITZ
- MEMBERSHIP CERTIFICATE
- KAMSTRA LIMITED EDITION BOOK
- SORCERERS POSTER
- PREMIUM CHOICE BOOK VOUCHER
- FREE DESIGN CONSULTATION TICKET
- POET-TREE FESTIVE-ALL POSTER
- LIMITED T. MIKE WALKER COLLAGE
- MYSTERY BROADSIDE
- COLLECTIBLE COMPACT DISK
- BEST OF SPARRING STUDENTS BOOK
- BOOKMARKS & BUTTONS
- 30% OFF AT SPARRINGARTISTS.COM

WATCH FOR IT IN 2025 AT SPARRINGARTISTS.COM

JIMMY VEGA
voicemail i ching

i leave the i ching in the car

      you ask   & i listen

some loves are ghosts

      you ask   & i carry three coins

who do you wish you could call

      a voicemail is letter in voice—

war is never over   in my pocket

      divinity ///

i reach for the i ching

      & i ask

--

i leave the i ching closed

      overflowing my mind

some transmissions are more sacred

      yellow flower   gaped

mouth, there is divinity in spit

an angel on the exit of the 90 sits,

      soaks sun, closed eyes

        gazing at me

"Once Again" artwork by
CATHYANN CUSIMANO

an insect leaves this realm & i hear

      a popping sound

quiet whisper, glorious & hitherto rever-

berating ///   divinity in sacrifice

--

ephemeral clashing bird song

     serene & ubiquitous

tell me about god cause i've almost forgotten

     as you milk sunrise into oblivion

feed every hungry atom of my body

     way a sleepy kiss murmurs

       forget-me-nots

& i listen—

--

i dream the i ching on my freeway bed

     pass the overpass pass my tortured

darlings   you ask   & i listen

some loves are sentences that keep repeating,

     —a coma splice hidden as run-on

cultivate technologies   an ofrenda

     is archive   is praxis

a folded ladder inside a gallery in shadow

a voicemail is letter   is voice

     i'd give a lot of everything to sit

     in your suffering   in your thirst

a voicemail is a letter   often unopened

     archival transubstantiation breath

melting inside your *fade into you* cosmic day-

dreaming   like the eudaimonia found intensely

     in staring into sunset-mirrored-ocean

     through a lens of glass-polymer

my own déjà vu revisiting me
my own déjà vu revisiting me
my own déjà vu revisiting me

     you ask…

& i listen—

Collage art by **MICHAEL C FORD**

T. MIKE WALKER
SMOKING!
A poem for jazz accompaniment

It was '53 in 'Frisco when I emerged at 16 from the fog of adolescence
Into the thick sooty smog of the city streets,
swimming through black smoke bellowing from a million
cars and trucks, planes and trains, gray smoke coiling from the lips
of 100 million people puffing King Size, Regular, filtered and flavored
cigarettes, cigars, and pipes…tobacco smoke swirling in restaurant fans
streaming from open car windows, smoke in most offices,
smoke before breakfast, smoke after lunch, smoke every coffee break,
smoke in back of school until they caught me,
but most especially smoke in bars like the jazz cellar…
*("A Train" starts w/sax intro)
down tobacco stained stairs beneath a north beach pizza pub,
smoke so thick I had to squint to see across the crowded room;
jazz musicians were blowing their brains out next to the bar,
Ellington's A-Train flying us to Harlem on a smooth tenor riff,
Piano, bass & drums driving the train while Brew Moor sipped
from a smoking cigarette clipped next to his mouthpiece
so he could smoke and blow at the same time…
And when he blew, white smoke swirled from the bell of his horn,
forming rings of soulful sounds with every exhaled phrase,
and I shivered, thrilled, pressing my 6 foot skinny body back against the
plush red lounge, silently sipping my coke, trying 2 lay low, 2 be cool, 2 just
dig the music and become like smoke, invisible…
Brew stopped blowing…
*(sax stops and bass solos)
and the bass soloed with a fretless plucking and slapping of strings
while Big Bill Wijon laid down rail-like chords, blues notes weeping
from his fingertips as a cigarette dangled from his lips,
the ash growing steadily longer, his head wreathed in a cloud of smoke…
Then the drummer rattled our bones *(bass)…and Brew returned
*(sax counts in last chorus of "A Train and out")
singing again through his smoking horn, and they were all blowing at once
a glorious free-for-all cacophony the audience joined by shouting
"Yes!" and "Say it, brother!" and "Go, man, Go!"…
as the band blew the A Train all the way back home,
gliding to a stop at the station… *(All Music Stops)
…and the waterfall of sound was silent.

Such wild applause! The musicians were sweating, smiling,
bowing to the audience, many of us on our feet, clapping in appreciation.
Across the room a cocktail waitress glanced my way. Oh, Shit!
I shook a Chesterfield from its cellophane pack and flamed it with a flick of
my dad's old silver army lighter, drawing in a breath while smoke curled out
of my nostrils into my mouth, my one suave trick to try and look older,
just as the waitress arrived and looked me up and down:
"Neat trick, kid," she said, "Can I see your ID?"
I coughed, and blew a smoke of words over her as I fumbled for my wallet:
"Gee, I already showed it at the door when I paid my cover…"
I passed her my fake ID and a $10 dollar bill. "I live for this music, don't

CONTINUED NEXT PAGE

you? And they're playing so beautiful tonight…I sure would like another
coke, my throat feels dry, and you can keep the change…"
"Now you're talking kid." She gave back my ID. "You want a cherry in it?"
"Yum," I grinned. "You guys are all alike!" She winked,
then turned and worked her way back across the room toward the bar.

As if on cue Brew finished his beer and placed the empty bottle on top of
Bill's upright piano, and the drummer said, "Let's pick up the pace!"
Brew sucked a long deep drag from his ever-burning butt:
"Out of nowhere, man--B flat," he said with in-held breath…
*(sax counts in "Out of Nowhere" …3, 4!)
Then he blew an explosion of smoke from his horn, plunging us all
 into nowhere at supersonic speed, the band racing to keep up with him.
The cramped room crackled with high electricity, the thick air swirled in dim
circles beneath the lonely ceiling fan, and then a cherry coke appeared,
I sipped, and once again the world was right, the band was smoking,
the whole house rocked like a train car smoking through time…
*(Music fades out, then percussive bass accompanies)
…and later that night, walking up market street alone at two in the morning,
smoking my last cigarette, I hummed & whistled as I walked,
snapping my fingers and stomping my feet, twitching my lips
to imitate trumpet and saxophone sounds, scatting immeasurable riffs
all the way back to our rented family flat on Hayes street…
smoking, yes, smoking that jazz!
*(sax cadenza, bass holds on Bb Maj.7)

Collage artwork by T. MIKE WALKER

MYSTIC BOXING COMMISSION PRESENTS

LOOK FOR IT AT SPARRINGARTISTS.COM

At any moment all of this could disappear, someone could come into this room and rub things out; my womanhood, my childlike point of view, my bleak and bizarre devotion to unfashionable fictions;

at any moment, at any moment, all the pots and pans of my honorable co-existence with reality rattling in the dark, the hall light flickering with horror or self-doubt; love, intention, respectability, sucked from the room;

at any moment, the dull ache in the belly resembling desire; at any moment, the emptiness that accompanies too much future and not enough now; at any moment the hole in my heart which will not close;

I am an amulet, I am a figurine, I am Loki the shape-shifter, dancing on the eyelids of sleep; I am a minotaur, a semi-precious stone; I am a fading rose in a faded dream;

at any moment, all of this could disappear, and be replaced by a promised land beyond the American guilt-consciousness;

sunlight pouring in from the western horizon, red brick rooftops and a stitchery of leaves;

a flutter of wings, a cage with no bird;

bourbon on ice, poured freely by hand, with a hint of Miles Davis to level things out.

Opposite page:

"Heart of the Matter" collage art by **T. MIKE WALKER**

SCOTT WANNBERG
I KILLED MY BROTHER

I killed my brother.
Why won't he die?
Everyone's in love
but nobody can drive.
I ate my belly
and now the food don't rise.
I don't want you
to guarantee me any more surprise

I killed my brother.
It was so easy
but he won't stay put
and it's getting
eerie
Oh I wish I could write you a song
but my heart
got lost
in the great large hole
I need to hit bottom
so my bones
will
know...

The strange clown
on everyone's smile
speaks in such a cryptic manner
it takes me days
to figure out

what I thought he
might have
meant to say.

I voted for your entree,
I shelved all your corpses,
but now the maître d
can't find my reservation,
and I'd love to trust you
but my lawyer
sweats every time
you cross his
threshold.

I killed my brother
because he refused my hand.
I just needed someone
to walk me across the
scary street,
but sometimes the scary streets
double back on their origins,
and all would be bets
are off.

I didn't really want to kill my brother,
I just needed something to occupy my time.
The volcano spews out only so much shit
before you have no resort
but to turn your ears in.

I should have killed your brother,
just to prove I'm an equal opportunity believer,

"Male Repression" collage artwork by T. MIKE WALKER

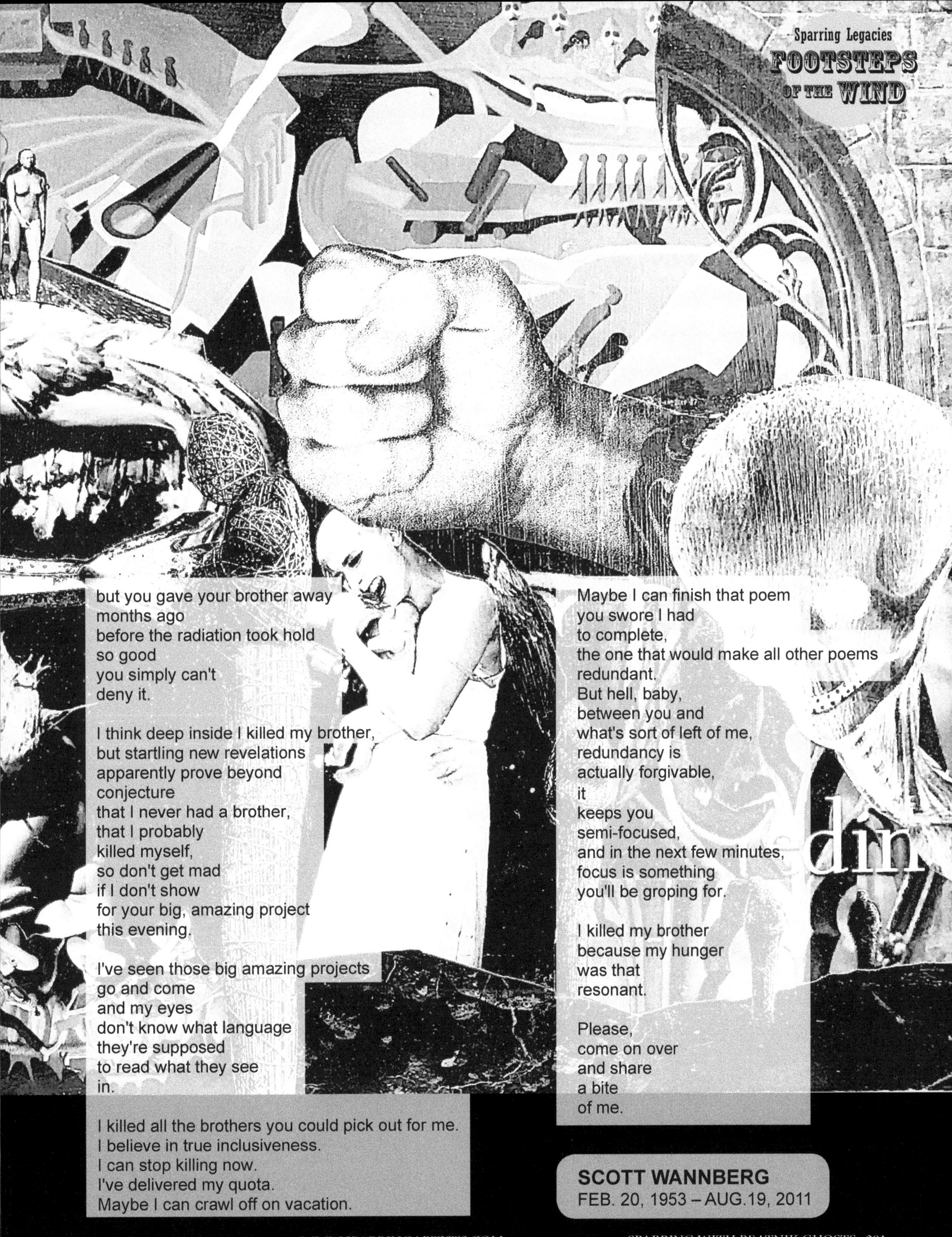

but you gave your brother away
months ago
before the radiation took hold
so good
you simply can't
deny it.

I think deep inside I killed my brother,
but startling new revelations
apparently prove beyond
conjecture
that I never had a brother,
that I probably
killed myself,
so don't get mad
if I don't show
for your big, amazing project
this evening.

I've seen those big amazing projects
go and come
and my eyes
don't know what language
they're supposed
to read what they see
in.

I killed all the brothers you could pick out for me.
I believe in true inclusiveness.
I can stop killing now.
I've delivered my quota.
Maybe I can crawl off on vacation.

Maybe I can finish that poem
you swore I had
to complete,
the one that would make all other poems
redundant.
But hell, baby,
between you and
what's sort of left of me,
redundancy is
actually forgivable,
it
keeps you
semi-focused,
and in the next few minutes,
focus is something
you'll be groping for.

I killed my brother
because my hunger
was that
resonant.

Please,
come on over
and share
a bite
of me.

SCOTT WANNBERG
FEB. 20, 1953 – AUG.19, 2011

DIG WAYNE
THIS POEM IS MARLON BRANDO

this poem doesn't care whether you like it or not

this poem is interested in everything
the engineering marvel of
ant hills
pyramids
bee hives
spider webs
woman's under garments
zip lines

the politics of word-foolery
the politics of mind-foolery
the politics of genocide
the politics of ignorance and its flag of dull eyes
the politics of lobotomies in 1950s America
the politics of Mulholland

the supposed honor
of the poet
the truth seeker
the visionary
the life inhaler

I say bring the poet's tragic flaw
the missed improvisation
the sour note that makes you pay attention

the roses are red mad man blowing you kisses with his butt hanging out
the violets are blue homeless woman screaming in Pig Latin in front of
the 7-11 after 11

let's make her the poet laureate of every
7-11 in Southern California
exploit her madness and call it art
too bad she's a white girl under the dirty face

this poem is Marlon Brando

it doesn't care whether you like it or not

this poem will be interrupted at any moment by the management
it will bite the hand that feeds it
repeatedly
this poem is praying for mistakes
this poem will test positive for Covid
this poem has a bad attitude
this poem is not a democracy
this poem is a panoramic dumpster fire
this poem will not come in out of the rain
this poem will not take responsibility for itself

I say, let's hear the executioner's poetry
as he smiles under his hood and sharpens his axe to grind

Design/collage by YARYAN

CONTINUED NEXT PAGE

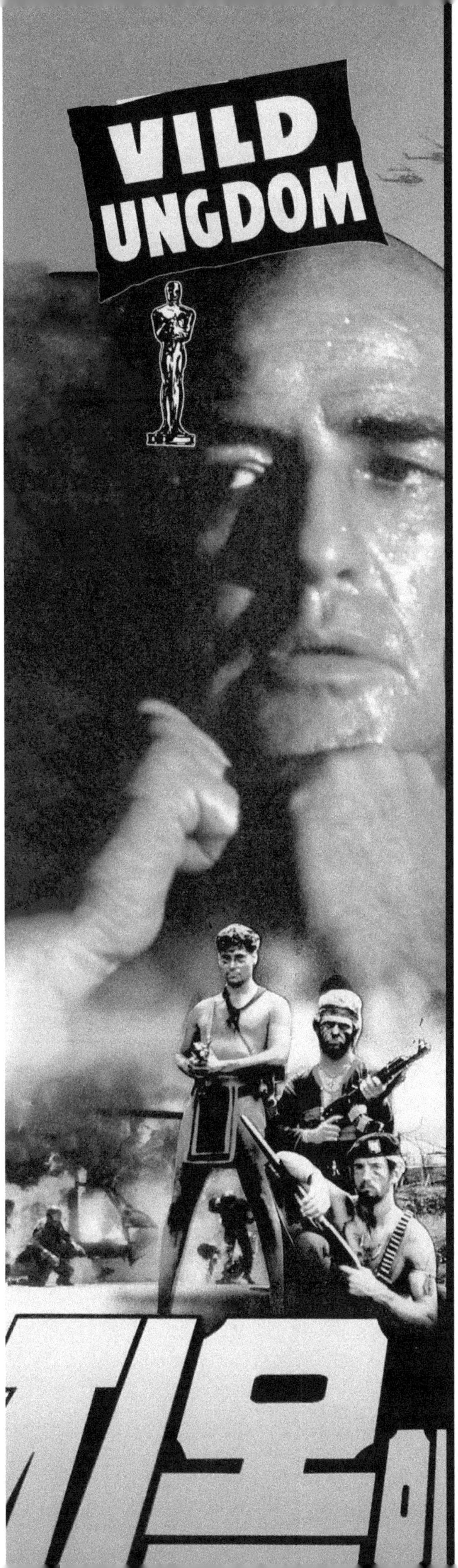

CONTINUED FROM LAST PAGE

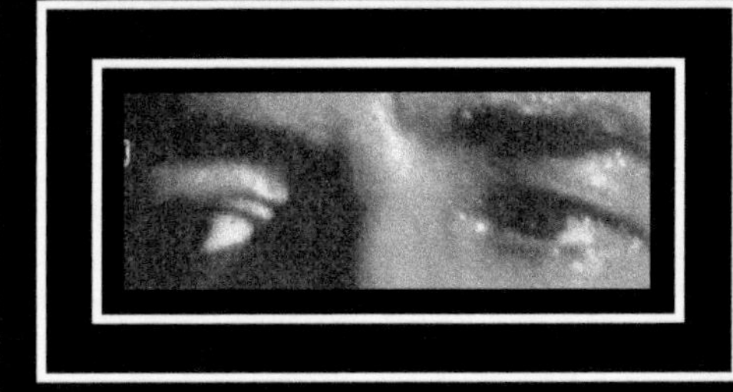

celebrate the pick-pocket poet
the plagiarist poet
the decapitated poet
the illiterate poet
they will see beyond the cliché
beat down moon and stars

hear the knell of academic spuddlery
chasing its tail for answers to everything
excavate the wormy poetry under your crusty socks
eating the eyes out of your slave owning ancestors
the grizzly poetry whipping four horses in a to-the-death chariot race
hoping to drag some Hollywood barbarian to his glorious end

read his verses as he disintegrates into a red mist

this poem is interested in everything
Denny's kids menu
the unseemly disappearance of McRib
smog checks
identity theft
walks on the beach

this poem is Marlon Brando

this poem doesn't care whether you like it or not

this poem is Bettie Page with a hard-on
this poem is a West Virginia coal mine in 1972
this poem will be burned as contraband
this poem is old dog teeth
this poem is rabbit ears
this poem is in glorious black and white
this poem is a genius
this poem will chew with its mouth open and its elbows on the table

bring the poet's tragic flaw
memorize the primal need
rebel against yourself, Johnny
read the back of empty cereal boxes
journey to Battle Creek, Michigan where all life began
with the philosophy of cruelty and
nutritional facts

this poem is for sale to the highest bidder
this poem is worth a million and a half dollars a day
this poem will refuse any accolades
this poem is looking for Sacheen Littlefeather
this poem will not make you an offer
this poem's potential is not up for discussion
this poem will not be recycled
this poem will self-destruct

what do you want this poem to do, buy you flowers?
tango with a knife in your back?
this poem is not here to impress you

CONTINUED NEXT PAGE

to help you discover your true self
to straighten you out
this poem is downtown Palookaville
this poem is Spit In The Ocean
this poem is interested in everything
mixed race conquistadors
Dad Longworth's whereabouts
cowboys on the beach
two-eyed Jacks
the divorce papers being finalized

this poem will fight injustice

let us screw our tragic flaws and dreams of perfection to
broken records and sail them into oblivion

this poem is a Cadillac up on blocks
this poem is a test of the emergency broadcast system
this poem is as American as the electric chair
this poem has been rejected by better people than you
this poem has spinach in its teeth
this poem has no will power
this poem has no discipline
this poem is grape Kool-Aid
this poem will eventually weigh 350 pounds
this poem is vanilla ice cream with hot fudge

this poem is Marlon Brando

© Dig Wayne

Design/collage by YARYAN

SUBMIT!
SEND YOUR
SHORT STORIES
AND ARTWORK TO
Venture
Illustrated
• Sci-fi, fantasy & horror
• 10-page max stories
• 300 dpi artwork
• Send to editor:
  dyaryan@gmail.com
MYSTIC BOXING COMMISSION
DEADLINE:
April 15, 2025
Artwork by RUBEN QUINTANA

*Artwork by **DAVID HUMBERT DE SUPERVILLE***

A.D. WINANS
IT COMES WITH THE TERRITORY

At eighty-eight
I receive far fewer letters
Then when I published Second Coming
Young writers wore my phone out
Filled my mailbox
Some were from women
But most from men
All of them wanted me to comment
On their poetry
Who saw me as a great writer
(their words not mine)
Most of them sought my advice
Wanted me to critique their work
Wanted to know the secret of my success
Which I told them was longevity.

Some compared me with Bukowski
A few with the Devil
But the truth is I am a longshot
In a fixed race
Too often left at the starter gate.

This poet is not Houdini
I have no tricks up my sleeve
No secrets to reveal.

Find yourself a good woman
I tell them
Don't obsess about being published.
Avoid the poetry politicians
"Stay away from the bars and cafes
Stay away from poets
Especially stay away from poets"
The same advice Bukowski gave me
I pass on to them.

Keep pounding the keyboard
Night and Day
Draw blood like a lab technician
Take a lesson from Joe Louis
And never settle for a draw.

Hang in there like Bukowski did
And maybe you'll make it
To the big show
More likely you won't
For d.a. levy was dead right
"Sum people can't beat the system
And poets can't even pretend
They are beating the system"

If you want advice
Ask Ann Landers
She doesn't have the answers either
But she gets paid for it.

"I Can Quit Whenever I Want" collage art by **FRANK T. RIOS**

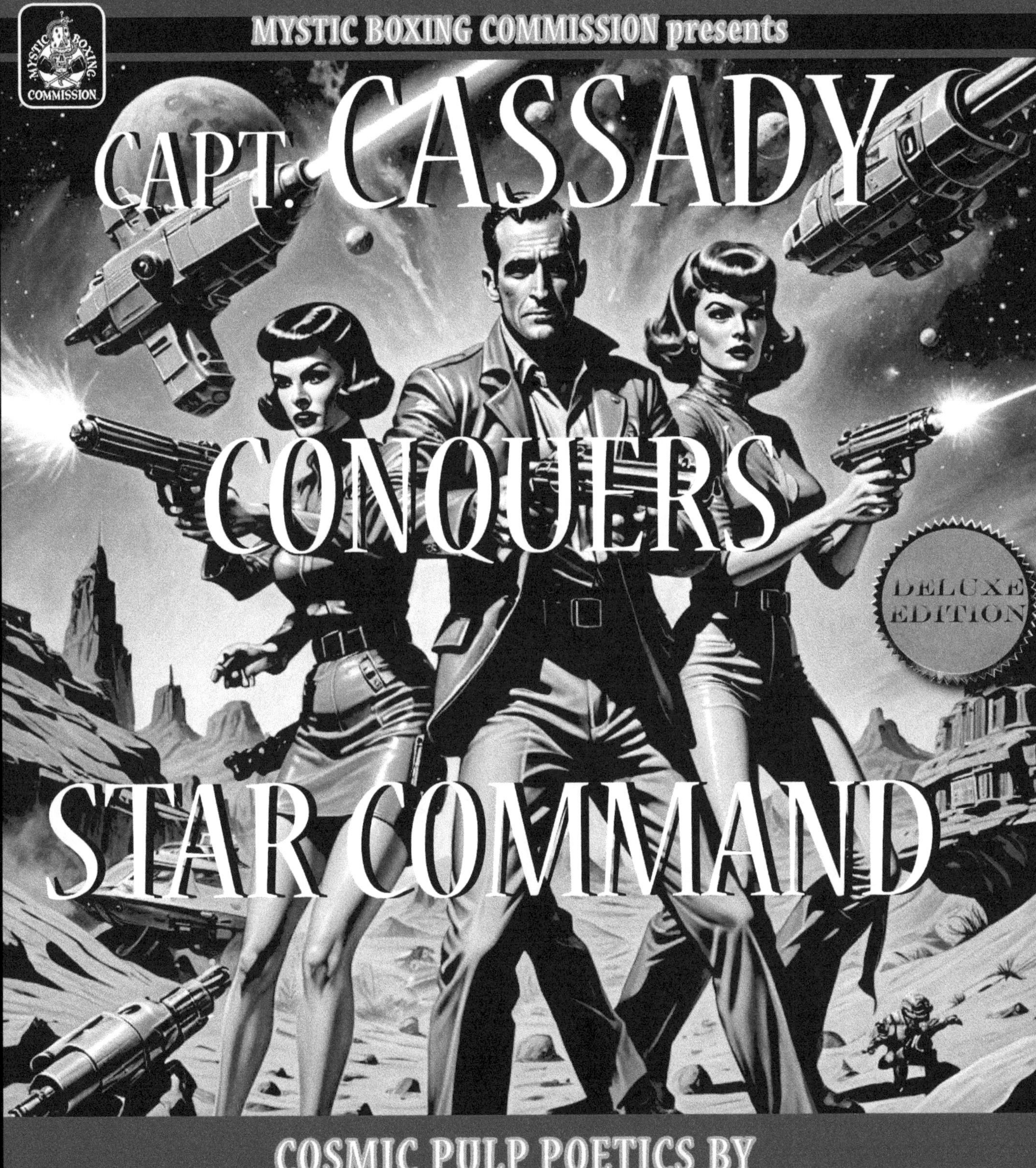
MYSTIC BOXING COMMISSION presents
CAPT. CASSADY
CONQUERS
STAR COMMAND
DELUXE EDITION
COSMIC PULP POETICS BY
DANIEL YARYAN

BOOKS FROM MBC!

WWW.SPARRINGARTISTS.COM

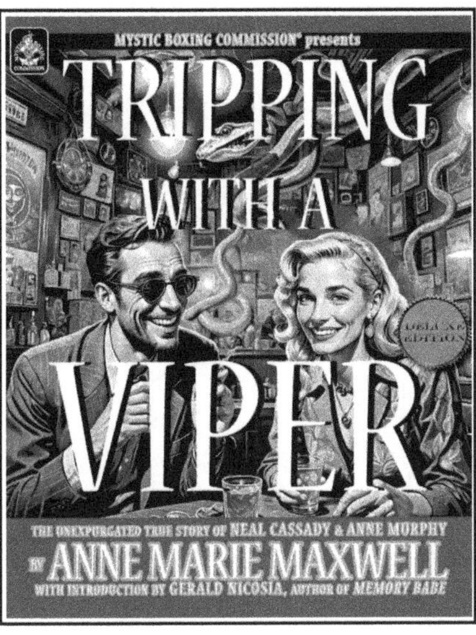

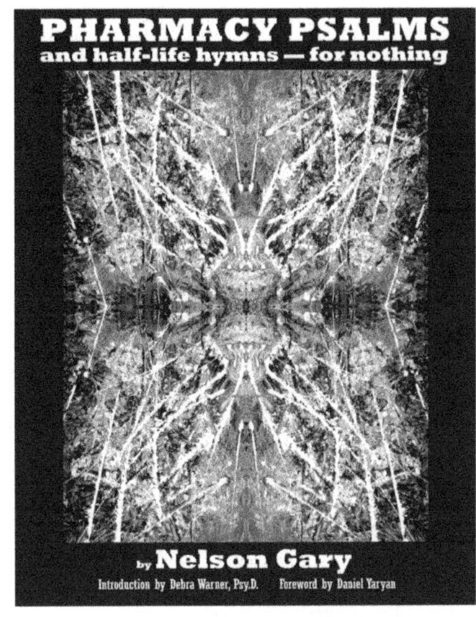

DELUXE LARGE (U.S. LETTER SIZE) BOOKS NOW AVAILABLE!

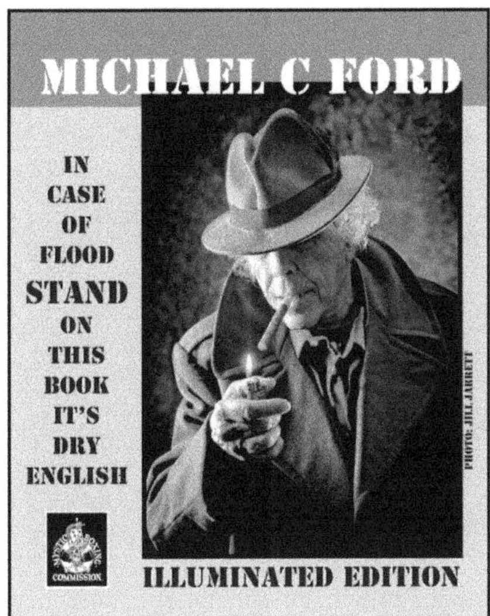

Collage artwork "Out of Bounds" by **T. MIKE WALKER**

Special recognition and thanks
to T. Mike Walker for all of his wonderful
contributions to Sparring With Beatnik Ghosts
in art and letters over the last 15 years!

—Daniel Yaryan